Praise for
THE WITCHES ARE COMING
by Lindy West

ONE OF THE BEST BOOKS OF FALL 2019
Amazon • *Book Riot* • Bustle • *E! News* • *Esquire* • Mashable •
Refinery29 • *USA TODAY*

"Searingly smart...[with an] overarching tone of swashbuckling courage: West knows what she wants to say, and she really doesn't care what you think...a stirring manifesto for honesty...and an exhortation to give a damn."

—*Los Angeles Times*

"A fiery book from an admirable author."

—Morgan Jerkins, *New York Times Book Review*

"With her signature wit, brio, and laser-like clarity of vision, one of our foremost thinkers on gender unveils her unifying theory of America: that our steady diet of pop culture created by and for embittered, entitled white men has stoked our sociopolitical moment. Adam Sandler, *South Park*, and Pepe the Frog all come under West's withering scrutiny in this funny, hyper-literate analysis of the link between meme culture and male mediocrity."

—*Esquire*

"West is back and funny as ever in...*The Witches Are Coming*, a cultural critique of American culture, the #MeToo movement and what it means to not be a mediocre white man—in a society that so often protects and promotes him."

—NBC News

"As a girl, Lindy West obsessed about pop culture. As a critic and columnist, she analyzed it. Now she's creating it…In her wise, witty new collection of essays, *The Witches Are Coming*…West blasts the misogyny lurking in the media we love."

—*Star Tribune*

"A thoughtful and funny examination of rape culture in media."

—Bustle

"*The Witches are Coming* is simultaneously whip smart, infuriating, a call to action and, of course, laugh-out-loud funny."

—Huffington Post

"The book made me simultaneously laugh out loud and want to pull my hair out. West's snappy writing is funny but full of anger, and I felt myself instantly sucked in."

—Steph Coelho, *Book Riot*

"[A] hilarious, astute essay collection chock-full of her signature wit and personal anecdotes."

—*BUST Magazine*

"Equal parts hilarious and sobering, West's words will help fellow witches articulate why they are so fired up (YES!)."

—*Booklist*

"From Facebook to Goop, cancel culture to climate change, the essays here add West's discerning and quick-witted voice to the conversation about what social and environmental justice looks like, and what it can look like in the future. So if you need a little magic in your Halloween reading, pick this one up."

—LitHub

"[This book] highlights one of West's greatest gifts, beyond her voice and humor—her ability to shine clarifying light on the dark, knotted bits of culture without divesting herself of that culture completely."

—Seattle Met

"When I have a hard time making sense of and finding the words to describe the complexities of women's issues, I turn to Lindy West. There's something about her sharp, steady, and ferociously funny writing that re-centers and refocuses my mind on what's in front of me and why it matters. West has a gift for packaging the truth into easily digestible sentences. And her latest collection of essays, *The Witches Are Coming* is no different... The next time you're feeling lost or can't find the words to describe why you're angry about a particular topic, pick up *The Witches Are Coming*. Lindy will lead the way."

—Hello Giggles

"In this time of great frustration, this collection is a clearing in the woods to meet, to reflect, to dance, and to cackle around the fire."

—Abbi Jacobson, creator of Broad City and *New York Times* bestselling author of *I Might Regret This*

"Lindy continues to be one of the funniest, smartest writers around."

—Jessica Valenti, *New York Times* bestselling author of *Full Frontal Feminism* and *Sex Object*

"GET ME A BROOM."

—Samantha Irby, *New York Times* bestselling author of *We're Never Meeting in Real Life* and *Wow, No Thank You*

Praise for *SHRILL* by Lindy West

"Read West's ferociously funny book and you'll be shouting her praises."
                                                      —*People*

"Stitch-inducing and searingly honest.... West takes readers through her journey from a self-effacing child working to keep her body and voice small to an unapologetic, fat-positive feminist, skewering the status quo one keyboard stroke at a time."
                                                      —*USA Today*

"Lindy West is the troll-fighting feminist warrior you've been waiting for.... *Shrill* treats feminism, fatness, and social change with rigorous attention without losing any of West's signature humor."
                                                      —*Los Angeles Times*

"[West is] one of the most distinctive voices advancing feminist politics through humor.... With patience, humor, and a wildly generous attitude toward her audience [West] meets readers at their point of prejudice so that she may, with little visible effort, shepherd them toward a more humane point of view."
                                                      —*New York Times Book Review*

"[B]eautiful, joyful writing.... West defies clichés both by being persistently hilarious and deeply loving."

—*Washington Post*

"Hilarious, biting, and wise."

—Huffington Post

"Lindy West's memoir is a witty and cathartic take on toxic misogyny and fat shaming. She comes to accept her body just as Internet trolls congregate en masse to try to rip this new confidence from her, but she's rearing to fight back.... In *Shrill*, West is our fat, ferocious, and funny avenging angel."

—NPR, Best Books of 2016

"Reading West's book is like taking a master class in inclusivity and cultural criticism, as taught by one of the funniest feminists alive today."

—Refinery29

"An emotional roller coaster. One moment you're snorting from laughter, trying to avoid all the weird looks you're getting on the train. The next you're silently absorbing a larger truth neatly packaged into the perfect sentence you didn't expect to read."

—*Mother Jones*

"With her clear-eyed insights into modern culture and her confidence in her own intelligence and personal worth, West appeals to the humanity of even the most parents' basement-dwelling, misogynistic, and casually hateful of trolls."

—*Esquire*

"[West's] writing is sharp, smart, hilarious, relatable, insightful, and memorable. She tackles serious and personal subjects—like being fat, getting an abortion, feeling lonely, or dealing with harassment online—and is just as capable of eliciting tears as laughter...I dare you to pick up a copy."

—*Newsweek*

"Poignant, hilarious, and contemplative."

—*Cosmopolitan*

"One of the most impressive aspects of this book is the level of nuance, self-reflection, and humanity that West displays in her analysis of her own writing and her relationships with others....It's the best kind of memoir, and it shows that Lindy West still has a lot more to say—and that we should all keep listening."

—Bitch Media

"West is utterly candid and totally hilarious...as funny as she is incisive."

—*Vogue*

"With *Shrill*, West cements her reputation as a woman unafraid to comfort (and confound) her critics....[*Shrill*] illustrates just how deeply sexism pervades our society while laughing at the absurdities that sexism somehow normalizes."

—*Elle*

"Lindy West can take almost any topic and write about it in a way that is smart, funny, warm, and unique."

—Bustle

"West is candid and funny, unafraid to criticize rape jokes or explain how airlines discriminate against fat people, and her fearlessness has made her one of the most notable voices on the Internet."

—Flavorwire

"Both sharp-toothed and fluid....West is propulsively entertaining."

—Slate

"Lindy West did not set out to be a feminist warrior against the forces that wish to silence and hurt women for doing things that men take for granted....*Someone* has to fight the misogynists, after all, and West is well-situated for the front lines, lacing her blunt sense of humor with a surprising amount of nuanced empathy, even for those out there who are the ugliest to women."

—Salon

"Lindy West is one of the Great Ladies of the Feminist Internet....250 pages of pure hilariousness."

—Feministing

"Incredible and insightful....What West ultimately strives for is to incrementally make those small changes that can lead to something so much bigger and better for us all."

—Amy Poehler's Smart Girls

"[West is] warm and cutting, vulnerable and funny in equal measures; her sense of self makes you yourself feel seen."

—BuzzFeed

"Hey reader! I thought I'd read enough in this lifetime about people's childhoods and feelings and such and I'd never want to do it again. But Lindy West is such a totally entertaining and original writer she kind of blew that thought out of my head halfway into the first chapter. I dare you to feel differently."

—Ira Glass, *This American Life*

"You have to be careful about what you read when you're writing, or you can end up in total despair, thinking, 'This is what I wanted to say, only she got there first and said it better.'"

—Jennifer Weiner, *New York Times* bestselling author of *Good in Bed* and *The Littlest Bigfoot*

"The surge of love and joy I felt while crylaughing through this book almost made my cold dead heart explode. Lindy is so smart and so funny that it almost hurts my little jealous-ass feelings. She is my most favorite writer ever."

—Samantha Irby, *New York Times* bestselling author of *We're Never Meeting in Real Life* and *Wow, No Thank You*

"It made me hurt, both from laughing and crying. Required reading if you are a feminist. Recommended reading if you aren't."

—Jenny Lawson, number one bestselling author of *Let's Pretend This Never Happened* and *Furiously Happy*

"It's literally the new *Bible*."

—Caitlin Moran, bestselling author of *How to Be a Woman*

"There's a reason Lindy West is such a beloved writer: she gets to the heart of impossible issues with humor and grace. West will have you cringing, laughing, and crying, all within one page. *Shrill* is a must-read for all women."

—Jessica Valenti, *New York Times* bestselling author of *Full Frontal Feminism* and *Sex Object*

Shit, Actually

Also by Lindy West:

The Witches Are Coming

Shrill

Shit,
Actually

The Definitive, 100% Objective
Guide to Modern Cinema

By Lindy West

hachette
BOOKS

New York

Hachette Books
Hachette Book Group
1290 Avenue of the Americas
New York, NY 10104
HachetteBooks.com
Twitter.com / HachetteBooks
Instagram.com / HachetteBooks

First Edition: October 2020

Some of the movie reviews in this book originally appeared on Jezebel.com and GQ.com.

Published by Hachette Books, an imprint of Perseus Books, LLC, a subsidiary of Hachette Book Group, Inc. The Hachette Books name and logo is a trademark of the Hachette Book Group.

The Hachette Speakers Bureau provides a wide range of authors for speaking events.

To find out more, go to www.hachettespeakersbureau.com or call (866) 376-6591.

The publisher is not responsible for websites (or their content) that are not owned by the publisher.

Print book interior design by Jeff Stiefel.

Library of Congress Cataloging-in-Publication Data has been applied for.

ISBNs: 978-0-316-44982-3 (hardcover); 978-0-316-44984-7 (ebook)

Library of Congress Control Number: 2020942010

Printed in the United States of America

LSC-C

10 9 8 7 6 5 4 3 2 1

To Dr. Richard Kimble,
who didn't kill his wife,
not that I care.

Contents

CONTENTS

Introduction

I love making fun of movies. I love turning a piece of criticism into a piece of entertainment. I love pointing out a plot hole that makes a superfan write me an angry e-mail. I love turning my unsophistication into a tool. I love being hyperbolically, cathartically angry for no reason. I love being flippant and careless and earnest and meticulous all at once.

Shit, Actually is inspired by a series of essays I started at Jezebel, in which I'd rewatch successful movies from the past to see how they hold up to our shifting modern sensibilities. That concept has grown even more relevant in recent years, as grappling with those shifts has become something of a national obsession. What do we do now with beloved cultural works that don't hold up? What do we do with the oeuvre of beloved people who fail us? Are we "allowed" to like imperfect things that mean something to us?

A few of those Jezebel pieces became extremely popular, none more so than my *Love Actually* rewatch, which to my great joy still makes the rounds online every December (I'm told that some families now read it aloud each year à la "'Twas the Night Before Christmas"). *Love Actually* is in here, along with some other favorites from that series, spruced up and expanded for freshness.

But I've also added a whole bunch of new ones! If you're wondering about my methodology for those, I selected movies that fit at least one of three categories: 1) cultural phenomena that took over the Earth, 2) movies I was personally obsessed with, or 3) movies I picked because it seemed like someone should talk about them. Lots of things are missing. Don't think about it too hard.

I started my career as a snotty twenty-three-year-old (!) film critic who was, to be honest, less interested in film than in exploiting my column inches to write jokes. As I grew older (I am thirty-eight now) and graduated from a local to a national platform, I shifted from writing about movies to writing about politics, and my writing, of necessity, became increasingly serious. After the bone-deep vulnerability of my memoir, *Shrill*, the exhaustion of writing political columns both during and after the 2016 election, and the careworn scream of my second essay collection, *The Witches Are Coming*, I am excited to be writing some goofy jokes about movies again.

And *Shit, Actually* is that! But what I began working on as a silly book for release into a darkness I understood—the demoralizing grind of public life under Donald Trump—is now to be a silly book for release into a darkness I don't.

I finished writing *Shit, Actually* six weeks into the COVID-19 stay-at-home order—six weeks of trying to think of funny things to say about *Face/Off* while worrying about a friend on a ventilator, six weeks of mustering comical outrage over Harry Potter plot holes while the president went on television to suggest that the ill try drinking bleach. Meanwhile, Trump and his party (whom, in a previous book, in a previous life, I might have described as morally bankrupt but now feel comfortable calling FULLY FUCK-ING DEMONIC) have been flagrantly funneling taxpayer-funded relief money to the richest and least deserving while the rest of us sit, isolated, trapped in our homes, as everything we know and love crumbles into uncertainty.

As shelter-in-place stretched on and I began adjusting to my new, smaller, lonelier life, I started to find a strange comfort in the task of making this book for you and thinking about it in your hands and homes—this silly, inconsequential, ornery, joyful, obsessive, rude, and extremely stupid book.

More than anything I want this book to make you feel like you are at a movie night with your best friend (me). I had no way of knowing, when I proposed *Shit, Actually* back in 2017, that I'd be writing it in a time when movie nights with your best friend no longer existed.

Writing this, in a way I could not have guessed, has made me feel less alone. Thank you for being my friends. It kept me afloat knowing you were there.

Love,
Lindy

Shit, Actually

The Fugitive Is
The Only Good Movie

O bjectively, there's only one good movie, and it's *The Fugi-tive*. *The Fugitive* is the only good movie. Now, if you think I'm being capricious, know that I have had this feeling before about other things—I remember when I first read *Island of the Blue Dolphins*, I was like, "Shut it down, no need to write more books." Ditto with "The Sign" by Ace of Base—but those feelings didn't last because eventually I heard "Poison" by Bell Biv DeVoe and read a little story you might have heard of called THE BIBLE? But when it comes to *The Fugitive*, I have never wavered. *The Fugitive* is the only good movie. We didn't need any more movies after *The Fugitive*. We didn't need any movies before it either. We should erase those.

I wanted to call this whole book *The Fugitive Is the Only Good Movie*, but my publisher wouldn't let me, probably because they're deep in the pocket of Big Gump. Undeterred, I shall be rating every movie in this book on a scale of zero to ten DVDs of *The Fugitive*. I rate *The Fugitive* thirteen out of ten DVDs of *The Fugitive*.

In case you haven't seen *The Fugitive* and have somehow escaped prosecution under my regime, *The Fugitive* is the terrible tale of Dr. Ser Richard Kimble, American hero, America's sweetheart, America's Next Top Daddy Doctor, Heir of Isildur and King of All the Dúnedain.

Richard Kimble is a respected Chicago vascular surgeon who, after a long day vasculating, is having a well-earned glamorous night out with his sexy '90s wife and his doctor friends at a sexy fashion show benefit for the Children's Research Fund. (You want a children's benefit to be as sexy as possible!) All the other doctors agree that Richard Kimble's wife, Helen, is the number-one coolest and hottest wife of all the doctor wives. Kimble is on top.

Kimble and Wife Helen head home, erotically, and they love each other very much in the car. Kimble touches his wife's face; it's so cute. Suddenly, Kimble is called in for emergency surgery! He's gotta go. "I'll wait up for you," says Wife Helen.

Flash-forward. What's this? Two cops are interrogating Kimble, and it is just like *The First 48*! Just like *The First 48* (and, incidentally, all police departments worldwide), there's two cops: glasses cop and grumpy cop. Also like *The First 48*, the cops arrest Kimble on the Husband Did It principle because—WOW—someone went and murdered Mrs. Helen in the night while Richard was at the hospital!

The cops ask Richard questions about what he remembers, insinuating that he, the Husband, Did It and is planning to collect megabucks from his Helen insurance. Things are not looking good: "His fingerprints are all over the lamp, gun, and the bullets. And the good doctor's skin is under her fingernails." Now, I watch a lot of murder shows if you have any questions about how murder works. Did you know that if your DNA is under a murder victim's fingernails, they don't even have to give you a trial? The sheriff just yells, "Geeee-ilty!" and then his dog chases you all the way to prison! Richard's boned!

Also, on Wife Helen's 911 call, she's like, "Richard, Richard, he's trying to kill me!" And the cops are like, "Hmmmm, YOUR name's Richard. Do you think maybe she meant...you?" Which, to be fair, and I know this is tacky because she's a corpse, but Helen could not have done a worse job here. Like, watch ONE *Dateline*, Helen! You have to say, "A large, upsetting Greek man with a perm, a large, upsetting Greek man with a perm, HE'S trying to kill me! Not Richard, who is nice!"

Fortunately, Richard has an extremely compelling explanation for the cops: "When I came home there was a man in my house. I fought with this man. He had a mechanical arm. You find this man. You find this man!"

They...don't love it.

Richard gets sentenced to death by lethal injection, and keep in mind that this is only twelve minutes and forty-nine seconds into the movie!!!!!!!!!!

Kimble boards the prisoner bus, which features all four types of prisoners: spooky white guy, great big Black guy, Latino guy, and Richard Kimble. Spooky white guy does a bad plan and stabs the guard with a whittled toothbrush, causing the bus to crash into the train tracks. A train is coming! Could this day get any worse???? The other guard reveals his cowardly heart by running away while Richard, an earth angel, is the only one who cares to stay and try to save toothbrush guard, which he DOES. Would a guy who killed his wife do something *nice* like that??? (Yes, absolutely, humanity is infinitely complex!)

Richard jumps from the bus right when it gets hit by the train, which derails the train, and now the train is chasing Richard down the hill. Richard runs in a straight line away from the train (idea: turn!). He manages to escape and get his handcuffs off, but I guess in vascular surgery school they don't teach you to THROW THE HANDCUFFS INTO THE RIVER SO THE COPS DON'T FIND THEM AND START MANHUNTING YOU INSTANTLY, GIVING YOU LITERALLY UNLIMITED NON-BEING-CHASED LEISURE TIME TO INVESTIGATE WHO KILLED YOUR WIFE, RICHARD.

Instead, US Marshal Tommy Lee Jones shows up to investigate, and he's like, "My, my, my, what a mess," and you just *know* he's thinking about Al Gore in the dorm room.

Here's a fun Tommy Lee Jones trivia game you can play with your friends: it's called "Is Tommy Lee Jones 20 or 100 in This Movie?"

As a person who is interested in someday becoming good at my job, it is inspiring how good US Marshal Tommy Lee Jones is at his job. He has assembled an incredible team, which he leads with a just, firm, fatherly hand. You know where nobody is ever competent or assembles an incredible team, which they lead with a just, firm, fatherly hand? Real life! Which makes this basically sci-fi, which I think maybe makes it okay to love a cop?

Kimble needs to get out of his prison jumpsuit ASAP, and luckily he sees a dude take off all his clothes and leave them in the front seat of his car with the windows down in the middle of winter in Chicago. He then sneaks into the hospital, sews up his wound, shaves his beard, steals Mr. Johnson's breakfast sandwich and big shirt, stops to save the life of toothbrush guard real quick AGAIN, and narrowly escapes detection with thrilling audacity.

I mean, is there a better moment in all of cinema than this???

> **State Trooper:** Hey, Doc! We're looking for a prisoner from that bus/train wreck a couple of hours ago. Might be hurt.
>
> **Dr. Richard Kimble:** Uh, what does he look like?
>
> **State Trooper:** 6'1", 180, brown hair, brown eyes, beard. See anyone like that around?
>
> **Dr. Richard Kimble:** Every time I look in the mirror, pal. Except for the beard, of course!

Reader, I just had sex with that dialogue!!!! And it rocked!

Kimble steals an ambulance to get away because when you're trying to escape detection, it's good to put your body inside something covered in flashing lights that is instantly missed. Now he's on the run in an ambulance!

Of course it must be acknowledged that *The Fugitive* is a movie all about men, where women don't do very much except die or sometimes hold a clipboard. It's all men who are the boss, but who is the most boss of the men??? Is it the Harrison Ford kind of boss, or the Tommy Lee Jones kind of boss? They're both your dad, but which is the best spanker?????

This is allowed because in 1993 it was still okay to make movies all about men, as their contract wasn't up yet.

Now Kimble is trapped in a tunnel, but he tricks the cops by crawling on the floor and into the sewer and the cops have never heard of holes before. But Tommy has! Now Tommy chases Richard through the sewers! Tommy drops the gun, now

Richard has the gun! Oops, now Tommy has another gun! He's a two-gun Jones!

THIS IS THE WHOLE MOVIE RIGHT HERE:

"I didn't kill my wife!"

"I don't care!"

Tommy Lee Jones is a guy that can tell you to shut up and you don't mind.

Okay, now the sewer is also a dam. Kimble is trapped and he's gotta make a choice. Get shot, get lethal injected, or jump off the dam. He jumps off the dam.

Tommy's team wants to go home and lie down straightaway, but Tommy says no. He's got a feeling this guy knows how to jump off a dam and be fine.

WELL, HE'S RIGHT.

Richard is very cold but he is alive. He wakes up and he knows what he has to do: You find that man! You find that man! Richard gets some hair dye and becomes Dark & Natural. Now Richard is on top again. And the one-armed man? Is on bottom.

Meanwhile, the marshals raid a house because they think Kimble is there, but whoops, it's one of the other guys from the prisoner bus, who they kill, which I hate. Wait, so someone called the cops and said, "There's a fugitive from that prison bus accident hiding at this address, but I WON'T TELL YOU WHICH ONE! Hee-hee!" Who's the whistleblower? Rumpelstiltskin?

Anyway, Tommy Lee Jones shoots the guy and it makes his friend Curly Boy deaf, which is confusing because surely Tommy was way closer to the gun? Because he was shooting it? Tommy hates it when people on his team get hurt, but also he lives by a code.

> **Curly Boy:** It's terrible. I'm going to have permanent hearing damage. [WHY??]
>
> **Tommy:** I don't bargain.

Tommy Lee Jones is the hero *and* the villain! This is the gorgeous umami flavor of *The Fugitive*!

Richard sneaks into another hospital to infiltrate the prosthetics department and steal their one-armed files. The marshals hear from Kimble's rat lawyer that Kimble hasn't left Chicago, which gets Tommy's Tommy sense aflame. He starts to wonder: What is this guy's deal? Why isn't he leaving Chicago? Why would he kill his wife in the first place? The dumb cops say it was for the money, but Tommy knows that a vascular king like Richard doesn't need insurance bucks: "What do you mean he did it for the money? He's a doctor, he's rich!" Haven't you seen his truly breathtaking modern staircase? At this point, on *The First 48*, one of the detectives would say, "I dunno, Fingerman, I don't like this guy for this." Tommy is starting to not like this guy for this. Unfortunately, that's not Tommy's job. He "don't care."

Or do he??????????????????????????????????

Tommy interviews Richard's colleague Chuck, who tells him, "If you want help, gentlemen, you've come to the wrong man. Richard is innocent." Wow! What a loyal and trustworthy best friend! I would happily place my liver in Chuck's tender care any day.

Kimble has rented a room from an old woman and he falls asleep reading *Atlas of Limb Prosthetics*, which sounds impossible,

I know. Suddenly, uh-oh! The cops are raiding another house, and this time it *is* Richard's! You think it's all over for Kimble, but it turns out they're just looking for the old woman's gross Polish son.

;) <————— tfw u think the cops found u but it's just the gross polish son

Rick heads back to the hospital, where he impersonates a janitor. Using his years of being janitored upon as reference, he does the job of janitor with surprising success. Way more successful than the time the janitor had to pretend to be a surgeon![1]

He sneaks into an office and searches a prosthetics database for one-armed men. Only five results. One of them has GOT to be Helen's murderer. Are you sure this is how computers work? What if the murderer got his prosthetic arm at a different hospital? Or not in Chicago? What if you remembered his number of arms wrong? Or which arm it was?

On his way out, he encounters an influx of trauma patients to the ER. There has been a school bus crash. Richard jumps in to help because even though he absolutely needs to get the heck out of there, his perfect heart won't let him! Dr. Julianne Moore conscripts him to bring a kid down to observation room 2, and on the way, Richard sneaks a cheeky look at the film and sees that he's been misdiagnosed. He changes the kid's chart, saving his damn life. Julianne Moore notices the janitor changing the chart and calls for security because normally janitors are not preeminent vascular surgeons in disguise, and I get that. Richard runs away.

Skreeeet! Here comes Jones!

---

1   If this joke is classist, my husband wrote it.

GODDAMN, THIS MOVIE'S GOOD. You know, I approached this essay from the semi-joking, hyperbolic premise that *The Fugitive* is the best movie ever made, and assumed I was setting myself up for disappointment. But then it turned out that I was right and it's literally true! *The Fugitive* IS the best movie ever made! I set myself up for appointment!!!!

Tommy talks to Julianne Moore about the mysterious janitor who changed the charts.

Tommy: How's the boy doing?
Jules: He saved his life.

This just isn't adding up for Tom-Tom. "What I can't figure is the place is crawling with cops, everybody's looking for Richard Kimble, so why would the guy be stupid enough to come hang out in a trauma ward, pretending like he's Mother Teresa?"

THEN A ONE-ARMED GUY GOES BY and he's like KABOI-IIIIING! Oh yeah! Richard said a one-armed man killed his wife, so now he is trying to find the one-armed man! Why would a guy who killed his wife go to so much risk and trouble trying to track down a fictional man he made up? He wouldn't, dumbass! Now Tommy is looking for the one-armed man too. That lil bitch doesn't stand a chance!

Kimble goes to the jail to visit Clive Driscoll, one of the one-armed men from the one-armed computer. When he gets there he realizes that Clive Driscoll is a Black person, and he definitely remembers Helen being murdered by a one-armed white. Wrong guy! Richard hops up to leave so he can move on to the next guy on his one-armed list. Clive Driscoll doesn't care that they don't know each other, though—he wants to chat! "Ain't no cable in this damn place!" But Richard (who is stressed out about being a fugitive in a building full of law enforcement I guess yeah whatever) is like, "Sorry, bye," and leaves Clive disappointed and lonely, right at the moment when his wounded heart thought he finally had a visitor. This is Richard's only flaw as a man.

Tommy Jones gets to the jail just as Richard is exiting and they do a chase. To buy some time, Richard yells, "There's a man waving a gun and screaming!" so the cops tackle Tommy instead of him. This is a good prank that you should try on your little brother the next time he's chasing you with a gun.

Richard escapes outside into the St. Patrick's Day parade, which is the one where they dye the Chicago River green, and this is unrelated to the movie but it seems like they shouldn't do that. Richard steals a green bowler hat from some idiot and joins the parade. He is having a blast.

He sneaks into the house of another one-armed man from his list, and bazinga, it's a spicy meatball. This is the guy. Not only that, but there are a bunch of pics of this dickhead hanging out with Richard's two best friends, Lenz and a big fish, without Richard! He doesn't let the hurt show on his face, but you know it stings. One time in middle school, my three best friends all went trick-or-treating together as Dorothy, the Tin Man, and the Scarecrow, and they didn't invite me, even though they *didn't even have a lion*. And then, crazy story, they murdered my wife!

Turns out, the one-armed man, Sykes, is on the payroll of Devlin MacGregor Pharmaceuticals, which is just about to launch a new drug called Provasic. VERY INTERESTING. Richard calls up Tommy. "I am trying to solve a puzzle and I just found a big piece."

Back when he was a doctor and not a doctor/fugitive,

Richard found out that Provasic caused liver damage and he told *everyone*. He told Chuck. He told Lenz. He told the big fish. He told the mayor of the Munchkin City. So why was Devlin MacGregor releasing Provasic to the public anyway? How did it get approved by the FDA? Richard goes back to the hospital and gets the old Provasic-damaged liver samples from his friend in the samples basement. He takes them to lanky cherub Jane Lynch, who discovers, "not only did they all come from healthy livers, they all came from the same liver." DANG! That's not how liver samples are supposed to work! Somebody must have switched the fucked-up samples with healthy samples so that Devlin MacGregor could make $7.5 billion in net sales last year alone! (Only a hunch, but maybe Devlin MacGregor?)

Co-inka-dinka, Richard runs into Sykes on the street and Sykes is like, "Bad news, Mr. Kimble! My gun works on husbands too!" They fight on a train and Sykes shoots a train cop, but ultimately Richard wins and handcuffs Sykes to the train. Then he says one of those zingers that were cool as hell in the '90s: "You missed your stop." It's so badass that Sykes's other arm falls off.

In another weird coincidence, Devlin MacGregor is having a Provasic gala literally right now. Richard toots over there. Crashing a pharmaceutical gala when you are a fugitive positively drenched in blood? This movie is from 1993, but that's a 2020 mood.

Richard gets to the gala and who's up there at the podium pampering Provasic's dong? Who just got appointed to the board of directors of Devlin MacGregor?? Wow, it's only CHUCK! Richard's "loyal" and "European" "best friend" who told Tommy Jones earlier that Richard is an innocent man. *I guess he would know, if you know what I mean.*

This bitch is literally like, "Provasic is remarkably effective and has no side effects whatsoever." Excuse me??? Richard can't take it and he recites the verse for which he became poet laureate of Chicago:

> *You almost got away with it, didn't you? I know all*
> *about it, I can prove it!*
> *You changed the samples,*
> *didn't you?*
> *You switched the samples after Lenz*
> *died!*
> Haha, Richard,
> I'm sorry, I'm in the middle
> of this speech.
> *After Lenz died, you were the only one who had the access.*
> *You switched the samples*
> *And the pathology report!*
> *He falsified*
> *his*
> *research!*
> *Did you kill Lenz too?*
> *So Devlin MacGregor could give you*
> *[witheringly] PROVASIC.*

Chuck is like, "Heh-heh, uh, hey, come back to the greenroom with me, Ricardo, heh-heh-heh," then as soon as they get back there he's like, U CANNOT DEFEAT ME I HAVE THE POWER OF PROVASIC!!!!! They fight and Richard chases Chuck up to the roof. They fall through a skylight and end up in the hotel's laundry dungeon. At this point, Tommy and Joey Pants show up

(I shouldn't have to tell you that Joey Pants is in this movie—you should always assume), and everyone is chasing one another around and around.

I was going to say that they don't make movies like this anymore, where the last thirty minutes is just one continuous incredible chase, except they do, all the time, but they make it all CGI so it's impossible to care about. Who cares about a drawing of a very fast exploding truck that a computer made? Not me! I care about Joey Pants getting bonked in his actual head with an actual steel beam on a zip line that is somehow an integral part of washing hotel sheets! Real cinema!

Tommy yells out to Richard to let him know that he figured it out about Chuck and how he sent the one-armed man to kill Richard to cover up the Provasic side effects so he could keep damaging people's livers for money, but then the one-armed man accidentally killed Helen instead, which turned into a whole *thing*.

Chuck tries to shoot Tommy, but Richard saves him by clonking Chuck with a metal pipe. Finally, it's over. Richard is happy because he didn't kill his wife. Tommy unlocks Richard's handcuffs in the police car and gives him an ice pack. Best friendship with Chuck over. Now Tommy is best friend.

"I thought you didn't care."

"I don't. Hahahahaha."

The Fugitive is the best movie because it has the best lines and is never scary, only interesting and exciting. All other movies should quit. Case closed. GAVEL.

RATING: 13 / 10 DVDs of *The Fugitive*.

Shit, Actually

We open in a fucking airport. A fucking airport!!! Of course *Love Actually*, the apex of cynically vacant cash-grab sentimentality, would hang its BIG METAPHOR on no less than an empathy-stripped cathedral of turgid, racist bureaucracy. Of course. Hugh Grant's voice pipes in to tell us how inspiring and magical the airport is, as though we've never been to one, because when you're at the airport you can't help but notice that "love actually IS all around." THE FUCKING AIRPORT!!!!!

If that's not the epitome of unexamined privilege—declaring that the airport is *your favorite place*—then I don't know what is. Welcome to *Love Actually*.

Bill Nighy and his technicolor dream-blouse are in the studio recording a shitty, vapid Christmas song in hopes of squeezing a few dollars out of idiots who will pay for any tatty garbage as long as it has a celebrity's name attached (*way* better metaphor for your movie than "the airport," BTW!). Bill Nighy keeps ruining perfectly good takes so he can yell about how shitty his shitty Christmas song is because Bill Nighy doesn't care about the valuable time of the hardworking professionals who are just trying to finish his bad record so they can get home to their families. Not Bill Nighy's problem! He's done *heroin* before!

Question: Why is Bill Nighy weirdly hovering over the stool like that? Can somebody please adjust Bill Nighy's microphone so he doesn't have to cop a weird squat? I should be able to watch a movie without my brain being forced to contemplate the current dilation of Bill Nighy's butthole. Thx.

Text appears on the screen to alert us that it's five weeks before Christmas. Why are you recording a Christmas single FIVE WEEKS BEFORE CHRISTMAS!?!? This movie is so fucking incompetently made that even the people doing their fake jobs inside the movie are incompetent.

Meanwhile, Colin Firth's girlfriend is sick. NBD, right!? WRONG. Turns out, she isn't sick with the flu—she's sick with ColinFirth'sBrother'sDongitis! Colin Firth cannot deal, so he runs off to France all sulky to fucking type a novel on a fucking typewriter in a mansion. Siiiigh! "Alone ah-GAYN!"

This old Frenchwoman shows up at Château de Firth and is like, "Bonjour, I found you a lady. I'm literally giving you this lady." Score! Free lady! The lady is named Aurelia, and she only speaks Portuguese, and so does her entire family, apparently, even though *all of them live in France*. It's irritating.

Colin Firth falls in "love" with Aurelia at first sight, establishing *Love Actually*'s central moral lesson: the less a woman talks, the more lovable she is.

None of the women in this movie fucking talk! All of the men in this movie "win" a woman at the end! This goddamn movie.

Liam Neeson is bummed out because his wife just died. The

grief-stricken Liam Neeson calls up Emma Thompson, who I guess is just some woman he knows (relationship NEVER EXPLAINED, and don't argue with me that they are brother and sister—I DID MY RESEARCH AND THEY NEVER SAY [and yes, of course, men and women can be platonic friends, but *could they in 2003?*]), to talk about how sad he is. Emma Thompson is *Love Actually*'s top female-personality-haver, which means that she's totally nice and bland 95 percent of the time and then every once in a while she'll say something horribly caustic and inappropriate and out of character. You know, like normal regular human woman who is not robot!

Emma Thompson tells Liam Neeson that she's obviously "terribly concerned that your wife just died but anywayz bye, LYLAS." Later, she tells him, "Get a grip. People hate sissies. And no one's going to shag you if you cry all the time." Oh, she's just *terrifically naughty*, isn't she? (Don't worry, though! She'll be punished later for her infernal personality!)

In an office building somewhere, some fucking guy is running around throwing sandwiches at people and asking female office workers if they want his "lovely nuts." It's possible that he says something important, but I couldn't tell you because the music is louder than the dialogue because #competence.

Oh, looks like his name is Colin, and he's terribly, terribly oppressed because no ladies want to sit upon his ginger ween (idea: could it possibly be because you wear a shirt that says SATISFACTION GUARANTEED and call complete strangers "my future wife" in a professional setting and then cry about not receiving immediate intercourse?). Colin decides to go to America in order to locate skanks. This is his entire plotline.

Hugh Grant plays the role of "horny prime minister," which raises the question: What percentage of Americans believe that

Hugh Grant *literally is the prime minister and/or boy king* of the UK? I'll bet you the number is not zero, and that is why we should all probably eat poison.

It's Hugh Grant's first day on the job, and he's saying hello to his new staff. One staffer is named Natalie, and as far as I can tell, her job is "woman." She's also incredibly, disgustingly fat, like a beanbag chair with feet, according to literally everyone else in the movie who apparently all have Natalie Dysmorphic Disorder (a silent killer). Natalie accidentally says some swears in front of the prime minister, and then she makes lemon-face for forty-five minutes. Actually, she's probably just thinking about delicious lemons because NATALIE HUNGRY!!!!!!!

Hugh Grant falls instantly in love with Natalie, which is understandable, because she hasn't yet exceeded her *Love Actually* attractiveness word quota. (The quota is twenty-seven words before you become Emma Thompson and must be composted.)

Keira Knightley is marrying Chiwetel Ejiofor while wearing some sort of terrible hairy cardigan. In the middle of their wedding, the best man reveals his "big surprise" (and no, it's not his penis...*kind of*): he arranged for a large choir/marching band flash mob to interrupt the ceremony that Knightley and Ejiofor carefully, painstakingly planned to celebrate their love in order to undermine their relationship and attempt to steal the bride for his own ON HER WEDDING DAY.

HEY. DUDE. YOU'RE A DICK. THIS ISN'T ROMANCE, IT'S CRIME.

Also, why did nobody notice those seventeen strangers with saxophones taking up half the audience? Fuck these people. And fuck Laura Linney for wearing her woolly hat during a fucking wedding ceremony in a fucking church.

Meanwhile, on the set of a movie that is supposedly not a porno but also apparently doesn't contain anything other than fucking, Martin Freeman and a blonde lady named Judy are simulating intercourse. The blonde lady has to take her top off so that Tony, who is also Colin's best friend, can light her nipples. (This is one of those movies where you're supposed to be impressed that the characters know each other.)

By the way, wasn't that guy JUST AT A WEDDING!? Like, twelve seconds ago?

Yep! There he was! Wearing a different outfit. Twelve seconds ago. Hanging out with Colin backstage at the Knightley-Ejiofor nuptials because Colin is both a sandwich deliveryman *and* a caterer. This is either horrible editing or a deliberate prank to make white people feel like they can't tell Black people apart.

Also, is there only one building in London? Is that what's going on? WHY ARE THE WEDDING AND THE FUNERAL AND THE PORNO ALL IN THE SAME WEIRD MILLIONAIRE CHURCH?

Anyway, then Tony asks Martin Freeman to massage Judy's breasts. "For the lighting."

Right.

Alan Rickman calls his employee Laura Linney into his office to talk about whether or not she "loves" her coworker Karl. Because apparently she's just constantly sitting around staring at Karl behind a veil of silent darkness because *everyone in this movie is a fucking creep.*

RUN LIKE THE WIND, KARL. RUN AND NEVER LOOK BACK.

Alan Rickman tells Laura Linney that "the time has come to do something about it." Like touch his genitals in the break room, I guess. Um, sorry, WHAT KIND OF BUSINESS MEETING IS THIS? Was the working title of this shit *Hostile Work Environment: The Movie?*

In keeping with that theme, Alan Rickman's secretary is just constantly pointing at her vagina and licking her own face like she's a porno actress who forgot she was doing a mainstream movie. Or, more accurately, like the *character* is a porno actress who forgot she was working in a real office. I don't mean that there's anything wrong with porno actresses, or that the actress who plays Alan Rickman's secretary is doing a bad actress job, I mean that *LOVE ACTUALLY* SEES NO PROBLEM WITH TREATING ITS FEMALE CHARACTERS LIKE GIANT BIPEDAL VAGINAS IN SWEATER VESTS.

(Also, she's *still* looking for a venue for the holiday party and it's only *three weeks before Christmas*!?!?! This is why you shouldn't hire any non-sentient organ to do clerical work.)

Anyway, the flirtation is a prob because Alan Rickman is married to Emma Thompson, but don't worry—she wears foundation garments and talks too much (see above) and therefore deserves to die alone with nothing but Joni Mitchell for comfort.

Laura Linney, the only other female character with some semblance of an inner life, meets a similar fate.

This is a movie made for women by a man.

Back at Hugh Grant's office, where Hugh Grant does his man-politics, Hugh Grant is like, "Who do you have to screw around here to get a cup of tea and a chocolate biscuit?" Then Natalie walks in with a cup of tea and a chocolate biscuit.

Her. That woman. That's what you have to screw.

Liam Neeson doesn't know what to do because his eleven-year-old stepkid (whose MOM JUST DIED) seems to sit around in his room being sad a lot (!?!!?!?!?). Emma Thompson drops by to cheer him up with her own signature combo of product placement, synth strings, and being a fucking asshole for no reason.

From now on, every time I see a box of Frosted Flakes, I will think of Liam Neeson crying.

To be perfectly honest, Liam Neeson is really acting the hell out of this movie.

Okay, turns out, the kid—whose name is Sam and who's played by Jojen Reed from *Game of Thrones* (what the fuck was the point of that character, BY THE WAY????? And I read the books!)—is "in love" with a girl named Joanna (which is his dead mom's name, which the movie could have just *not done*!!!!!!!!!), but she doesn't know he exists. Probably because he's been hanging out with the men of *Love Actually* too much, so he just sits around feeling sorry for himself instead of talking to her like a human being.

When Sam tells Liam Neeson that's why he's depressed, Liam Neeson laughs in his face. Then they come up with nine hundred different strategies to "make" Joanna fall in love with him. Weirdly, none of the strategies are "Say hi to her." Also not considered: "You're eleven. Calm down, baby boy."

(Ugh, Jojen, just put this movie out of its misery with your frog spear already.)

Hugh Grant offers to have Natalie's ex-boyfriend murdered for telling her that her thighs are too large—which is an especially *adorable flirtation* when you consider that he's a major world leader whose office has historically colonized half the world and bombed and murdered countless actual human beings. BUT IT'S

PRETTY FUNNY IN THIS CONTEXT BECAUSE HE WANTS
TO GET SOME HOT SNATCH.

Then he looks up at a photograph of Margaret Thatcher and
calls her a "saucy minx."

Hey, idea: I'm no Thatcher stan, but could someone respect a
woman for *one second* in this movie? Or could we at least confine
the misogyny to women who are actual characters in the film?

Okay. Seriously. Is this Colin Firth story line actually about
human trafficking? Colin Firth shows up in France and this
90 Day Fiancé just gets dropped off at his house and he "falls
in love with her" even though they cannot communicate and
the only thing he knows about her is that he's really, really
into her butt. But it's "love"! So he just "has" her now! She's
"his"! Colin Firth decided they should be together without ever
saying a single word to each other, *and so that's what happens.*
Congratulations, now you have a weird stranger who lives in
your house and fat-shames you in Portuguese. "Love."

This entire movie is just straight white men acting upon
women that they think they "deserve." This entire movie is just
men doing things!

Also, who writes their novel on loose pages on a typewriter in
an open-air shack next to a pond? Amelia Bedelia?

Billy Bob Thornton, the president of America, comes to visit
Hugh Grant. In the hallway, they run into ~~Natalie~~ Fatalie, and
this exchange occurs:

> **Billy Bob Thornton:** How's your day so far?
> **Natalie:** [Indistinguishable giggle.]
> **Billy Bob Thornton:** Excellent.

First of all, how are you not gonna answer the president of the United States when he asks you how your day's going, Natalie!? Too busy thinking about ham, I bet.

And second of all, once again, IT NEVER FUCKING MATTERS WHAT WOMEN SAY. THE WRITERS LITERALLY JUST TOOK A LINE AWAY FROM A WOMAN AND RE-PLACED IT WITH A NONSENSE SYLLABLE. SHE COULD HAVE ACTUALLY SAID SOMETHING, AND INSTEAD SHE JUST GOES "MEEP MEEP" AND BILLY BOB THORNTON POPS A BONER.

Third of all, it kind of seems like less a depiction of our president and more like Billy Bob Thornton just broke character when that girl walked by.

I find it personally insulting to imply that I belong to a species this simple.

Later, at a press conference, Hugh Grant causes a major international incident because Billy Bob sexually assaulted a property he likes:

> I love that word *relationship*. Covers all manner of sins, doesn't it? I fear that this has become a bad relationship. A relationship based on the president taking exactly what he wants and casually ignoring all those things that really matter to, erm...Britain. We may be a small country, but we're a great one, too. The country of William Shakespeare, Churchill, the Beatles, Sean Connery, Harry Potter. David Beck-ham's right foot. David Beckham's left foot, come to that. And a friend who bullies us is no longer a friend. And since bullies only respond to strength, from now

onward, I will be prepared to be much stronger. And the president should be prepared for that.

HE'S TALKING ABOUT HIS PENIS, YOU GUYS. It might be a small penis, but it wrote Harry Potter.

Everything in this movie is fucking insane. That's not how press conferences work. That's not how diplomacy works. That's not how prime ministers work. NOTHING IS HOW ANY-THING WORKS. That's not how weddings work, that's not how audio recording works, that's not how saxophones work, that's not how hair works, that's not how business meetings work, that's not how art works, that's not how grief works, that's not how primary school Christmas concerts work, that's not how airports work, that's not how music charts work, that's not how fat works, and none of it is how "love" works.

Keira Knightley, wearing an unacceptable hat, goes over to the best man's house to look at his video of her wedding.

Turns out, the wedding video he took is 100 percent close-ups of her face because the dude is a fucking psychopath.

Keira Knightley: They're all of me.
Worst Guy: Yeah.

Yeah, I took it so I could watch it later over and over when I'm alone in my house thinking about your skin.

Instead of calling British 911, *she's flattered.*

Thanks, *Love Actually.* Thank you for telling a generation of men that their intrusiveness and obsessions are "romantic," and that women are secretly flattered no matter what their body language (or mouth!) says.

Was the score to this movie just a page with "doo dee doo dee doo doo dee doo dee doo doo dee doo dee doo doo dee doo dee doo" scribbled all over it?

Hugh Grant decides he needs to fire Natalie because she's 2 tempting 2 believe. Then he has this Actual Conversation with his secretary:

> **Secretary:** The chubby girl?
> **Hugh Grant:** Would we call her chubby?
> **Secretary:** I think there's a pretty sizable ass there, yes, sir. Huge thighs.

Can we not refer to a woman who worked her way up to a job in the prime minister's office as "the chubby girl"? Also, can we fire the entire government for sexual harassment?

Liam Neeson and Jojen Reed relax and watch *Titanic* to regroup because that's something middle-aged men and little kids do together. Jojen is still totally stumped about the best way to force Joanna to love him against her will. I mean, he's tried everything. He tried staring at her, he tried never talking to her, he tried complaining to his dad, he tried watching *Titanic*...seriously, what is it going to TAKE, Joanna!?

Then, light bulb! "There's this big concert at the end of term, and Joanna's in it, and I thought that if I was in the band and played absolutely superbly, there's a chance that she might fall in love with me."

OH MY GOD, OR YOU COULD JUST GO TALK TO HER.

TALK TO HER.

TALK TO HER.

Despite *still* never having had a conversation with him, Laura

Linney finally gets her coworker Karl back to her house for intercourse. They get in the door and go straight to the bed (wouldn't want to wander into the living room and accidentally have a conversation), where we finally find out Laura Linney's TERRIBLE SECRET.

She has a brother.

And he calls sometimes.

To be more specific, Laura Linney has a mentally ill brother who lives in a facility and calls her frequently for reassurance and comfort, and she always takes his calls because she loves him deeply and feels responsible for his well-being now that their parents are dead.

DEAL BREAKER. Karl's out.

I can't believe Laura Linney showed her boobs for this.

Alan Rickman buys a fancy sex necklace for vagina-secretary and Emma Thompson finds it in his pocket and gets all excited and then cries when all she gets for Christmas is a Joni Mitchell CD that I'm sure she already had because she said earlier in the movie that Joni Mitchell is her fucking favorite singer. But yeah, I'm sure you found a SECRET JONI MITCHELL CD she'd never heard of, asshole!

Anyway, I hope Emma Thompson learned her lesson about being a human being made of perishable cells. Guh-ross.

Love Actually puts a lot of stock in the idea that people are either good or bad. People either love or they don't, reciprocate or they don't. The grander the gesture, the greater the crime of not reciprocating. LOVE GOOD. NOT-LOVE BAD. It's a nice fantasy because if, instead, you accept the difficult truth that people are more than just good or bad, then you have to question whether or not happiness really exists. Because if people are more complicated, then happiness must be more complicated, and at that point, is it really happiness?

Oh, god, why am I bothering. Actually.

Liam Neeson tries to explain to Jojen Reed what love is by describing his sex life: "Wanton sex in every room of the house, including yours."

Hey, why are you always talking to that kid about sex like that? Like, get a friend.

That best man guy shows up at Keira Knightley's house and spawns a decade of nice-guy emotional manipulation reframed as "romance." And Keira Knightley *fucking kisses him* for it.

I know it's early, but I'm calling it. Artistic low point of the twenty-first century.

Meanwhile, Hugh Grant realizes he should never have fired Natalie for having too much juice in the caboose (MAINLY BECAUSE THAT IS ILLEGAL), and so it's grand gesture time!!! He hops in the misuse-of-government-funds-mobile and has the driver take him to Natalie's street, where he *knocks on every door looking for her*, because apparently the UK government does not keep records of the contact information of recent employees AND ALSO THE PRIME MINISTER DOES NOT HAVE A CELL PHONE.

When Hugh Grant finally tracks Natalie down, her horrible family bullies him into accompanying them to the school Christmas play, but not before Natalie's dad calls her "Plumpy" in front of the prime minister.

They begin to profess their "love" for one another in the car but don't get very far because there's a kid dressed as a papier-mâché octopus crammed in between them. Thanks for nothing, cock-blocktopus!

The pair sneaks backstage and starts making out during the big finale, only to have their "secret" tryst revealed when the curtain rises and they're kissing in the middle of the set. Hey, prime minister, we all like making out with fat chicks, but WHY DON'T YOU EVER GO TO WORK? DON'T YOU HAVE AN ENGLAND TO RUN?

Colin Firth goes all the way home to London, but as soon as he gets there, he realizes he forgot his Portuguese sex maid on the baggage carousel or something. So he abandons Christmas dinner with his loving family and flies back to France. The one expression of genuine love in this movie and Colin Firth peaces out to go hump a stranger.

He shows up at Aurelia's front door and starts yelling at her father in shitty Portuguese. He's like, "I am here to ask your daughter for her hand in marriage," and the dad is like, "Say what!?" because he thinks Colin Firth means his *other* daughter, who is fat and gross, and that would obviously make no sense because women who are slightly larger than some other women deserve to be in the garbage. Then the dad offers to *pay* Colin Firth to take fat daughter off his hands. Colin Firth is like, "Ew, no. I only want to purchase/marry HOT women I've never spoken to in my life."

Once the truth gets sorted out, fat daughter says, "Father is about to sell Aurelia as a slave to this Englishman."

FIRST SENSIBLE LINE ANYONE'S SAID FOR THIS EN-TIRE MOVIE.

Fat Daughter: You'd better not say yes, Father.
The Dad: Shut up, Miss Dunkin' Donuts 2003.

DAD, I WON A CONTEST. BE HAPPY FOR ME.

Oh, also Jojen Reed has now chased Joanna all the way to the airport, where he's broken through security and is leading agents on a "wacky" chase to the gate. Do I need to mention that this kid is white?

Colin Firth and this entire French village (who, again, apparently *all* speak only Portuguese) finally arrive at the restaurant where Aurelia works. Rumors are running wild among the crowd at this point:

> "Apparently, he is going to kill Aurelia!"
> "Cool!"

GOOD JOKE.

When they get there, Aurelia looks horrified and is like, "What the fuck are you doing at my work!? I don't even know you, dude! Get out of here! Oh my god, I'M TRYING TO RUN A RESTAURANT HERE. GO AWAY, YOU CREEPY ENGLISHMAN."

No. Just kidding. She agrees to marry the guy. Forever. Even though they have never spoken.

In a painfully fitting finale, Colin returns from America with the woman he got, and it's Shannon freaking Elizabeth. He literally brings her back to England with him like an airport souvenir. But don't worry, Tony, HE IMPORTED AN OBJECT WITH NO AGENCY FOR YOU TOO. HERE, PUT YOUR MOUTH ON IT.

That's love, kids.

Oh, wait. Actually, it's shit.

RATING: 0/10 DVDs of *The Fugitive*.

On Marriage

We're taught, from when we are very young, that the ultimate purpose of marriage—the work of love—is to become one of those elderly couples you see in *People* magazine, who met in the one-room schoolhouse when they were eleven, who were each other's first kiss, who stayed true through the war, who never said an unkind word, who died holding hands in their sleep at one hundred. Aren't they sweet? Look at how he looked at her. Look at her little hat.

I already know that I'm not going to die in a bonnet in *People* magazine because I'm nearly forty, and that's not my marriage. I married a difficult, crazy guy. My husband married an anxious, insecure woman. Sometimes our shortcomings rub against each other painfully. Sometimes things get dark—occasionally in an active, explosive way, but more often in a passive, resentful way, where you snap to and realize you haven't really looked at each other in months. He creates chaos. I micromanage. We've both had to forgive each other for a lot of things.

Having been through a real marriage, it's hard for me not to feel like those perfect old dead couples are lying, or in denial, or maybe they just didn't go deep enough, maybe they were always too scared. The truth is that you simply can't make it into adulthood unscathed. And if somehow you did, you wouldn't have the perspective and empathy to properly care for another human being for the rest of both your lives. It's impossible. Everyone's going to have their shit.

My husband and I met when we were twenty-three, became best friends and started dating when we were twenty-nine, and got married when we were thirty-three. We're thirty-eight now, and that means we've seen each other through selfish youth and the onset of back pain and the deaths of parents and the disorienting transition from fun to tired, and somehow we still want to be together. Even in our worst moments, we still crack each other up and hold each other at night.

The true work of love isn't staying together when things are perfect; it's staying together even when things are awful, weathering catastrophic mistakes (within reason) because, well, you decided to, and because you know the potential is as real as the now. It turns your partnership into something that grows instead of something that atrophies. You're promising another person not just passion and love but a safety net, some degree of stability and certainty in a fucking terrible world. You're saying, "I promise I will stay with you even if you suck for a while," an almost narcotic comfort that we all deserve.

I don't dream of dying adorable; I dream of dying calloused and wise, of looking my husband in the eyes and saying, "Remember that thing we almost didn't survive? Aren't you so glad we did?"

At the same time, though.

I cannot fucking imagine.

The look.

On my face.

If my husband came to me and said...

"Honey..."

"Yeah?"

"Honey."

"What is it?"

"Honey, I have something to tell you."

"Just tell me!"

"Honey...I shrunk the kids."

You did *what*???? YOU DID FUCKING WHAT!?!?!?!?!???!??

Imagine the years of frustration. Imagine how much she's already had to forgive to stay in this marriage. How many times she must have needed his help carrying in the groceries, vacuuming the stairs, weeding the flower beds, not to mention the subtler, more invisible tasks that so often fall to women— scheduling, delegating, nurturing, knowing what's done and what needs doing. She probably tried every angle with him: asking, at first, then "joking," scolding, begging.

But no, don't bother Wayne, the genius! Don't ask anything of Wayne, the world's foremost expert in...size science(??)! He's *busy*. He's in his fucking lab, working on his precious *machine*—as though Diane's time isn't innately as valuable as his, her energy just as precious. What about *her* career? What about the untapped greatness that lies inside *her*? What passions did she shove aside to be the caregiver for this gibbering little turkey boy?

And for what? For WHAT??

I'm sure they fought once in a while. I'm sure she'd lose her temper: WHY DO WE EVEN NEED A SHRINK RAY, WAYNE? Seriously, literally, what need does this fill? You're sick, Wayne! Sick! EVERYTHING IS ALREADY THE RIGHT SIZE!

Mostly, though, I'm sure she breathed deeply and smiled, for him, for years, because she loved him, and because she took a vow—and, hey, he forgave her for the way she tended to nag. Night after night, she lost him to the lab, the empty bed cold beside her, but this was his *thing*, and she loved him, and he promised her it would be "worth it."

WELL, GUESS WHAT, WAYNE? IT HAS NOT BEEN WORTH IT.

YOU SHRUNK THE KIDS.

YOU SHRUNK 'EM.

And now, I'm sorry, you want me to what? Climb into this harness so you can dangle me over our lawn with a magnifying glass in hopes of saving our only two living children—whom I fed with my blood and pushed out of my body and WHOM YOU SHRUNK—from being killed by a scorpion?? Why do we even have scorpions in our lawn, Wayne? WHERE THE FUCK DO WE LIVE????

It's survivable, though. Again, this is the work of love. Any good couples therapist will tell you: sometimes the dork you married accidentally shrinks the kids and they get imprisoned in a Lego by a scorpion and their pet ant sacrifices himself to save them and they ride the dog into the house and then your son falls into the Cheerios and your husband almost eats him for breakfast and then your husband reverses the shrink ray and re-biggens them all again and you all eat a big turkey.

She could do it. They could make it.

But now imagine.

Now imagine.

You've gone through the Herculean task of forgiving your husband for all of that. You've healed, slowly, with trepidation but also with grace. You've made it through. You've moved to a new town, had a new baby, found a fresh start. Parts of you are still raw, but you know that forgiveness is growth and those scars will make the pair of you stronger than before. This is your person, and he's worth it, and he's learned.

And then. After all that. Just three years later. Only three! Your husband comes to you.

Again.

"Honey."

"Yeah?"

"Honey."

" . . . "

"I blew up the baby."

RATING: 3 / 10 DVDs of *The Fugitive*.

Dude, You Gotta Stop Listening to Your Mom

We open with a feather, which is a metaphor. You see, because it's white, like Tom Hanks, and you want it to stay away from you, like the Vietnam War. Also this feather shot JFK.

After falling off a disgusting bird somewhere, the feather floats over and lands on Tom Hanks's foot. Tom Hanks plays Forrest Gump, our hero, currently waiting for the bus with childlike wonder and also bothering this elderly woman who is just trying to live. Gump picks up the feather (UGH, DON'T TOUCH IT) and presses it between the pages of *Curious George*, his favorite book. Congrats. Now your suitcase has bird mites.

"Hello!" Gump says to the lady. "My name's Forrest. Forrest Gump. You want a chock-lit? I could eat about a million of these. My momma always said life is like a box of chock-lits. You never know what you're gonna get." I mean, you mostly know. They write it on the lid.

Then the lady tells Gump that her feet hurt and she JUST WANTS TO GO HOME, so, naturally, he launches into his entire life story.

Small Gump goes to the doctor with his mom (Sally Field, who apparently gave birth to him when she was ten) to get fitted with some leg braces because "his back's as crooked as a politician." Gump reminisces about his ancestral namesake, General Nathan Bedford Forrest, who was the first Grand Wizard of the Ku Klux Klan. Fortunately, Gump, much like that filthy feather, is too pure to understand what racism is, so he thinks that the Klan was a sort of slumber party club where "they'd even put bedsheets on they horses and ride around."

Now, I guess that little rhetorical loophole (which serves the twofold goals of emphasizing Gump's naivete and keeping this feel-good movie *max digestible*) is better than just *not* addressing how fucking racist Alabama was in the 1950s, but I can't help feeling like Gump was AGGRESSIVELY failed by the system. Like, he's no brainiac, but he's capable of understanding basic concepts! If he can follow the rules of Ping-Pong to the letter, he can grasp the idea that some white people think they're better than Black people. Instead, apparently everyone just tapped out hard on Forrest's education, like, "Oh, he's a little slow. Let's NEVER TELL HIM ANYTHING."

Then, the worst character from *Lost* (FUCKING BERNARD) shows up (WILL YOU NEVER LEAVE ME BE, FELL GHOUL?) and tells Sally Field that if she wants Gump to go to his school, she's going to have to build a giant SOS sign out of rocks...*IN HIS PANTS.*

Actually, the interaction goes like this:

Bernard: Is there a Mr. Gump, Mrs. Gump?
Sally Field: He's on vacation.
Bernard: [SEXUAL GRUNTING THAT WILL HAUNT LINDY WEST TO THE GRAVE]

35

Later, Forrest is like, "Mom, what's 'vacation' mean? Where Daddy went?" and Sally Field goes, "Vacation's where you go somewhere and you don't ever come back."

Again. Um. Respectfully, maybe the issue here isn't that Forrest is a bumbling simpleton, it's that his mom keeps telling him that life is chocolate and vacation means that you never come back??? Maybe he's just an average dude who's spent his whole life being lied to by freaks about the definitions of basic words.

On the first day of school, Gump meets his school bus driver:

> **Gump:** Mama said not to be taking rides from strangers.
> **Bus Driver:** This is the bus to school.
> **Gump:** I'm Forrest, Forrest Gump.
> **Bus Driver:** I'm Dorothy Harris.
> **Gump:** Well, now we ain't strangers anymore. [gets on bus]

I think I see a couple of holes in your security system there, Mrs. Gump, but okeydokey.

Once aboard the school bus, Gump becomes acquainted with a great Southern tradition: white people being territorial about bus seats. "This seeeyit's taayyykuuhn." "Cayn't sit heeeeyuuuhhhhh." But like a bolt from the heavens, Jennay appears with a fateful scooch. She lets Forrest sit by her, and, kicking off their "adorable" decades-long abuse pattern of Jennay being a complete dickhead and Forrest accepting it because he feels like he has no other options, she immediately goes, "Are you stupid or something?"

"Mama says stupid is as stupid does."

YO. GUMP. WHAT does that mean.

Dude, you *gotta* stop listening to your mom.

One day, some mean kids on bikes start throwing rocks at Gump because of his leg braces, so Jennay's like, "Run, Forrest! Ruuuuuuunnn!!!" (The fact that this took off as a catchphrase means we should all be in prison.) Forrest runs so hard that his LEGS EXPLODE and his leg braces scatter all over the road, which I guess is supposed to be triumphant even though I'm pretty sure those things are expensive and it's not like Mrs. Gump is flush with leg-brace cash (or, as she calls it, "green chocolate").

"From that day on," Gump says, "if I was going somewhere, I was running."

Then miniature Forrest and Jennay shape-shift into Tom Hanks and Robin Wright, and then those same shithead kids come to throw rocks at Forrest again, only their bikes have shape-shifted into a truck!!! So Jennay's like, "Run, Forrest, ruuuuuuuuuuun!" again, and I guess you're supposed to be like "CLAP CLAP CLAP CLAP CLAP CLAP OH HO HO A PHRASE I HAVE HEARD BEFORE! DEE-LIGHTFUL!!!"

Forrest run-Forrest-runs right through a college football game and the football coaches are like, "Gwuuuuuhhhhhh!???!!?!?!" and they hire him to play football for their college even though he is clearly forty-five years old. There's a brief Mr. Ernst cameo, Forrest invents desegregation, and then Forrest uses punching to save Jennay from intercourse. Gump: The College Years.

Jennay takes Forrest to her dorm room for sexual gratitude and is like, "I want to be famous. I want to be a singer like Joan Baez." And Forrest is like, "Is Joan Baez a kind of chock-lit?" And then Jennay's like, CHECK OUT THESE CANS, and Forrest loses consciousness due to the cans (and probably control of his bladder on Jennay's bed if we're being honest?).

Speaking of bladders, Forrest gets to meet JFK because he's so good at football-running, and tells the president that he is full up with urine. "Sometime later," Gump says, "for no particular reason, somebody shot that nice young president when he was riding in his car."

HOW DID YOU GRADUATE FROM COLLEGE? Also, could somebody answer, like, ONE of Forrest's questions? *You're a college.*

Then Gump joins the army, but on the army bus, eh-vuh-rayyee see-yuhht's tayyy-kuhhhh UH-GEEEEE-YIN!!!!! That's when Gump meets Bubba. Literally the only thing Bubba does is list different shrimp preparations, which Forrest interprets as "best friendship."

One day, in the army, someone throws a dirty magazine at Forrest and goes, "Hey, Gump! Get a load of the tits on her!"

Gump gets a load.

OH NO! IT'S JENNAY! THOSE ARE JENNAY'S TITS UPON WHICH GUMP IS GETTING A LOAD!!!

Clearly, Jennay needs Forrest's help. He finds her doing naked Joan Baez at a strip club, which is not going over that well because the patrons came to get a load of the tits on her, not listen to mediocre folk covers. So Forrest punches everyone and Jennay is, again, a real dick about it. "You can't keep doing this, Forrest. You can't keep trying to rescue me all the time."

Then Forrest is like, "Say bye-bye, Jennay. They sending me to Vietnam. It's this whole other country." And Jennay is like, awwww, bye!

So Forrest goes to Vietnam. Right away, Gump and Bubba meet Lieutenant Dan "The Toolman" Taylor, an irascible shithead who will literally follow Gump around being awful until death. Lieutenant Dan tells Bubba not to get his lip caught on a trip wire, which is racist. Then he delivers his signature Lieutenant Dan socks lecture. LIEUTENANT DAN LOVES SOCKS. This becomes something of a tragic irony later.

The only thing Lieutenant Dan loves more than socks is getting blown up in a war. "Somebody in his family had fought and died in every single American war. I guess you could say he had a lot to live up to." (Again, I kind of feel like Forrest's problem isn't that he's stupid, it's that *literally everyone he ever meets is a fucking weirdo who makes no sense.*)

One day, everybody blows up, and Forrest finds Bubba dying in the jungle.

> **Bubba:** Forrest. I got one last thing to say.
> **Forrest:** What is it, Bubba?
> **Bubba:** I forgot...shrimp...ceviche.
> **Forrest:** Bubba, please don't die!
> **Bubba:** Camarones...del...diablo.

Then Forrest goes, "Bubba was going to be a shrimpin' boat captain, but instead he died right there by that river in Vietnam," and if you claim you didn't squeeze out at least ONE TEAR at that moment, then you're a lying sack of shrimp! Sorry!!!

Gump gets shot in the butt while rescuing all his army friends from the exploding jungle, so he gets to go live in the hospital and eat ice cream 24-7. Turns out, Lieutenant Dan is in the bed next to him! ("FUUUUUUUUUUUUUUCK!!!"—Lieutenant Dan.) Lieutenant Dan may have lost his legs, but he didn't lose his horrible attitude! He mostly hangs around and verbally abuses Forrest for being an eternally optimistic font of pure joy.

One day, Jennay sends back all the letters Gump wrote her

from Vietnam in one huge bundle. Like, Jennay, you didn't need to SEND THEM BACK. You could have just thrown them in the garbage. You literally went to extra effort just to be a dickhead. Jennay sucks.

Gump picks up Ping-Pong while trying to kill time in the hospital, and it turns out he is a Ping-Pong wizard. Lieutenant Dan is so proud of Gump's Pong skills that he throws him out of bed in the middle of the night to scream in his face about how much he wants to die. And it's all Gump's fault: "You cheated me! I had a destiny. I was supposed to die in the field, with honor."

"This movie's kinda weird."—my kid.

Gump wins the Medal of Honor, affording him the opportunity to show Lyndon Johnson his ass wound. Because talking to American presidents about his genitals[2] is *kind* of his thing.

Then Gump accidentally wanders into an anti-war rally on the Mall in Washington, and Jennay is at the protest OF COURSE and she's like, "Forrest! Forrest!" and he's like, "Jennay!" and they run out into that stank duck pond and hug. Then Jennay takes Gump to a Black Panther meeting, where her boyfriend Wesley (DIFFERENT WESLEY) slaps her in the face for no reason, so Gump is like GUUUUUUMP ATTAAAACK and punches him. Wesley explains that it's actually Lyndon Johnson's fault that he is violent toward women, so Jennay forgives him and goes off with him in a bus.

Forrest becomes an incredibly famous international Ping-Pong star (yes, a thing, I'm sure) and goes on Dick Cavett, where he meets John Lennon.

---

2   Butts are genitals! Change my mind!!!

Gump: In the land of China, people hardly got nothing at all.

Lennon: No possessions?

Gump: And in China, they never go to church.

Lennon: No religion too?

Cavett: Wow, hard to imagine.

Lennon: Well, it's easy if you try, Dick.

This is the most terrible scene ever to appear in any film.

Gump reunites with Lieutenant Dan and vows to use his Ping-Pong endorsement money to fulfill Bubba's dream of being a shrimp boat captain. Lieutenant Dan, for some reason, is EXTREMELY SKEPTICAL that this dude who's already met three presidents, won a Congressional Medal of Honor, wrote John Lennon's "Imagine," blew the whistle on Watergate, and made tens of thousands of dollars PLAYING PING-PONG could possibly achieve the famously insurmountable dream of buying a medium-size boat in Alabama and riding around on it looking for shrimp. "If you're ever a shrimp boat captain, that's the day I'm an astronaut."

DUDE. HE IS THE MOST SUCCESSFUL MAN IN THE WORLD.

Meanwhile, Jennay is off somewhere having a shitty vibe because of the '70s.

So, Gump moves back to Alabama to do the shrimp-boat thing, but it turns out that catching shrimp is his only weakness. He fucking sucks at it. He mostly catches garbage. But then, one day, there's Lieutenant Dan sitting on the dock! He wants to join the shrimpin' crew! Gump gets so excited that he jumps from the helm into the water, allowing the boat to run rogue and destroy the entire marina. This is never spoken of again.

Lieutenant Dan doesn't turn out to be much help with catching shrimp, so Gump starts going to church every Sunday while Lieutenant Dan sits in the back glaring at people and drinking whiskey. Then, one day, Gump's prayers are answered! An ENORMOUS HURRICANE comes and destroys the entire Louisiana shrimping industry!!!!! EXCEPT FOR THEIR BOAT!

YAY! YAY! YAY FOR IMPOVERISHED BLACK PEOPLE WHOSE HOMES, LIVELIHOODS, AND FUTURES HAVE BEEN OBLITERATED BECAUSE NOW THESE TWO RANDOM WHITE DUDES WHO ARE *LITERALLY JUST DOING THIS AS A HOBBY* CAN BECOME FUCKING MILLIONAIRES! YAAAAAAAYYYYY!!!

Then Lieutenant Dan finally becomes nice and thanks Forrest for saving him from blowing up to death in Vietnam. Then Forrest gets a call that his mom is dying, so he swims home. Then she dies. Then Lieutenant Dan invests the Bubba Gump Shrimp money in Apple Computers, so Forrest is able to buy his church a funky new bass player and Bubba's mom gets a white slave. Then Jennay comes home to visit, buys him new shoes, does sex with him, and then leaves again. So Forrest runs back and forth across the country a few times.

And then we're caught up!!! We're back on the bus bench! Forrest is like, "Yep, I got this letter that I should come visit Jennay, so I'm on my way to her apartment," and the people on the bench are like, "FUCKING FINALLY, MY FAMILY THINKS I'M DEAD," and then some old lady gives him directions and it's denouement o'clock.

He shows up at Jennay's house and she introduces him to her new kid.

Jennay: His name's Forrest.

Forrest: Like me!

Jennay: I named him after his daddy.

Forrest: He got a daddy named Forrest too?

Jennay: You're his daddy, Forrest.

Not the coolest way to deliver that news, but I get it. You're Jennay.

They get married and she wears the worst wedding dress I've ever seen and she tells Forrest she has HIV. But they don't say HIV. They just say "a virus."

And then they have this Meaningful Conversation about life's majesty:

Forrest: And then, in the desert, when the sun comes up, I couldn't tell where heaven stopped and the earth began. It was so beautiful.

Jennay: I wish I could have been there with you.

Forrest: You were. [But you were really high and you don't remember.]

Then Jennay dies and turns into a feather and THE WHOLE MOVIE STARTS OVER AGAIN FROM THE BEGINNING.

RATING: 5 / 10 DVDs of *The Fugitive*.

Literally a Bird's Diary

W e open at some kind of fancy old folks' convalescence palace. "Simple guy" James Garner shows up to read out loud to senile silver fox Gena Rowlands, but Gena Rowlands's nurse is like, "She's really not into it today. Thanks anyway." Kicking off a trend of men-Red-Rovering-through-women's-boundaries-like-Ram-Man-but-horny that will come to define the entire film, James Garner is like, "SUCKS 2 SUCK," and barges in there anyway. He begins reading some of his Ryan Gosling fanfic out of *a notebook* (that's a reference), and it goes a little something like this:

It's June 6, 1940, in Seabrook Island, South Carolina, and Ryan Gosling is at a carnival. Suddenly, he spots a sexy babe on the bumper cars and his nostrils flare so wide you can see his brain.

She's perfect! She's so beautiful! She's said, like, four syllables so far and none of them have been just a faucet of hot drool! She probably has other qualities that are also valuable in a woman and I will get back to you ASAP as soon as I think of any! He has got to have her. (Literally. He literally says, "When I see something that I like, I gotta have it.") Unfortunately, the lady—Rachel McAdams—turns out to be a human being, kind of, so she's like, "Get away from me, weirdly aggressive nostril man."

Goz, like all red-blooded Real American alpha males, is allergic to the Friendzone, so he comes up with a charming scheme to win McAdams over. Approach #47, the Untreated Personality Disorder Gambit: he simply climbs on to the spokes of a moving Ferris wheel and threatens to throw himself into the deadly, grinding machinery unless she agrees to go on a date with him! Cute!!! Instead of fucking screaming in terror at the unhinged stranger coercing her into touching his penis by blaming her for his imminent gory public suicide (THE ULTIMATE NEG) and then waiting for the police to arrive after which Gosling can hopefully get the psychiatric and emotional help he needs, Rachel McAdams is like, "Okeydokey! But I'm getting an appeteaser AND an entree!!!"

Much like *Love Actually*, this is a movie made for women by a man.

Thanks, men.

For their big first date, Goz knows he needs to turn the romance up a notch, but he *kind* of shot his wad at the carnival. Finally, though, he gets it. What's hotter than a suicide? How about a *double suicide*? (Math: it is literally TWICE AS HOT!)

"Just relax," he says as he leads McAdams out into the middle of a main thoroughfare. "You need to learn how to trust." Then he has her lie down next to him in the street, underneath the traffic light. He points up. At the light. That's the date. Lie in the crosswalk and look at the traffic light.

Now, I don't mean to get all Microsoft Encarta on you, Goz, but I'm pretty sure the word you're looking for here isn't *trust*, it's *hope*. We *trust* that pedestrians and cars will obey the traffic laws designed to keep everyone safe, such as "don't drive on the sidewalk" and "don't fucking take a nap in the middle of the fucking street because that's where the fucking cars go." And we *hope* that creepy jackasses don't do reckless shit to impress their girlfriends, such as placing their vulnerable skulls in the paths of oncoming Chryslers whose drivers are just trying to get home from the factory without squishing any teenage brains. Also, you know you can see the traffic lights from the sidewalk, right? It is arguably a *better angle*. COULD YOU PLEASE GO OVER THE COST-BENEFIT ANALYSIS OF THIS ACTIVITY ONE MORE TIME.

But apparently Gosling's 'stincts are right on because McAdams is so exhilarated by almost getting run over that she presses her boday against his in a sensual dance.

"BLAH BLAH BLAH," James Garner cuts in, "BLAH BLAH BLAH BLAH BLAH."

Oh, cool, this part's back. Old Guy Reads Out Loud: The Movie.

"It was an improbable romance," James Garner Garn-splains. Yes. How can a beautiful white woman ever be with a beautiful white man!?!??!?! (Speaking of white people, BTW, this movie would be a lot less sympathetic if they made the characters as racist as those people would have been IRL. Kudos on totally whitewashing this region and time period while scoring it mostly with music by Black artists! Do you know how hard it is to give a shit about Ryan Gosling's teenage crush while listening to Billie Holiday?)

Next, this actual dialogue happens:

> **McAdams:** You think in another life I coulda been a bird?
>
> **Goz:** What do you mean?
>
> **McAdams:** CAW CAW SAY I'M A BIRD!!! SAY IT!
>
> **Goz:** You're a bird.
>
> **McAdams:** Now say you're a bird too.
>
> **Goz:** If you're a bird, I'm a bird.

Is this screenplay literally a bird's diary?

McAdams makes Goz go to a rich-people dinner so she can introduce him to her dad's mustache. Some fancy-lad asks Goz how much money he makes at the dirty skritchy poor-hole where he works, and Goz, in that horrible poor way he has, is like, "Forty cents an hour!" (Then McAdams's mom is like POOOOOOOOOR RAAAAAAAAAAGE!!! and nickels shoot out of her ears on jets of steam.)

After dinner, Goz takes McAdams to a haunted house in the woods and goes, "It's time." Now I'm going to fuck you on a ghost. But before they get down to it, McAdams insists on talking about shutters for an hour because women love interior design, until he promises to build her a mansion LITERALLY COVERED IN SHUTTERS so she'll shut up. Then she's like, "OKAY, DO ME ON THIS DERELICT MOUSE PIANO!"

(Question: In olden times, how did they even know how to do it? Like, before sex ed, when everything was supposed to be a secret? It's not like now, when a man Gosling's age would have watched literally ten thousand hours of instructional video by this point [porno]. Vintage intercourse must have been THE DRYEST WORST.)

McAdams takes her shirt off and Gosling's like, "I knew you had boobs. I knew all along."

Then Gosling takes his pants off and is like, "And yes. I have one. One penis."

Then McAdams takes off her underpants and is like, "Well, are you ready for this? My lower part?"

But then, right at penetration o'clock, Kevin Connolly busts in all, "YOU GOTTA PUT IT AWAY, MAN! HER PARENTS CALLED THE SEX COPS!!!"

So they all get hauled back to the McAdams plantation for a lecture about why rich penises are better than poor penises, and Mom gets major harsh: "He's a nice boy, but he is TRASH TRASH TRASH NOT FOR YOU" (that is a real sentence, not a sentence I made up for a joke). Goz runs outside all wounded-masculine and tells McAdams that they can't be together because he knows he'll NEVER BE ABLE TO BUY HER THE SHUT-TERS SHE DESERVES, so McAdams gets all defensive and *Harry and the Hendersons*es him and he runs away to cry in his swamp until death. Romance is abolished.

McAdams moves to New York to go to Sarah Lawrence, and Gosling moves to Atlanta to go to army. He writes her one letter every day for a year ("That's 365 letters"—thanks, movie), but little does he know, Mother McAdams is squirreling all of his letters away in her secret hex box lined with poor-people skin! Apparently, McAdams is incapable of looking up Gosling's address and sending *him* a letter, which would be a fucking irritating plot hole except I'm not sure if you can make a hole in a perpetual sucking void.

At this point, James Garner pipes up to say, "If summer romances have one thing in common, it's that they're shooting stars!" Let me stop you there. Because they have at least two things in common right up front, which are 1) they're romances . . . 2) that happen in the summer. Who are you, Forrest Gump's mom?

Meanwhile, in World War II, Kevin Connolly dies. Like, four seconds after he gets there. It is not a good part of the movie, as parts of movies go.

McAdams goes to work at a hospital for wounded soldiers. "To her," Garner intones, "the broken men with shattered bodies who filled the ward were all [Goz], or someone who fought beside him in the jungle or the frozen snow-swept road." YOU GUYS. FOR FUCK'S SAKE. SHE DOESN'T EVEN KNOW HE'S IN THE ARMY. SHE HASN'T GOTTEN ANY OF HIS 365 BORING LETTERS, REMEMBER? THIS NOT-GETTING-THE-LETTERS MIX-'EM-UP IS, LIKE, THE DETAIL THAT YOUR WHOLE MOVIE HINGES ON.

One of her patients, James Marsden, starts hitting on her at work even though he's heavily medicated, they've never had a real conversation, and she's just trying to do her fucking job without some dude in a full-body cast constantly pointing at his papier-mâché boner. After he recovers, he tracks her down at her school and is like, "Look! I got my cast off! [WINK] Let's date!" And so they do. And then he proposes. So she says yes. Because why not.

Yo, does this really have to be McAdams's life? Just endlessly stalked and followed and watched and obsessed over by every man she ever meets? And then she has to say, "Thank you," and call it "love"?

This sucks!

Gosling comes home from the war and—being the king of

healthy impulses—decides to buy that pile of rotten boards where he almost put it in McAdams all those years earlier and fix it up. PRETTY sure that guy's a teardown, but okay, buddy.

Goz spends all of his time obsessively working on the house. One time he sees McAdams out of the bus window and chases her down the street, only to discover her making out with Marsden in a cafe. So instead of talking to her or being normal, he just breathes heavily behind a bush and then goes home and has cry-sex with a war widow whom he's TOO BROKEN TO LOVE. (Note to my partner: if I ever get dementia, and you show up to read to me from your diary every fucking day, feel free to leave out the part where you bang the war widow.)

One day, McAdams is trying on literally the world's ugliest harlequin jester vampire wedding sack when she spots a photo of Gosling and his stupid house in the newspaper.

She rushes into Marsden's office and is like, "Listen. Bro. I have to go on a trip that definitely has 100 percent absolutely zero to do with Ryan Gosling's magnificent penis. Also, I never paint anymore, which apparently is a beloved hobby of mine that has barely been mentioned once in this entire film but is now a major emotional sticking point. The fact that I've quit painting is somehow your Ryan Gosling's penis. I MEAN FAULT."

She goes to Ryan Gosling's house and immediately drives her car through his fence like a classic woman.

Then we have to spend twenty minutes watching footage from James Garner's actual doctor's appointment. The doctor asks James Garner why he spends so much time reading out loud to Gena Rowlands. "Science only takes you so far," Garner says. "And then comes God." I wonder if there are audience members, at this point in the movie, who are still wondering how the

Garner/Rowlands story line relates to the Gosling/McAdams story line. If so, I think those people should have to go live on an island and weave their own shoes. Like, I find it hard to believe that *Gena Rowlands the character* didn't see where this was going by minute three.

Gosling and McAdams have dinner and then he asks her to come back in the morning. "There's something I'd like to show you."

IT'S MY PENIS. It's always been my penis.

Meanwhile, James Garner's kids show up at the old folks' home and are like, "Daaaaaad, stop reading your notebook to this old lady over and over. She doesn't even like you." But Garner refuses: "That's my sweetheart in there. This is my home now. Your mother is my home." I live in your mom. I'll never forget the first time I "lived" in your mom. Here's a fucking four-hour movie about it.

In the morning, Marsden calls McAdams's hotel room and she's like, OH GAH GOO GOO GAR GAR NO NOTH-ING'S WRONG I'M NOT BEING WEIRD YOU'RE THE ONE BEING WEIRD, and then goes back to Gosling's house for her "surprise." He rows her out into this goose-infested swamp (the part this movie leaves out is that geese are rank, shit-covered, hissing demons, but I guess it's okay because they are his kin), even though he knows it's about to start pouring down rain *and says so before they get in the boat.*

When it starts raining, both of them are like, "HAHAHAHA-HAHAHAHAHA!"

OH MY GOD, THE RAIN TOLD THE FUNNIEST JOKE.

And then she's like, why didn't you write me, and he's like, I wrote you 365 letters, and she's like, oh okay I forgive you, and they lick each other's faces, and geese are watching, which is weird because one of those is his mom, and then it's time for penis-in-vagina (for best results, as you watch the sex scene, remember that James Garner is describing it all to an old lady with dementia). In the morning, McAdams wakes up to a special gift from Gosling. He got her some painting stuff!!! Because he's not like James Marsden, who made PAINTING ILLEGAL.

Mom shows up and warns them that Marsden is coming, and then drives McAdams over to the quarry and is like, "See that dirty laborer? I used to love him, but I abandoned him because I'm a classist shithead who loved shutters. JUST LIKE YOU. So now I just come here sometimes and stare at him and masturbate in my car. Just kidding, I am repressed." Then she finally hands over all the letters she intercepted from Gosling, and literally says—as far as I can discern—"I've been keeping these inside my ball bag for seven years."

I've been keeping these inside my ball bag for seven years. I'VE BEEN KEEPING THESE INSIDE MY BALL BAG FOR SEVEN YEARS.

I was confused at first, but later I googled it and found out that "ball bag" was 1940s Southern slang for nutsack.

Then Gosling and McAdams get in one last fight because this movie needed to be longer, and he tells her that she's "a pain in the ass 99 percent of the time." That means that he loves her approximately three and a half days per year. The rest of the time she makes him feel like a spear or dagger is literally stabbing him in his asshole.

So McAdams is like, "I have to go." (Whispering: "Number two.")

Feeling conflicted, she goes to hang out with Marsden, hoping that it'll help her make up her mind. Marsden tells her, "In spite of everything, I love you," which is almost as hot a pickup line as "You are a pain in the ass 99 percent of the time." HOW WILL SHE CHOOSE BETWEEN THESE CASANOVAS? WAS THIS DIALOGUE WRITTEN BY MYSTERY?

Uuuuuuuugh, anyway, she chooses Gosling, OF COURSE, and then they animorph into James Garner and Gena Rowlands, and then James Garner's magic notebook cures Gena Rowlands's dementia for five minutes—you know, like medical science—but every time the skeptical doctor comes in, she goes back to being senile again because she's the Michigan J. Frog of dementia, and then we find out that the title of the notebook is *The Story of Our Lives* (HEY, WHY NOT JUST CALL IT *BOOK*), and it turns out the notebook was Tom Riddle's diary all along, and then Gena Rowlands is like, "Do you think we could just die together real quick?" and he's like, "Yeah, prolly," so then they do. Cause of death: felt like it. Cause of death: hospital food, amirite? Cause of death: basilisk.

And that's how Ryan Gosling got laid one time.

RATING: 3/10 DVDs of *The Fugitive*.

Harry Plot Hole

I would call myself a so-so Harry Potter freak. I couldn't recite the names of everyone on the Slytherin Quidditch team from a random Slytherin vs. Ravenclaw match on page 217 in book three (trust me, SOME KIDS CAN), but I can tell you the wizard who thought the world was ready for a cheese cauldron (Humphrey Belcher), the general gist of Gamp's Law of Elemental Transfiguration (you can't turn poop into food), and the best kiss Ron ever had (Auntie Muriel). In other words, I could not beat your niece at a Harry Potter trivia pub quiz, but I could maybe beat you. Relative to other Harry Potter people, I'm in it medium.

As it is for, I assume, plenty of other adults with emotional problems, Harry Potter is a reliable security blanket for me—during challenging periods in my life, listening to the (Jim Dale) audiobooks has been the only thing that gets me to sleep. It's low-stakes and goofy, but also high-stakes and I care about the characters, plus there's magic. Those are all of my needs.

However, the best thing about Harry Potter, the thing that keeps me hooked year after year, is that the internal logic *barely* hangs together. None of it makes any sense! The best thing about Harry Potter is that I hate it!!!

My best friend and I have a decade-long text thread where we send each other new Harry Potter plot holes we discover (or forget and then remember again) and then become magnificent with rage over each one. And we discover new ones literally every day! If you could run a light bulb on Harry Potter plot holes, we could solve the climate crisis because Harry Potter plot holes are AN INEXHAUSTIBLE RESOURCE.

For starters, because it's at the start of this movie, can we talk about the Deluminator? Both the book and movie versions of *Harry Potter and the Sorcerer's Stone* open with Dumbledore clicking his "put-outer" and sucking up all the streetlights on Privet Drive so Hagrid can land his flying motorcycle. First of all, how useful is this? How often do you specifically need to put out ten to twelve Muggle streetlights? Often enough that you needed to make a dedicated invention for it? *A magic wand isn't enough?* And who fabricated the Deluminator? House elf slave labor? Or was Dumbledore up in his office—right in the middle of Voldemort's rise to power—hunched over a soldering iron(?) fashioning a tiny hinge for his magic cigarette lighter that sucks up Muggle light-balls? Mightn't his time have been better spent making, I don't know, A GUN? Also, if Dumbledore forgets to put the light-balls back in the lamps, how do the Muggles get the lights back on? Does it work to just change the bulbs? Is he stealing the electricity? Or the concept of light itself?

(Then, in book seven, suddenly the Deluminator is also...a radio? That tells you when your friends are talking shit about you and kind of leads you to them anywhere in England? So, it sucks up balls of light and also helps you find your friends' tent. HOW IS THAT AN INVENTION???? That's like if I went on *Shark Tank* with a shoe that was also a dialysis machine, but I didn't tell Mark Cuban about the dialysis thing until we'd already been in the shoe business for like twenty years. Why????????? People's kidneys are failing, man!!!!!)

Anyway, Dumbledore walks past a cat sitting on the curb, just a regular cat like you might see in a neighborhood. WRONG! IT'S AN OLD HUMAN WOMAN.

Why is it that *at no point* in this entire book and/or film series does Professor McGonagall use her turn-into-a-cat power for anything helpful? She never uses it to sneak into the Ministry of Magic and eavesdrop, she never uses it to see Voldemort naked, she never uses it to give Lucius Malfoy cat scratch fever of the dick. They say it's excruciatingly difficult to become an animagus and takes years and years of study (except that even flushable wipe Peter Pettigrew figured it out in, like, one year as a teenager, but okay[3]), yet McGonagall uses it *literally exclusively* to blow kids' minds on the first day of Transfiguration class. Ma'am, you are engaged in guerilla warfare against a shadow army of fascists that can do magic. Turn into a cat one time?

It's cute that they try to make pointy wizard hats a workable fashion choice in this first movie and then by number two they're like, "Yeah, this is fucking stupid, no one would wear this, it's so tall, I can't get through a door." The pointy hats are the most implausible thing in the whole series, and

---

3   OHOHOHO, but he had the help of *two other teenagers*!!!!!!! Truly incredible counterargument, Casey Novak.

that includes someone whose last name is Lupin coincidentally getting bit by a werewolf.

Dumbledore and McGonagall arrive at the Dursleys' house where they're about to dump Harry, an infant, for eleven years. McGonagall is like, "Where's the baby?" and Dumbledore is like, "Hagrid is bringing him," and she's like, "Uh, excuse me?" and he's like, "I would trust Hagrid with my life." R U sure? He is the most bumbling person you've ever met!

They leave the baby on the porch in the dark and go back...home? Where do Hogwarts teachers live? Do they have to, like, live in their offices? Are they allowed to get married and have children? Let the teachers live in Hogsmeade, at least! That way the students wouldn't constantly have to see McGonagall in her tartan dressing gown, and the teachers could achieve some work-life balance. Can someone please start unionizing at Hogwarts? I nominate Madam Hooch—she's not busy (how is "occasional referee" a full-time job??????).

Flash-forward eleven years: Harry is now a severely traumatized tween who is forced to live in an airless cupboard and do unpaid domestic labor for his abusive (and worse, FAT) family because Dumbledore, "the only wizard you-know-who was ever afraid of," who *lives in a castle*, thought it was "safer" for Harry there, even though as far as everyone knew at the time Voldemort had exploded. And yeah, I'm aware of the freaking magic power of a mother's love, but couldn't Harry just put the Dursleys' as his registered address and then go "on vacation" to Hogwarts all year? He lives there most of the year anyway! And as far as I can tell, magic is all semantics! It doesn't seem to be a problem when he leaves Privet Drive early to go to the Burrow for the last month of summer holiday every year. And anyway, what about Harry's *emotional* safety?

AAAAAAAAALSOOOOOOOO WHAT THE FUCK HAP-
PENED TO *ALL FOUR* OF HARRY'S GRANDPARENTS? DID
YOU KNOW THAT IF YOU DO THE MATH, LILY AND
JAMES POTTER WERE ONLY TWENTY-ONE WHEN THEY
DIED???? ALL FOUR OF THEIR PARENTS WERE ALREADY
DEAD!?!?!? DO YOU KNOW ANYONE LIKE THAT IN REAL
LIFE WHO DIDN'T LIVE THROUGH A WAR OR PLAGUE?

JUSTICE

FOR

NANA

AND

GRAMPO

EVANS

AND

MUNGA

AND

POP

POP

POTTER[4]

You know, it's like actually insane to make Harry sleep in the
cupboard under the stairs when you have an entire extra bedroom. And don't you need the storage? I would NEVER give up
my linen closet no matter how much I hated my shitty nephew!
Take the master, Grayson! I expected better logic out of Aunt
Petunia, being the only non-fat in the family.

---

4   I know this information is almost certainly available on like Weasleys-
    Wizard-Wiki-dot-toadspot-dot-cauldron because J. K. scrambled for an
    answer in a Pottermore interview once or something, but, paradoxically,
    the word of J. K. "Wizards Used to Shit in Their Robes and Then Vanish
    the Diarrhea" Rowling is actually not canon! Sorry!

Harry's cousin Dudley has his parents totally cucked. He screams at them that he didn't get enough birthday presents, and instead of giving him the present of a ride to the orphanage, his dad starts crying and takes him to the zoo. They're in the reptile house when Harry just starts talking to a snake, and his only vibe is like, "Huh, I've never talked to a snake before." Dude, you're essentially a Muggle right now! It's not like you live in the wizarding world where a cat is a person and sometimes a book will slice your jugular. This chill is psychopathic.

Harry and the snake bond over their shared traumas. The snake tells Harry he was bred in captivity, and Harry goes, "That's me too. I never knew my parents either." Which had to have bugged the shit out of the snake because that's not what "bred in captivity" means at all. That's like when you tell someone your dad died and they nod and say they understand how you feel because they really miss their cat when they're at work. Like, sorry your parents got murdered by a magician, but "bred in captivity" involves the kidnapping, imprisonment, forced insemination, and slavery of your entire family, sweetie! Look it up!

Harry uses his secret wizard emotions to make the glass disappear, so the snake is like, "Bye, I'm going to slither to Burma." Okay, good luck with all of Europe, the Middle East, Central Asia, and the Indian subcontinent. I'm sure you'll make it, though!

Now it's Harry's birthday, and for the first time in his life, he gets a letter in the mail. Mesmerized, this dumbass brings the letter into the dining room like he's never met his own family before. Uncle Vernon of course confiscates it, fatly, but the letters keep coming! Thousands and thousands of them! Uncle Vernon has no choice but to Airbnb a shack on a crag in the middle of the ocean and drag his weeping family there because no wizard could possibly check his browser history and figure out where they went. (Actually, that is true. Wizards are constantly roasting "Muggle technology," meanwhile their best method of long-distance communication is sticking your face in a fire and hoping your friend happens to be in the kitchen at the time. But yeah, fellytones are stupid!)

The Dursleys are all asleep. Harry's making himself a birthday cake out of dirt, which is also his bed. Just then, a giant wild man rips the door off its hinges and barges into the crag shack, which we're expected to think is very cool! (IDK, I kind of feel like Muggles should have some rights, even if they're dicks?) It's Hagrid, and he's brought Harry a real cake and an invitation to Hogwarts.

"Of course you know all about Hogwarts."

"I'm sorry, no."

If you thought Harry knew all about Hogwarts, then why did you hunt this family down and break into their house????

Even in the moment when his whole family is being terrorized by a giant, fatboy Dudley can't stop himself from plunging his face directly into the cake and omph momph gromph skromph. As a fat woman, this moment of cultural representation moved me deeply. My uncle got straight up killed by a dog at his own wedding and I was still like, "So, uh, when we gonna slice into this baby?? Don't keep Mama waiting!!!!!!"

Hagrid takes Harry back-to-school shopping in Diagon Alley, which is a top-secret wizards-only neighborhood in London. Here's another thing I don't get: If wizards live in London (and as we know, Hogsmeade is the only all-wizard village in England, so most wizards must live in Muggle settlements!), why don't they understand *anything about Muggle culture*? They're surrounded by millions of Muggles every day! You're telling me they never need to use Muggle money to get a sandwich or take a bus? They can't get a basic handle on Muggle clothes? Mr. Weasley walks through giant crowds of Muggles every day on his way to work and still thinks he needs to wear an umpire's chest protector and teal yoga pants and a baby's christening bonnet and a Hula-Hoop just to pick Harry up from the bus stop? What are all the kids wearing on the Hogwarts Express before they "change into their school robes"? I am going to die of this.

Harry buys a magic wand from John Hurt, considered by many to be the greatest actor of his generation, who really takes his twelve seconds of screen time talking nonsense to a child TO THE LIMIT. Hagrid buys Harry an owl as a present. They visit the bank, which is run by hook-nosed goblins with rubber hands (YIKES), so Hagrid can do some secret Hogwarts business. Harry admires the Nimbus 2000 in a shop window even though four seconds ago he didn't know that flying brooms existed. He is taking all of this in stride to a degree that, again, is disturbing.

That trend continues when Hagrid casually tells Harry that his parents were murdered by an evil wizard named Voldemort, who also tried to murder Harry, and probably still wants to ASAP. Harry's like, "Wow." Then Hagrid takes him to the train station and dumps him there! Alone! With no information except for "platform 9 and ¾" and "the evilest wizard of all time wants you dead, bye." Because he's "gotta meet Dumbledore." Oh, yeah, if only there was a train *named after Dumbledore's house* that was going directly from where you're standing to Dumbledore's house!

So, does the Hogwarts Express run year-round? Who operates

it? Hogwarts? The Ministry of Magic? Do the residents of Hogsmeade get to use it? Or is it just an entire steam train (WHO MINES THE COAL?) dedicated solely to taking one hundred children to and from Hogwarts twice a year? And if that's the case, how the fuck does the witch who runs the snack trolley pay her bills? Do wizards have bills? If they don't, then WHAT DOES IT MEAN THAT THE WEASLEYS ARE POOR?

Harry is wandering around looking for platform 9 and ¾, and if this were *Lindy West and the Sorcerer's Stone*, I would have literally stood on that platform until the Hogwarts Express came back at the beginning of summer holiday because I hate asking people questions, *especially train conductors*. But Harry spies a weathered railwayman and marches right up to him carrying a live owl like, "Excuse me, guv'nah, where is platform 9 and ¾?" and I tell you I would DIE before doing that!!!!!!!! Luckily, just as this uniformed authority figure starts yelling at Harry for being a wise guy (CORPSIFY ME FIRST), the entire Weasley clan walks by talking about "Muggles" and "Hogwarts" and Harry runs off to bug them instead.

Fred's and George's haircuts are literally disgusting.

Mrs. Weasley teaches Harry how to get on the train, and then Ron teaches Harry about all the different kinds of wizard candy. I'm sorry for constantly digressing, but who invented chocolate? Wizards or Muggles? Are house elves down in Brazil harvesting, roasting, grinding, and exporting cacao beans? Or did Muggles figure all that out, and then wizards just buy Muggle chocolate from Muggle chocolate factories (with WHAT KIND OF MONEY?) and then bewitch it to jump around like a frog? Because wizards literally treat Muggles like dumb trash, but there's no way they don't benefit constantly from Muggle invention.

Not to be a capitalist, but don't tell me wizards had any incentive to invent trains when they can already teleport.

Harry gets a Dumbledore trading card with his chocolate frog and is confused when Dumbledore just walks out of the frame. Ron is like, "Well, you can't expect him to hang around all day," and I'm sure you know what I'm going to ask. Is there just ONE SIMULACRUM DUMBLEDORE FOR ALL PAINTINGS AND CARDS? The odds of ever catching him on your chocolate frog card would be basically zero, but this is the least fucked-up thing about the internal logic of the sentient portraits in Harry Potter, so I will back down.

Ron introduces Harry to his hand-me-down rat, Scabbers, who blows (and is secretly a man, and has definitely seen multiple Weasley brothers masturbate????), and then Ron announces he's going to try out a new spell that Fred and George taught him. It goes like this:

"Sunshine, daisies, butter mellow, turn this stupid fat rat yellow."

Setting aside why anyone would possess the drive to turn a rat yellow, this is clearly not a real spell. We know this because a) the rat does not turn yellow, b) Hermione shows up and is like, "That's not a real spell," and c) Ron, your parents are wizards! You're eleven years old! Haven't you ever heard a real spell before? The spell for turning a rat yellow would be, like, "Rattonius yellowus" because let's be honest, sometimes the writing in these books is bad.

BTW, Hermione should 100 percent be the protagonist of this whole shit and I cannot wait for this series to root deep enough into the public memory to produce a bona fide literary fiction retelling from Hermione's POV and I'd like to put pre-dibs on the TV adaptation option for that property, please! Thx! I'm avail!

Thoughts on sorting:

First of all, reminder that *Harry Potter* presupposes that every witch and wizard in England went to the same high school except for a handful of full-KKK wizards who shipped their kids to Durmstrang. And there are only like fifty children in Harry's year! Everyone in the country would know each other! There's this part in book six where Harry holds Quidditch tryouts for Gryffindors only and is like, "Yeah, I don't know any of these people." HOW? There are 150 of you tops and you all live in a tower together and eat treacle tart family style *every day*! You've never met Cormac McLaggen before?

Second of all, the Sorting Hat. So it's a sentient hat, and they stick the kids' heads up its asshole so it can tell them whether they're brave, smart, evil, or other (the four genders). What does the Sorting Hat *do* the rest of the year? Does it have to sit in a cupboard in the dark? That seems cruel and unusual for a living hat. Does it ever get to fuck a woman hat? Freedom for Sorting Hat.

Third of all, I'm sure this is a hacky thing to say in Harry Potter fandom and many of you are sharpening your quills to send me letters about what "cunning" means, but disband Slytherin! Why keep it? Do we need it? Why have one house that's evil? Especially when your whole society is so scared of evil wizards they can't even say one guy's name out loud? Wizard hack: don't send fully one-quarter of your children to Evil School, and maybe end up with 100 percent fewer evil wizards.

Harry gets sorted into Gryffindor and goes up to his dorm room where he sits in his window seat petting his owl. Does anyone else find it weird how no parents ever come visit Hogwarts? It's weird, right? These kids don't even have phones! It is weird to be ten and only talk to your parents once a year, sorry.

Now is the time for wizard school to start!

I know that "Dumbledore trusts him," and I get the whole Harry's parents' backstory, but the way that Snape treats Harry throughout this series is absolutely off the rails and would be illegal in Muggle society (but yeah, wizards are "better"!). You're telling me the students have absolutely no recourse if they're being abused by staff? You're telling me there aren't any wizard helicopter parents (or as Mr. Weasley calls them, "smellyhopper" parents) who would complain? Harry is verbally and emotionally abused, not to mention held back academically, for *six years*, because Snape, an adult male authority figure, has such poor coping skills he can't stop himself from vindictively projecting his resentments onto an innocent child! It's truly a dystopian vision of an education system with no community oversight!

That said, Alan Rickman!!!!!!! The acting in this movie so vastly outstrips the script and direction it is frankly problematic and I'm telling cancel culture.

I hate how they sometimes crimp sections of Hermione's hair like that's part of her natural hair texture like we've never seen hair before.

The kids go outside for their first flying lesson. Neville immediately loses control of his broom and crunches to the ground, and Madam Hooch is like, "Oh, weird," as though that's a completely unexpected outcome when you give a child a flying machine and no instruction. "Oh dear, it's a broken wrist." Yeah, because you did a really bad job supervising them!

She takes Neville to the hospital wing, so Malfoy seizes the opportunity to be a dick. He steals Neville's Remembrall (a ball filled with smoke that turns red when you've forgotten something, more a torture device than a convenience, really, worse than not having one, IMO!) and flies high up into the air with it, taunting Harry.

Harry takes the bait: "Give it here, Malfoy, or I'll knock you off your broom!" Wow, you'll KILL HIM???? For Neville's Remembrall? What a psycho! #Maybe! #Snape! #Was! #Right!

Malfoy throws the Remembrall into the sky and Harry executes a flawless catch to save it and Professor McGonagall spies him out the window. You think he's going to get in trouble for breaking the rules, but fortunately, the only thing McGonagall cares about more than rules is balls of yarn, and the only thing she cares about more than balls of yarn is laser pointers and the only thing she cares about more than laser pointers is tuna water and the only thing she cares about more than tuna water is SPORTS. She makes Harry the seeker on the Gryffindor Quidditch team. Hermione informs Harry that his dad was the Gryffindor seeker in 1972 because this freak has already memorized every trophy in the castle.

Harry, Ron, and Hermione inadvertently wander into the forbidden corridor on the third floor, and when they're nearly caught by Mrs. Norris (...a cat), they run deeper and deeper into the forbidden corridor where they're nearly mangled and mutilated by Fluffy, a three-headed giant dog. See, this is what happens when children are given no foundation of safety and consistency—when they're just as likely to be publicly humiliated by an adult goth as they are to be heard and believed if they're caught in apparent misbehavior and tell the truth. Kids should be able to say, "The staircase moved so we accidentally went down the wrong hallway, sorry," without Filch beating them with a chain!

Anyway, Ron is like, "What do they think they're doing, keeping a thing like that locked up in a school?" and it does seem like a significant liability just to protect a rock that Dumbledore could easily keep in his underpants.

Oliver Wood teaches Harry the rules of Quidditch in his turtleneck. Is that what cool clothes and hair were like in 2001? Can I have all my crushes back?

They go to Charms class and we meet Professor Flitwick, the only professor who matters, who should be making a billion galleons a year but instead is only ever referred to as "tiny Professor Flitwick." Charms is basically ALL SPELLS. Name one useful thing they learn in Transfiguration! Oh, finally, a solution to my teacup surplus / mouse shortage!

Hermione is (rightfully) condescending about "wingardium leviosa," so Harry and Ron hurt her feelings and she goes to cry in the bathroom. Professor Quirrell comes running into the lunchroom screaming that there's a troll in the dungeon, so Dumbledore sends all the kids to their dormitories to hide. Harry and Ron remember that Hermione doesn't know about the troll because she's boo-hooing in the shitter! They race to get her and discover that somehow in the maddening, thousand-room maze that is Hogwarts Castle, the troll has wandered into the random girls' bathroom where Hermione is crying. Sure, okay!

Why does a troll wear a loincloth? It can't talk, but it feels shame about its genitals?

Harry and Ron defeat the troll by sticking Harry's wand up its nose and into its brain, and then Ron wingardium leviosas the troll's club so it knocks him out—yet another instance of

Hermione saving everyone's ass by being the only competent person in the building. Not only that, then she does them a huge solid. In the toilet!!!!!!! Just kidding, she does them a huge solid by taking the blame for hunting down the troll while being children. And McGonagall *awards them points for it*, yet another example of the completely destabilizing systemic inconsistency allowed to flourish at Hogwarts! (This is why Harry never goes to an authority figure about any of his many outrageous and deadly problems. What does authority even mean in such a context?)

It's time for Harry's first Quidditch match of the season. Snape approaches him. "Good luck today, Potter. Then again, now that you've proven yourself against a troll, a little Quidditch match should be no problem, even if it is against Slytherin." Dude, you're an ADULT. GO TO THERAPY.

Harry and the Gryffindors square off against Marcus Flint and his magnum dentures. If Quidditch were real, every single one of these Quidditch players would be dead. In the middle of the match, Harry's broom—a.k.a. a stick that a child is riding in the sky—goes rogue and tries to throw him off. Hermione spies Snape (seemingly) muttering a curse in the stands, so she sets him on fire, the only recourse available to a student at a school where chaos is king! Then Harry catches the golden snitch in his mouth and wins.

Yeah, there are technically Black characters in Harry Potter, but tell me one thing about Dean Thomas.

The kids visit Hagrid and trick him into telling them the deal with Fluffy. "Bought him off an Irish fellow down the pub." Wait, you believe in Ireland? Why would wizards care about Muggle borders? Hagrid, bumbling, says that Fluffy is there to guard something "between Dumbledore and Nicolas Flamel." This is great news for Harry, Ron, and Hermione, who are always looking for some fucking beeswax that's none of theirs!

Now it's Christmas at Hogwarts! What the fuck is Christmas! If you're a wizard! Wizards! Are! Christian! I! Guess!

Harry gets presents for the first time in his life, and now I want presents.

An anonymous gifter sends Harry his dad's old invisibility cloak, which the kids quickly realize they can use to sneak into the restricted section of the library under cover of night to research Nicolas Flamel. OR, you could…ask Madam Pince, the literal full-time librarian? Did you ever think that maybe she's a bitch because no one has ever engaged her help on a research project (i.e., respected her enough to let her do her job)?? Instead of doing that, Harry gets a lantern and the cloak and creeps over there himself.

Again, I know that magic is "better" than technology, but maybe the Wizengamot could revisit the no-computers thing? There's no internet, so these kids can't google Nicolas Flamel, and there's apparently not even a library catalog? You just have to pull books off the shelves at random? And you don't even have a fucking flashlight? You have to bring *fire* into the library?

Harry finds no information (OF COURSE) and nearly burns down the building. On the way back to bed, under the invisibility cloak, he encounters Snape threatening Professor Quirrell. "You don't want me as your enemy, Quirrell." Okay, so, what does Snape know here? Does he suspect that Quirrell is working with Voldemort at this point? HOW? And if so, don't just wedgie him in the hallway, man—Floo powder 911!!! (I apologize for the bone-chilling granularity of this parenthetical, but the only explanation that makes any sense is that Snape just thinks Quirrell is trying to steal the Sorcerer's Stone for non-Voldemort-related reasons, but then what about the part when Quirrell was trying to murder Harry during the Quidditch match? Who did Snape think was doing that? Also, why was there no formal investigation into that ATTEMPTED CHILD MURDER?? And why didn't Snape just tell Dumbledore that Quirrell was after the stone, so they could have, just brainstorming here, *fired him for being evil??????*)

Harry ducks into a random classroom where he finds the Mirror of Erised, a magical artifact that shows you a reflection of the thing you most desire, which is *erised* backward, please kill me. If I looked into that mirror, I would see myself blissfully smiling in a universe where I'd never heard writing as bad as "Mirror of Erised"!!! (See also: "Death Eaters." PLEASE, is this a scary story I wrote when I was nine?) In that universe I also have amazing jugs. :) Harry sees himself reunited with his dead parents. :(

They go visit Hagrid again, who is in the process of hatching an illegal baby dragon named Norbert. Norbert is only in this movie because fans would have been mad if he weren't, which is not a good way to make a movie. Dumbledore ships Norbert off to Romania instantly with zero complications. Norbert story line concluded!

While they're meeting Norbert, Malfoy spies them out of bed after hours and tattles to McGonagall, who gives them all (including Malfoy, haha) detention with Hagrid. Hagrid takes them into the Dark Forest in the middle of the night to investigate what kind of eldritch horror is killing unicorns and drinking their blood. HAGRID, ARE YOU SURE THE CHILDREN SHOULD BE ON THIS TRIP?

He sends Harry and Malfoy off by themselves (SURE!), so

of course they run into Lord Voldemort sucking a unicorn dry. Okay, what IS Voldemort at this point? I truly don't know. Because he walks toward Harry like a dude, but then he flies away like a tiny ghost. And also I thought his whole *deal* was that he didn't have a body?

Anyways, they're saved by a centaur. Centaurs are irritating. It seems like if they're really half-man/half-horse they should either have no arms or they should have to balance on two horse legs. This is a half-man/two-thirds-horse. Disrespectful.

FINALLY they go try and tell Dumbledore that someone's trying to steal the Sorcerer's Stone, but McGonagall tells them he's not home, so they decide that the ONLY WAY is to go get the stone themselves. (WHYYYYYYYYYY?) Neville stands up to them because they are breathtakingly selfish and he's sick of getting in trouble for it, and Hermione petrifies him! *Petrificus totalus!* Such a brutal spell to use on a person who is ostensibly your friend, and then she just LEAVES THIS CHILD PARALYZED ON THE COLD FLOOR ALL NIGHT. I'm a Hermione loyalist, but this move is insane. Way worse than stealing his Remembrall!

They head to the forbidden corridor on the third floor only to discover that somebody got there before them (presumably Snape). Now would be a great time to go back to McGonagall and be like, "SERIOUSLY," but instead they just squeak past Fluffy and jump down into a trapdoor. The Sorcerer's Stone is guarded by a series of trials, each designed by a different teacher at the school. They have to escape from an evil plant. They have to catch a little flying key. They have to figure out which potion to drink. It goes without saying that Harry and Ron would have been instantaneously deceased without Hermione, but as usual, Harry's the fucking hero.

The second-to-last trial is a game of giant wizard chess, where they each have to ride around on a giant chess piece while they beat the shit out of each other. Fortunately, just as Harry's singular talent is flying and Hermione's singular talent is literally everything else, Ron's singular talent is chess. Convenient! Hermione is injured, and Ron sacrifices himself to win the game, so Harry has to carry on alone.

"You'll be okay, Harry!" cries Hermione. "You're a great wizard." Um, he's had one semester of wizard elementary school.

Harry gets to the final trial and finds not Professor Snape but Professor Quirrell trying to steal the Sorcerer's Stone! Wow! What an upset! He's staring at the Mirror of Erised and stomping his little foot. Why won't the stone come out of the mirror?? A creepy voice tells Quirrell to make Harry get the stone. Who is that creepy voice? Oh, it's only VOLDEMORT HIDING UNDER QUIRRELL'S HAT! Quirrell's got male pattern VOLDNESS.

Voldemort explains to Harry that he needs the stone so he can get his body back and return to being evil full time, okay?? Harry uses his pure heart to erised the stone out of the mirror and then Quirrell jumps on him. But it turns out that Voldemort can't touch Harry's skin because it's infused with the power of a mother's love! Quirrell catches on fire! Then Voldemort turns into smoke and flies straight through Harry's chest, which I guess is no problem.

Harry wakes up in the hospital wing. Dumbledore awards each of them a ton of points for being blisteringly stupid and reckless. No one is punished for the torture of Neville Longbottom. They all live to see another six years of being absolutely maddening impulsive narcissists! Cheers!

RATING: 6/10 DVDs of *The Fugitive*.

Big Boy Freaky Friday

I rewatched a lot of movies for this book, and going into it, I thought I had a handle on which movie characters I hated the most. Jason Biggs in *American Pie*. Bernard from *Lost* in *Forrest Gump*. Scorpion in *Honey I Fed Our Kids to a Scorpion*. But that's what happens when you go twenty years without rewatching *Face/Off*, you idiot! You forget about the number-one biggest dud of a fuckin' guy ever made, America's Next Top Worst Best Friend, and that includes Elsa from *Frozen*:[5] FBI Special Agent Sean Archer, as portrayed by John Travolta and Nicolas Cage but *especially John Travolta*. BOO, SEAN ARCHER, BOOOOOOOOOOOOOO.

In case you don't know what *Face/Off* is about (hold on to your face!!!!!!), it's the story of a straight-laced FBI agent named Sean Archer who has to go undercover as his nemesis, master

---

5 You lived alone in a castle with your sister for like *ten years* and you never talked to her????

criminal Castor Troy. How do you go undercover AS somebody else? WELL, THE TITLE OF THIS MOVIE IS A CLUE, BUT I WILL TELL YOU IN A MINUTE.

We open in the past, when Special Agent Sean Archer is enjoying a nice carousel ride with his son. I have never understood what is so fun about a carousel, sorry. I already have a fake horse with a long pole that I ride around in circles for hours—it's called YOUR DAD. Just kidding!!!! Your dad's pole is only medium. *Just kidding!!!!!!!!!!!!!! Don't worry!!!! I am repressed!!!!!!!!*

Sean Archer (John Travolta) is on the carousel with his son, and they have this positively pestilential face thing they do where Sean Archer drags his big unwashed mushy palm down over the kid's entire face—eyeballs, nose, lips, teeth, and tongue. The kid loves it. They hug. Just then, Castor Troy (Nicolas Cage and, *wow*, his mustache) pops up and shoots Sean Archer in the back. Aaaaaaargh! Then some loose balloons drift away into the sky, which is international semaphore for "a kid died."

It's six years later. Archer survived the shooting, but if he had any good personality traits before, those tragically did not make it. To put it kindly, Sean Archer is an uptight lil weenie. He neglects his family and he is mean to his employees and he has no sense of humor and he is no fun. He only cares about one thing, which is crushing, killing, and destroying Castor Troy, and he is not even very good at that! Like, I can tolerate a workaholic with a shitty attitude if he is some kind of interesting genius (Sherlock Holmes[6]), or I can tolerate a big uptight dork if his devotion to his family comes into some kind of interesting tension with his

---

6   Okay, he is sometimes in a good mood, I guess, but if a person ever said "elementary" to me, I would stab them.

74

job (Ned Stark). But Sean is a shitty boss AND a shitty husband! I hate him!

Meanwhile, Castor Troy is smoking a cigarette while dressed like a priest, which was the kind of edgy shit we incinerated our panties for in the '90s. He's an indie terrorist with extremely opaque goals (uh, being a bitch?), who is arming some kind of big sexy bomb in order to kill Los Angeles with it.

It is madness, by the way, that every director does not do whatever it takes—financially, spiritually, erotically—to put Nicolas Cage in everything they make. He is the only person who ever does anything interesting in any movie. Yeah, I said it! Do I mean it? I don't know. But I do know that sometimes I forget about Nicolas Cage for weeks or even years at a time, and then I watch a Nicolas Cage movie again and it feels like coming home—to a house where your dad is cocaine and your mom licks your face if you've been good AND if you've been bad. I'm happy there!

Archer gets intel that Pollux Troy, Castor Troy's little brother, has chartered a private jet, which can only mean one thing: Castor is *at this very moment* walking toward it in slow motion! What's that??? The source also says he's wearing a shiny maroon suit and the world's worst tiny octagonal sunglasses!?!? This is more serious than I thought. The entire FBI races for the airport.

Castor boards the plane and starts sexually assaulting the flight attendant before they even take off, making her sit on his lap so that he can whisper what is scientifically the worst phrase utterable by the human mouth: "You know, I can eat a peach for hours." This combination of sounds is profane even in alien languages from the coldest depths of deep space, and is actually used as an emetic by the worm lords of Xooxoo-12. If you say, "You know, I can eat a peach for hours," in the presence of a gaseous one from Quabzab 971bb7cx80001, he will straight up ruin your face.

Archer gets to the airport and begins chasing the rapidly accelerating jet in his FBI car. On board, unaware that the feds are closing in, Castor is like, "Hey, if I were to let you suck my tongue, would you be grateful?" and the flight attendant is like, "YUM YUM, OH BOY," and she does it!!! She does it! Even worse, it turns out that she's not a horny flight attendant at all—she's in the FBI. She's an undercover FBI tongue-sucker! Are there really civil servants out there sucking terrorist tongues for *my freedom*? I didn't ask for this! Castor shoots her.

It would be a real letdown if the last thing you did in your life was suck Nicolas Cage's tongue. And I say that respectfully, as a fan.

Okay, I looked away from the screen for one second and John Travolta is somehow flying a helicopter.

Helicopter Sean shoots out an engine on the plane, so Castor kills the pilot, and now he will drive the plane himself. But instead he just crashes it into a building, which doesn't help at all.

The FBI storms the hangar where the jet is on fire, so Castor jumps out of the plane sideways shooting his two golden pants-guns, which is absolutely the most functional maneuver and truly his only option at this point. Margaret Cho captures Pollux, which Castor hates, because Pollux is his baby, so he shoots many more FBI agents to death. A flawless operation.

Now Sean Archer and Castor Troy face off. It is just Travolta vs. Cage. (Chilling to remember that these were the two biggest movie stars in the world in 1997, which by my reckoning was about two weeks ago, but my kids have absolutely no idea who Nicolas Cage is and John Travolta is "the mom from *Hairspray*.")

The guys chase each other around the place for a while until Castor gets blown down a wind tunnel by a big jet engine—by far the coolest way to arrest someone. Sean Archer's life's work is achieved at last. Now he can finally go home, have sex with his wife for the first time, and stop his daughter from being goth.

A happy ending, right?? Yeah, for like ONE MILLISECOND.

Sean goes back to work where everyone claps for him because they are nice and he just fulfilled his singular all-consuming quest to avenge his son, and he, a dick, yells at them for it. In his office, he opens up his son's murder file to stare at it meaningfully (the file is under "carousel sniper victim"—what filing system is that??), when, uh-oh, Special Ops want a word! And it's not "keep your face on"!

The Special Ops agents, CCH Pounder and Tito, show Sean a zip drive containing a horny cartoon who's like, "My name is Sinclaire, and I am going to *blow you* . . . . *AWAY!!!!!!!*" because in the '90s we were really worried that bad guys were going to use computers to do scary stuff to us like send sarcastic e-cards about bombs. We didn't realize they'd just trick us into using our own computers to voluntarily destroy ourselves! Sinclaire is the name of that big bomb I mentioned earlier—"enough [bomb] to flatten a square mile and unleash a biblical plague on LA"—and Pollux is refusing to tell the FBI anything about the bomb unless they let him see Castor.

So, okay, let him. Problem solved, right?

No? You guys have a different idea? I assume it won't interfere with my 2:00 p.m. lovemaking appointment with my angry wife, haha, right, guys?

Guys?

CCH Pounder and Tito take Sean to a top-secret underground

medical facility. Castor Troy is there, asleep in a hospital bed, and apparently Sean thought he had died? He screams, "Oh, god, you're keeping him alive!" And instead of saying, "Yes, Sean, even incarcerated criminals have a right to lifesaving medical intervention," they're like, "Relax, Archer, he's a turnip."

Now the secret lab doctor explains the plan. Pollux Troy will only talk to his brother, right? So what we're gonna do is take this turnip's face off, and take your face off, and then put his face on your face. Then you're the turnip and you can talk to the brother! It's the only way to save Los Angeles, sorry.

Sean Archer is like, "Exqueese me?" And the doctor is like, "A sphincter says, 'No, thank you, I do not want to have my face taken off,'" and Sean is like, "Touché," because nobody wants to be a sphincter! So now he has to do it because in the '90s this qualified as a binding contract. Only the highest court in the land can overrule a sphincter clause!

Sean Archer has to take his *face...off*.

It's the only way. It's literally the only way. No one in the entire FBI can possibly think of any other way. There's obviously no other way! And Sean is definitely the only one who can do it. They can take someone's face...off, but it would be absolutely impossible for anyone else in the FBI to memorize some stuff about Castor Troy's life! Come on, Sean! "If you don't, the bomb will blow, and Castor Troy will win." Love 2 be emotionally abused by my job into taking my *face...off!*

"You're asking me to break the law, risk my neck, and you're asking me to put in the dark all the people that love me and trust me...I'll do it." You dick.

He heads home to break the news to his wife that, sorry, he's just going to disappear for an undisclosed period of time and almost definitely die on one last secret mission that he can't tell her anything about, but before he can get to all that, she jumps in: "I'm glad it's you that woke me, and not a phone call telling me you won't be coming home. But that's a fear I can finally let go of."

He looks at her like a golden retriever that just ate a whole beef Wellington. "Well.........."

DUDE.

GO DIE.

MA'AM, THERE ARE OTHER SEANS WITH BAD PERSONALITIES OUT THERE. PLEASE UNCHAIN YOURSELF FROM THIS FUNGUS.

It's time for the procedure. Archer shows the doc the hole from the bullet that killed his son and asks if he can "put his scar back on" after he's done being Castor Troy. I don't even know why they're bothering to take it off (or how?), but doc says no prob. Sean takes his wedding ring off and gives it to Tito.

Then they take his face...off.

And they take Nicolas Cage's face...off.

They cut around the face and then they use the face vacuum to slurp up the face.

Now Travolta's face is in a tub.

Now they give John Travolta the horrible baby bangs of Cage.

Now Cage face go on Travolta.

They put a chip in his throat so now he has the voice of Nicolas Cage.

Are you following this?

Then Sean Archer wakes up and he just is Castor Troy! And he loves it! And he hates it! He screams in agony and he smashes the mirror. "Fuck you! Fuck you! Fuck you! Fuck you! When this is over, I want you to take this face and burn it!"

There is no other movie where they do less to explain the science.

It doesn't seem possible, but the next phase of the plan is even stupider and worse. Now, I'm not in the Lady FBI, I didn't graduate from QUEENtico, so what do I know, but it SEEMS LIKE if you need to get information from Pollux Troy, you could just have him in a room, like maybe the room where you interviewed him before, and then put Sean-Archer-as-Castor in the room also, and have them talk to each other? Are you actually worried that Pollux is going to see right through this insane fucking plan? I know that whenever my brother's acting a little weird, my first assumption is that the FBI has taken his face... off and glued it to the skull of an FBI agent.

(I mean, this would 100 percent be a concern in real life because in real life fake Castor would still have the wide, lumpen torso of John Travolta and a big, loose face like Vincent D'Onofrio in *Men in Black*, and, yes, Pollux would absolutely scream and scream at a skin-suit demon made from his brother's mutilated body strolling into interrogation room 2 like, "How do you do, fellow brother?" But in this movie, IT'S JUST THE REAL NICOLAS CAGE. POLLUX WOULD BUY IT. I PROMISE.)

Instead, and I'm getting reports that this is actually the *only way*, you could drop Sean Archer into a secret prison and not tell anybody about the fact that he took his face... off, not even the guards there, so he just has to fend for himself with the face and bangs of the most hated guy on earth inside of a lawless cage filled with murderers who hate that guy extra because he 69ed all of their sisters. This is way better than the two guys talking in a room idea!

Sean is in prison now and a mean man in a little hat is

yelling at him. "YOU ARE NOW A CITIZEN OF EREHWON PRISON, YOU BELONG TO NOWHERE." Erehwon is *nowhere* backward, so kindly reanimate my corpse from where it lies in front of the Mirror of Erised and kill me again.

It turns out, in EREHWON, all the prisoners have to wear giant metal knee-high boots because they make it very hard to walk and also, "This entire prison's one big magnetic field. Your boots tell us where you are." This is kind of the signature *thing* of the prison, and it's pretty fucked up, but, silver lining—those inmates are *stacked*. They should do a THIGHS OF EREHWON calendar to raise money for more cattle prods!

Sean gets bullied by a mean prisoner in the lunchroom, and at first he just lets the guy whale on him, but then he remembers to be Castor Troy and be good at fighting. To make sure everyone knows he's Castor Troy and not an FBI agent with a face, bangs, chest hair, voice, and height transplant, he starts screaming, "I'M CASTOR TROY! I'M CASTOR TROY! WOOOOOOOOO!"

That is what he'd say. He always said that.

Meanwhile, back at the lab, the real Castor Troy wakes up without a face. (I'm sorry, they just left him there without a guard? The world's most wanted supercriminal and freelance dickhead? Not even a night nurse or a drip sedative?) He touches his raw skull, confused for one second, and then is like, "Ohhhhhh, I see what they did."

You do????????????????????????????

Castor phones his henchmen and has them kidnap the doc and bring him back to the lab.

Doc: What do you want?

I DON'T KNOW, DOC.

DOES HE SEEM TO BE MISSING ANYTHING IMPORTANT?

Back in prison, Sean is finally getting the goods from Pollux.

> **Pollux:** We're gonna blow up LA, bro, it's gonna be
> cool. [Not a good enough reason, IMO!]
> **Sean:** That bomb you built belongs in the Louvre.
> **Pollux:** Oh, well, I guess the LA Convention Center will
> have to do, giggle giggle.

Oh, great! Now Sean can get out of here and save LA just in time! Oops, he has a visitor, so the guards take him to a metal room and lock his boots to the floor. Who's it gonna be? Tito, I hope!

OH, it's only Castor Troy, wearing Sean's face! And, bad news, he killed the doc. He killed Tito. He killed CCH Pounder. Now there's nobody left who knows that they took their faces............... OFF! Sean's stuck in boot prison till death!

Castor's like, "I have got to go, I've got a government job to abuse and a lonely wife to fuck," and, I'm sorry—did they change your dick too? Because I am over 70 percent sure that she will notice!

Okay, now Castor Troy is just running WILD all over Sean Archer's life, and aside from the part where he aggressively hits on Sean's teenage daughter, which I cannot type about because I had to flush my brain down the toilet, it's tough to find fault with any of it! Sean sucked, and Castor is fun, and what does he really do that's so bad? He defuses his own bomb and becomes a national hero! He jokes around with his employees and is nice to them for once! He takes Sean's wife on an actual date night (he made lobster, tiny artichokes, and spaghetti) and rocks her world in the sack! Okay, that is rape, actually, and I am moving it to the "bad" column. But everything else—*pretty cool*! What has the real Sean ever done that is actually helpful? Seriously?

For some reason, they show the news on a giant screen at the prison, so Sean has to sit there all day and watch his greatest nemesis be way better at his life than he is. He has got to get out of there.

Here's his escape plan, which he appears to make up and execute on the fly: Sean asks a guard for a cigarette, then gets himself beat up and sent to shock therapy. They take your metal boots off when you get shock therapy, which he knew somehow, and the shock therapy protocol is that once a guy is done getting shocked they just throw him on the floor next to the shock therapy chair. So Sean gets in there, and they're just finishing shocking the last guy—a guy who hates Castor because Castor had a "sex sandwich" with his wife and sister. Sean knows how to use the sex sandwich to his advantage because they teach you that in the FBI. As they're strapping him into the chair, Sean says to the guy, "I didn't fuck your wife, I didn't fuck your sister, so let's get out of here."

The guy, who one second ago was unconscious and twitching and foaming at the mouth, is healed by the holy knowledge that Castor Troy did not have a sex sandwich with his wife and sister. He hops up and clonks the guard! Now it's a riot! Sean manages to turn off all the prisoners' magnetic boots, and in the chaos, he escapes to the roof. But then, "NOOOO! NOOOOOO!" Turns out, EREHWON is actually EREHWEMOS, and that erehwemos is in the middle of the ocean! Sorry, man, you gotta jump in the wawa!

Castor is at the cemetery visiting the grave of Sean's son (booooooooring!), when Margaret Cho calls to tell him Castor Troy escaped from Erehwon. But don't worry, she says, he definitely died jumping into the wawa.

Castor freaks out and insists he has to see the dead body,

and Margaret Cho is like, "Even if he is alive, he wouldn't be stupid enough to come back to the city!" Ma'am, respectfully, who cares??? He is the world's number-one worst terrorist! You absolutely need to take a couple of hours to find that bod and make sure he's actually dead!

Wait, no worries—Sean immediately calls Castor on the phone to taunt him and relinquish his one major advantage. "Well, if you're Sean Archer, I guess I'm Castor Troy."

Now it is the time for Sean Archer and Castor Troy to face off at last. They took their faces...off, AND THEY FACE OFF. DO YOU GET IT? You know this pun was the entire pitch!

Sean goes to Castor's friend's tacky casino loft for a party. He gets super high on pills and tells his crime team that he's going to get Sean Archer.

"I want to take his face...off."

"You want to take his face...off?"

"Yes, I want to take his face.......off. Now if you'll excuse me, I have to use the little boys' weewee room."

Meanwhile, while Sean is using the little boys' weewee room, Castor is over at Sean's house doing some extreme parenting. He sees Danny Masterson (yikes) trying to rape Sean's teen daughter, Jamie, in the driveway, so he fucking murders him! Heck yes! The old Sean would have cupped his balls probably!!

Then he lectures Jamie on dressing sluttily (actually, he says, "Dress up like Halloween and ghouls will try to get in your pants," but I assume that's what he means?), and Jamie is like, "Someone tries to rape me and I'm to blame?" and he's like, "Fair point, do you have protection?" and she's like, "You mean like condoms?" and he's like, "NO, LIKE A WIGGLY KNIFE." And he gives her a wiggly knife.

Back in the crime loft, Sean is having a sensual extramarital moment with Gina Gershon. "Gina Gershon," he says, "I'm not the same person you remember."

Yeah, I know, you have a completely different body.

Gershon decides this is the number-one hot moment to inform Castor (Sean) that he's the father of her son, Adam, who unfortunately looks a lot like Sean's real dead son. She's like, "Adam, I want you to meet your father," and the kid comes over and Sean, who is very high, has a complete meltdown about it. He grabs this kid and is just crying and screaming, "Michael? Michael? Michael?" Just then, the FBI shoots one million bullets into the building, killing everyone. ("Thank god!"—Adam, probably.)

Sean grabs Adam to rescue him from the FBI (yeah, me, the guy they're trying to shoot the most—let me carry the kid!) and hides him in a corner of the crime loft.

> **Sean:** Don't be scared, okay?
> **Adam:** Okay.

Yeah, I'm not scared now. This isn't scary at all. I'll just sit here and listen to my headphones while my mom and all her friends are massacred by the cops.

Sean and Castor end up in a *face-off* on either side of a two-sided mirror.

> **Castor:** I don't know what I hate wearing worse. Your face or your body. I mean, I enjoy boning your wife, but let's face it—we both like it better the other way, yes? So why don't we just trade back?
> **Sean:** You can't give back what you've taken from me.
> **Castor:** Oh, well, plan B, let's just kill each other.

Then they each have to SHOOT THEIR OWN REFLECTION. Wow! It means something!

Sean kills Pollux, which Castor hates. Now neither of them can give back what they've taken from them! Nobody escapes except for Sean, Gina Gershon, and Adam.

Archer's boss at the FBI, Victor (who is not enough of an FBI boss to be aware of the face/off scenario), is rightfully pissed that Sean got numerous FBI agents slaughtered for no reason and tries to take him off the anti-terrorism team. But since Sean is actually Castor, instead of saying sorry, he just murders Victor by surprising him real bad and then punching him in the chest so he has a heart attack.

A desperate and injured Sean breaks into his own house so he can explain everything to his wife. From where she's sitting, though, the terrorist who murdered her son is currently bleeding all over her bed. But don't worry, Sean has prepared an explanation so she doesn't freak out: "I'm Sean!" Good save!

He tells her to test his blood against fake Sean's. They might have identical dicks, but they have different blood types.

Sean goes back to Gina Gershon and tenderly promises her, "Whatever happens, I promise Sean Archer is off your back for good." Are you sure? She shot like twelve FBI agents in that last scene! Those were your friends!

Next there is a signature John Woo slow-motion bird shot with seagulls, and then immediately after there is a signature John Woo slow-motion bird shot with pigeons! Now the seagulls and the pigeons are going to FACE/OFF.

At last, it's time for the final face/off in the church after Victor's funeral. Everyone is pointing guns at everyone, and everyone shoots everyone, mostly. Gina Gershon clings to Sean and is like, "Take care of our boy, I love him so much, don't let him grow up to be like us," and then she dies. And Sean's wife is jealous, like that's her biggest problem right now??

Jamie shows up, and she doesn't know yet that her dad and his nemesis took their faces . . . off, so she shoots Sean Archer in the arm. Then Castor takes her hostage, but guess who remembered to bring her wiggly knife??? She stabs Castor in the leg, just like he taught her—truly the only real dad she ever had.

Okay, now there's a boat chase. A stuntman water-skis in his dress shoes while holding on to a chain attached to a speedboat. The boat crashes into the dock, and Archer and Troy both fly through the air and *land on their feet on the shore.* But it's still not over! More punching! Sean spear-guns Castor in the leg. But he can't spear-gun him to death because he still needs to take his FACE/OFF!

Just to be a dick, Castor starts fucking up Sean's face with a piece of glass so that he can't have it back, so then Sean just kills him with the spear gun anyway. Hopefully, the FBI can decapitate him and get his severed head in a fridge, ASAP! The only doctor who knew how to do the face/off surgery is dead and all the equipment blew up, but I'm sure it'll be fine!

Sean takes his wedding ring back from Castor's dead finger and goes home with his wife and daughter. Later that day, ding-dong! Who's that? Oh, it's just ADAM, THE ORPHANED SON OF THE TERRORIST I KILLED WITH A SPEAR GUN AT WORK THE OTHER DAY. "He needs a place to live."

The most unrealistic part of this whole movie is that Sean's wife does not beat him to death.

Face/Off is just Big Boy Freaky Friday.

RATING: 6/10 DVDs of *The Fugitive*.

Time Travel Doesn't Make Sense and I Think We Should Make It Illegal

Here we sit, grizzled and pandemic-worn, already five years beyond 2015—the dazzling, neon-lit vision that Doc Brown and Marty McFly drive to in *Back to the Future Part II* in search of [question mark?????]. With the gift of hindsight, this crossroads in real and cinematic time generates much hilarity, as it means that in 1989 (the year the film was made), Robert Zemeckis and Steven Spielberg were pretty sure that just twenty-five years in the future we'd have flying cars and bionic high-tops and robot Michael Jacksons would bring us all of our nanomilkshakes. What a coupla bozos! The coolest pieces of technology I have in 2020 are a windshield scraper with a mitten attached and a $400 flashlight that I'm told some people use as a "phone."

But let us examine.

We open in a garage. It is 1985. Marty McFly, having just returned from going back to the future once, is caressing his Jeep in an unpleasantly erotic way when Elizabeth Shue shows up. Sensing Marty is in the mood, she's all, "Shue-d we intercourse?"

and he's like, "Well, I kind of had a side thing going here with my Jeep, but I GUESS." (Hey, quick aside: Maybe if Elizabeth Shue is in your movie, don't name her character "Jennifer"? I already think that eleven out of ten blondes from the '80s are Jennifer Jason Leigh, and this is not helping. I don't come down to where you work and name David Niven's character "White Flavor Flav"—GOOGLE DAVID NIVEN AND TELL ME I'M WRONG.)

Marty's acting a little weird, so Jennifer's like, "Is everything all right?" Marty glances around furtively, catching a glimpse of the shadow-shrouded, reanimated corpse of Crispin Glover watching him from behind a screen door, as if to say, "I am in your house and I have your mom." "Yeah, I'm great!" Marty lies.

They're just about to tongue face when VROOOOOOOM, out of nowhere, HERE COMES DOC BROWN WEARING PHYLLIS NEFLER'S FOURTH-BEST SILKEN BED CLOAK.

"BLRRBLRRBRRBRRRRRBRBBBBBBRRR!" Doc explains, "MARTY! YOU GOTTA COME BACK WITH ME!"

"Where?"

"Back . . . to the FUTUBLLRRRRBRBRBRBRRRR!!"

When Marty expresses concern at not having been able to tongue Jennifer, like, at all, Doc Brown says, fine, they can take her to the future too. Marty and Jennifer, you see, have to drive to the year 2015 to stop their horrible toilet children from going to prison and ruining everything. (Yo, just a thought, but I kind of feel like it might be time to let this genetic line peter out? Marty's really the only borderline competent one out of *three generations*. Pick your battles.)

When they get to 2015, Jennifer is like, "Why am I in this flying garbage car?" and Marty goes, "Uhhh, Jennifer, ummm, I

don't know how to tell you this, but you're in a time machine."
So then, of course (WOMAN) literally the only thing Jennifer can
think of to do when confronted with the fucking miracle of time
travel is to *babble incessantly about her wedding*. Doc Brown is like,
"WHO IS THIS TERRIBLE PERFUMED YAPPER I THOUGHT
THIS WAS A BOY MOVIE," and immediately blasts her in the
face with a shut-up ray. "She was asking too many questions," he
tells Marty. "No one should know too much about their future."
Also, I thought dragging a lifeless corpse around would really
speed up our important mission.

Not to worry, though, because then Doc and Marty *literally
throw Jennifer in the garbage*.

It's raining outside, and Marty is like, "Ew," but then Doc is
like, "Hold up—just wait five seconds and it'll change, because I
have the rain memorized in the future for reasons unexplained."
Doc gives Marty some electric shoes and this terrible future-
jacket, and tells him to go to a nearby diner and pretend to be
his own son and then a man named Griff will come in and ask
him a question. "Say no, NO MATTER WHAT." If Marty fails
to say no, no matter what, "this one event starts a chain reaction
that completely destroys your entire family." Yo, is this really a
situation that justifies the use of a technology as fraught and
risky as time travel? One family has kind of a crappy time for a
few years? That's your emergency? Reminder: Marty and Doc go
on to fuck up this "mission" so egregiously that they *endanger the
fabric of time and space itself*. Cool. Worth it.

The future is sort of like the present but more bitchin'. Like,
they still mail things by having a literal guy pick them up and
carry them from one place to another (LOL), but the mailbox
has a COMPUTER ATTACHED, so, impressive. Everyone is

wearing wacky pants, the gas station is a robot, and all the cars look like logs of dook. Also, instead of skateboards they have these things that are exactly like skateboards except 400 percent more dangerous. It is just a trip, I tell you.

Marty heads to Café '80s, which is an '80s-themed cafe where all the patrons are dressed up in "vintage" '80s clothes. (Uh, you know people don't actually wear period costume when they go to novelty restaurants, right? I also don't dress like a toucan when I go to the Rainforest Café.) Their special today is "mesquite grilled sushi," which is just crazy, because who has ever heard of such a thing!? Only in 2015!!! Marty runs into Biff, who is old now, but not too old to call Marty a butthead.

Then another Biff comes in! Except it's not Biff, it's GRIFF, Biff's grandson! He looks exactly like Biff, just like Marty looks exactly like his own son, because apparently this universe has that *Lady and the Tramp* disease where all the boy babies look like the dad and all the girl babies look like the mom. "Genetics." Hey, I have a question. Who's the Biff of Marty's generation? Who's Griff's dad? Does he look like Biff too? Or does the Biff skip a generation? Doesn't anyone in this world ever fucking notice that there are only, like, *four guys*?

While Griff yells at Biff, Marty takes a sec to get clowned on by Elijah Wood and some other terrible urchin. Just then, Marty Jr.—who is a shambling simpleton, for reasons unexplained— comes in for his afternoon bullying appointment. Griff and his hench-griffs offer the customary 2015 pleasantries, inquiring after Marty's scrote, etc., and then try to persuade him to do this mysterious crime that's going to end his days. Old Marty, listening from his hiding place behind the counter, is appalled to discover that his future son is a "complete wimp" who can't even say no to a large, violent gang of *Lost Boys* extras with mercury poisoning. For shame.

Luckily, Griff tosses Young Marty over the counter in a murderous rage, so Old Marty is able to do a switcheroo, hop up, and take the place of his wimpy, terrible son. And double luckily, Griff calls Marty "chicken" almost immediately, triggering the ancient warlock's hex moste foule that causes Marty to morph into ULTRA-MARTY. He now has the strength of both a teenage boy and a chicken.

Marty punches Griff in the tooth and then steals a little child's hoverboard, which she probably got for her birthday, and zooms away. The hooligans chase him, but Marty is the lithest and craftiest hoverboarder of them all, so he wins. Then, the character of Griff, along with this entire save-Young-Marty-from-making-a-horrible-mistake story line, is abandoned and NEVER SEEN AGAIN.

Instead, Marty goes to the antique store and buys a sports almanac, determined to take it back to 1985 so he can become a billionaire and eradicate chickens. Doc is like, "BR-RRRLLRRLBBLBBBLLBLBBLLLBLLBLBL, YOU DILDO, NO SPORTS ALMANACS IS THE NUMBER-TWO RULE OF TIME TRAVEL!" (The number-one rule of time travel, as far as I can discern from time travel movies, is to never, ever use it to correct any of the catastrophic sins of history, such as by killing Hitler or giving a machine gun to every enslaved person in the antebellum South, but instead mainly just try to pass your history report and hornily scam on babes.) Marty, however, does not care about the fabric of space-time; he cares only for diamonds and rubies.

Just then, the cops find Jennifer's corpse in the garbage, scan her DNA, and get the address where Future Adult Jennifer lives with Marty and their garbage kids. They drop her off there, which is hella dangerous, Doc explains, because if she meets her future self it could "unravel the very fabric of the space-time continuum." It was totally worth it to bring her, though! And thanks, by the way, for having literally two female characters in this entire movie—one of whom spends it either comatose in the garbage or yapping about wedding dresses, and the other who's trapped in a sham marriage being abused by a sweaty gargoyle for sixty years.

Old Biff overhears Marty and Doc talking about the time machine, so he follows them to Jennifer's house and then steals the DeLorean, along with the sports almanac, while Marty's just wandering aimlessly around in the street for no reason. Biff drives back to 1955—he doesn't understand basic words and phrases, but he can intuit how to use a ramshackle time machine?—and gives the sports almanac to Young Biff so that Young Biff can become Rich Biff. Then Old Biff comes back to 2015, puts the time machine back, and sneaks away like everything's cool.

Now, here's my question. If Future Biff gives the sports almanac to Past Biff, and Past Biff uses it to get mega-rich, then doesn't Future Biff turn into Rich Biff? How does he go back to the same regular Hill Valley where Doc and Marty are searching for Jennifer? Wouldn't he instantly transform into Rich Biff? And doesn't that Hill Valley not exist anymore? And, like, at some point in the Rich Biff timeline, shouldn't Rich Biff have to travel back to 1955 to give the almanac to Young Biff? But where would Rich Biff get a time machine? TIME TRAVEL DOESN'T MAKE SENSE, AND I THINK WE SHOULD MAKE IT ILLEGAL.

Meanwhile, at Jennifer and Marty's house, Young Jennifer is hiding in the closet and learning tons of boring secrets. For example, "About thirty years ago," says Lorraine (who's really supposed to be at Rich Biff's velveteen sex casino right now, but okeydokey), "[Marty] tried to prove that he wasn't chicken and he ended up in an automobile accident...that accident caused a chain reaction that sent Marty's life right down the tubes!" Specifically, he injured his hand, and therefore never had the chance to teach Black people how to play rock and roll! *Quelle horreur!*

Then Middle-Aged Marty comes home and we see that he is beige and ineffectual, like a puddle, or a dry chicken breast (JUST KIDDING, MARTY, OH MY GOD, PLEASE KEEP IT TO-GETHER). At this point, you assume that stopping Old Young Marty from injuring his hand, thereby making his family hella pathetic, is going to become one of the objectives of the movie, but it's not. In fact, as far as I noticed, it's never mentioned again. I guess, once Marty and Doc fix the whole Rich Biff situation, the McFly family is just left to wallow in mediocrity forevermore? Which, don't get me wrong—I AGREE WITH. If time travel ever becomes a reality, I don't think its primary utility should be for middle-class white families to erase the minor consequences of their own incompetence. But couldn't we get some resolution here? Anywhere?

Anyway, then Flea's big face appears on a screen to cyberbully Middle-Aged Marty into doing some illegal money business. Marty's boss immediately notices the money crime and fires Marty via one hundred faxes (because in the future, they still send things by fax, just less efficiently). Then Old Jennifer comes home and sees Young Jennifer and they both scream and nothing comes of it, even though Doc said it could potentially END THE UNIVERSE, because the internal logic of this movie is nonexistent.

Doc, Marty, and Young Jennifer go back to the past, and Doc vows that he's going to destroy the time machine "and tackle the other greatest mystery of the universe: WOMEN." Yes, I can understand why you think of women as a great mystery because if the gender composition of this movie is any indication, you have never talked to one.

Doc and Marty abandon an unconscious-again Jennifer in public for a second time, this time just dumping her limp body on her porch. Marty goes to his house and discovers that a completely different family lives there! And Hill Valley has been transformed into a lawless wasteland full of bikers, tanks, slackers, neon bail bonds, and toxic waste! And everybody worships Rich Biff, "Hill Valley's number-one citizen and America's greatest living folk hero!" Marty swings by the Biff Museum and learns that Young Biff used the sports almanac to win every single sports bet in history, and then used the money to buy Marty's mom, and uses Marty's mom as a place to keep his penis. Bogus.

All of a sudden, Billy Zane comes out of nowhere, like Billy Zane does, and bonks Marty on the head and puts him to bed in his mommy's scarlet boudoir. When Marty comes to, he thinks he's back at his regular house, but instead, OOPS. SEXUAL MOM. After remarking upon the size of his mom's cans (attention, men: YOU DO NOT ALWAYS HAVE TO WEIGH IN), Marty comes face-to-face with Rich Biff for the first time. Rich Biff is mad because Marty is a lazy bum who is supposed to be in Switzerland, and Biff has invested many Biff-bucks in Marty being in Switzerland, so WHY IS MARTY HANGING OUT IN BIFF'S SEX-CLAM!?

Here commences a scene that I found so traumatizing as a child that I believe it rerouted the development of my entire worldview. Biff calls Marty a "butthead, just like his old man was," and Lorraine is like, "Don't you dare speak that way about George! You're not even half the man he was!" and says she's going to leave Biff once and for all, and then Biff throws Lorraine violently to the high-end sex-linoleum and sneers, "Who's gonna pay for your cosmetic surgery, Lorraine?" And Lorraine, gesturing to her magnum jugs, goes, "You were the one who wanted me to get these things. IF YOU WANT 'EM BACK, YOU CAN HAVE 'EM."

Okay. Now. When I first saw this movie at age...seven?, I misunderstood Biff's next line so egregiously that it has traumatized me for life—such that, despite having seen this movie multiple times since 1989, I never noticed until now. What Biff *actually* says is, "I'll cut off your kids," an effective threat because Lorraine is a devoted mother and Marty is a hapless butthead who can't even be in Switzerland properly. Solid leverage. But what seven-year-old Lindy *thought* Biff said was, "I'll cut off your TITS."

BECAUSE THEY WERE JUST TALKING ABOUT HER TITS IN THE PREVIOUS SENTENCE, YOU KNOW??? CAN I EVEN BE BLAMED?

Anyway, if you want to turn your little girl into a wet-blanket feminazi killjoy, just make sure that, once in a while, a male character in one of her beloved PG movies uses the threat of sexual mutilation to keep a female character trapped in a physically, sexually, and emotionally abusive relationship for life! It works!

Lorraine opts to stay with Biff (which made way more sense when it was her tits she was going to lose, not Marty's trust fund, TBH), and tells Marty that his dad is dead. Marty barges in on Biff while he's getting sensual with babes in his hot tub hot water machine to ask him where and when he got the dang sports almanac, and then Biff just reveals his entire sinister scheme for no reason and then tries to murder Marty. Doc rescues Marty in the DeLorean, beefs Biff in the face, and they fly to the middle of *Back to the Future I* to yoink the sports almanac and stop a shitty person from becoming rich (because woe betide us all if THAT EVER HAPPENS).

Okay, so then there's a whole bunch of malarkey wherein Young Marty number two runs around trying to slip his little fingers into Young Biff's warm, almanac-filled butt-pocket, while avoiding Young Marty number one, Young Lorraine, and Young Crispin Glover's Reanimated Lawsuit Corpse so that he doesn't accidentally ruin time again (like you give a fuck, you cavalier goofball!). He finally gets the almanac, drops some sandbags upon Biff's goons, killing them instantly, loses the almanac again, gets the almanac back again, and then drowns Biff in manure again, killing him instantly.

Then Joe Flaherty shows up with a special delivery: it's an advertisement for the next movie! Then time marches on, killing us all eventually.

RATING: 5 / 10 DVDs of *The Fugitive*.

I'd Prefer a Highway Away from the Danger Zone, but Okay

Controversial yet objectively factual opinion: Anthony Edwards is hotter than Tom Cruise in *Top Gun*. First of all, the mustache? WORKS. Second of all, he's fun! Third of all, Maverick is such a desperate, narcissistic, posturing, alienating, twerpy little prince that I find myself disorientingly at odds with a former self who long ago considered Tom Cruise to be attractive. Who was she? That woman who could look at a picture of young Tom and not flash immediately to this jittery rat terrier with a barely contained rage problem, a monomaniacal fixation on personal glory at the expense of the safety of everyone around him, and an approach to women that can charitably be described as Biff-esque? I don't know her.[7] Fourth of all, Maverick's hair is bad! It needs to be EITHER SHORTER OR LONGER.[8]

---

7   Paradoxically, I do think that Tom Cruise is an excellent movie star, and I enjoy his movies!
8   ALSO ICEMAN'S HAIR.

Maverick is the villain of *Top Gun*.

I hadn't seen *Top Gun* as an adult, and what I found watching it in my thirties was equal parts bloodcurdling and blood...emulsifying. Like, yes, watching movie stars in their electric youth will never not be life-affirming, as close to the pure beating heart of art as you can get, even if they are just yelling nonsense about planes, and the unapologetic homoeroticism is, frankly, woke as hell (?). Also, Meg Ryan is so good in this! So louche and alive! But, on the other hand, like I said, if he were a real person I would shoot Maverick with a crossbow.

Maverick is a navy pilot who's out flying around with his friends in their planes when they encounter some...Russians? Who are the enemies in this movie? They never say! Maverick can't shoot this son of a bitch, so he decides to see if he can have a lil fun with him. He goes upside down and takes a Polaroid giving the son of a bitch the finger. Dude, that jet is really expensive. How about you be a maverick in your own plane that you buy with your own allowance?

Meanwhile, Maverick's wingman, Cougar, is buggin'. He almost got missiled by one of the enemies, and now he's too freaked out to land, which, is that a real disease? The navy's take appears to be, "We'll just let him fly around until he runs out of fuel and crashes into the sea, oh well," (???) but Maverick goes against orders and escorts Cougar back down to the aircraft carrier. In the first of about infinity times that Maverick breaks the rules and is rewarded for it, he and his friend Goose get picked to go to TOPGUN, an elite fighter pilot combat weapons academy training fly gun bad boy bang bang school in San Diego.

Maverick is so excited about San Diego that he rides his motorcycle next to the fighter plane runway and he is racing the plane and the plane takes off and Maverick does a big fist pump!! Yeah!!!! Boys rock!

At TOPGUN, Maverick and Goose meet their instructor, Viper (Tom Skerrit), their nemesis, Iceman (Val Kilmer), and all the other guys in the program: Sniffer, Stinky, Stumpy, Candle, Bandit, Bratwurst, Rapunzel, LilHorsie, Dustpan, Corncob, Marge, PeePeeBoy, Flipper, and Bingbong. Maverick is pretty arrogant, but Viper likes that in a pilot (WHY?). Maverick is positive that he will be the number-one top gun (WHY?).

> **Goose:** The list is long but distinguished.
> **Bingbong:** Yeah, so's my johnson.

I want to hate it, but "Yeah, so's my johnson" is a real workhorse of a phrase. It goes with anything, like using florals as a neutral. Try it!

They go out to a bar to bother women—"this is what I call a target-rich environment"—and Maverick spots a bangin' blonde he can't wait to alienate with his long johnson. He and Goose ambush her and sing, "You've Lost That Loving Feeling" extremely aggressively into her face while the whole bar watches and laughs, and I tell you I would legitimately fucking catch on fire from embarrassment, but she's just like, "Oh, you GUUUU-UUYSSSSS," as though this is a normal-adjacent thing to do. "I love that song! I've never seen that approach." Truly praise be 2 the cinema for giving me this lifetime of extremely lifelike and believable female human characters!

Maverick's like, "I'm Maverick" (why would you introduce yourself as your call sign!?!? She's not a PLANE), and she's like, "I'm Charlie," and then she just kind of laughs at him and goes off to the little girls' weewee room. And he follows her in there to ask her out!!!!!!!!!!!!!!!!!!! He's so gross!

The next day, at plane Hogwarts, they're having their first lesson with a civilian contractor who's there to teach them about how planes stay up, and—OH SHIT. BATHROOM CHARLIE IS THE CIVILIAN CONTRACTOR. Maverick, did you sexually harass the civilian contractor AGAIN!?!? This happens every time we go to a new fighter boy pew pew school!

They discuss Maverick's upside-down Polaroid maneuver, and Iceman asks, VALIDLY, "Who was covering Cougar while you were showboating?" Maverick is like, "Cougar was doing just fine," but we know he wasn't! He almost crashed and died and then literally quit the navy! Why is nobody but Iceman fact-checking Maverick here!?

We're clearly supposed to resent Iceman for trying to stifle Maverick's unbelievably bitching bad-boy flying skills in the name of "SAFETY" and "REGARD FOR OTHERS" (boooooo!), but, you know what? I actually think being exceptional is bad. It's dangerous and unfriendly and it prevents us from building robust systems of aid and care. It precludes forethought and planning (oh, a hero will save us!), and it undercuts accountability when talented people do bad things (oh, but he's so *special*). My Norwegian mom always told me, "You're not special—never think you're better than anybody else," and I'm glad she did! Now I listen to other people and treat them with respect and wear a mask at the grocery store! Exceptionalism is a grift!

Maverick defeats one of his other instructors, Jester, in a sortie exercise, but breaks the rules of engagement, which kind of seems like it should not count as winning? In celebration, he buzzes the tower and makes the tower man spill his coffee.

Maverick loves to buzz the tower. (That's what he calls it when he shaves his pubes.)

Iceman confronts Maverick afterward for breaking the rules, being reckless, and abandoning other pilots to do whatever he thinks will get him the most attention.

> **Iceman:** You're everyone's problem. That's because every time you go up in the air you're unsafe. I don't like you because you're dangerous.

Wow, some very clear and constructive communication there from Iceman!

> **Maverick:** That's right. Ice...man. I am dangerous.

MAVERICK. IT IS BAD TO BE DANGEROUS. YOU ARE FLY-ING A MULTIMILLION-DOLLAR WARPLANE PRESUMABLY CHUNKY-STUFFED WITH WEAPONS THAT COULD KILL LOTS OF PEOPLE AND POTENTIALLY CAUSE A GLOBAL WAR IF USED IMPROPERLY.

HOW IS ICEMAN THE VILLAIN OF THIS MOVIE???????
BECAUSE HE LIKES SAFETY????????????????????????

THIS IS HOW AMERICA BECAME A HOTSPOT OF A GLOBAL PANDEMIC.

Because my generation was raised to believe not just that safety is for dweebs but that it's EVIL! Maverick is a full psycho and would definitely be at the "reopen America" protests because he wants the RIGHT to get his b-hole waxed even if he isn't actually GOING to go get his b-hole waxed and even though he knows that many thousands more marginalized and high-risk people will die and many b-hole waxing businesses will ultimately fail because you cannot sustain an economy on a handful of slobbering fascists who feel the need, the need for a Jamba Juice. Goose alludes to some dark past involving Maverick's dad, who was also a fighter pilot: "Every time we go up there, it's like you're flyin' against a ghost." And I'm sorry, but that is not an excuse! Go to therapy! You can be in a men's group with Snape!

After several days of doing heavy sex innuendo during class, the civilian contractor invites Maverick over for dinner at 5:00 p.m. But before dinner, it's . . . . beach volleyball time!

This is the famous volleyball scene, where all the guys—Goose, Maverick, Iceman, Pickle, Scabby, Shredder, Splinter, Bebop, Rocksteady, Dave, and Cornholio—oil up and spike the hogskin for a few days. Ohhhhhh, do I ever I wish I were that volleyball! Yeah, hit me with the tops of both of your wrists, boys! Unghhhh!

Maverick is late to dinner because he volleyballed too hard-core, but when he tells her he's "just gonna take a quick shower" (it's HER HOUSE!), she's like, "No, I'm hungry, and I prefer you very wet from volleyball on my furniture." A parrot watches. They decide to date even though she's his teacher and, let's be honest, reads . . . fifteen years older? Which, to be clear, is only because Tom Cruise looks a full Dennis the Menace twelve here.

In class, Charlie uses one of Maverick's dumb maneuvers as an example of what NOT to do while flying a plane, so he flounces off angrily to his motorbikey. She tries to explain to him that she's still gotta be his teacher, but he's like VROOM VROOM VROOM away into the twilight! She chases him in her car, and they jeopardize many lives. When she finally catches up, she insists, "My review of your flight performance was right on,"

(YES), but then admits that she sees some real genius in his flying but she couldn't say that in there because she's afraid that they'll see that she's falling for him. UGH! ET TU, CHARLIE!?

Indeed, it is incredibly inappropriate, and as we have just seen, dangerous, that you are falling for your student! You already can't give him necessary and valid feedback on his flying because of his lacy-crispy-wafer-thin ego! This is bad!

Then they do it. Sex.

Another day, another flying exercise where Maverick abandons his wingman to chase individual glory because he thinks he's the only person who matters. Maverick and Goose feel the need, the need for speed, but I wish they would feel the need for weed and maybe take a nap once in a while?

Iceman once again confronts Maverick for being dangerous and foolish and is once again correct.

Goose's wife, Meg Ryan, comes to town and they all have a great party and get wasted and Goose plays "Great Balls of Fire" on the piano. Meg Ryan tells Charlie all about Maverick's many previous erotique lovers, but assures her that he is extremely hot for teacher now and, yes, don't worry, you should definitely trust that guy! He's absolutely not the exact floor model of a dude who would fat-shame you while you're pregnant and then bang your couples counselor because he's a "super-feeler." For sure marry this unhinged tween!

It's the next day. They're out flying again. Something goes wrong. (I forget.) Maverick and Goose start to crash. They have to eject. But Goose's hatch thingy doesn't detach properly and he blasts straight into the dome exactly like a goose flying into a plate glass window! They parachute into the sea, but Maverick can tell that Goose already died. It was Goose's last honk.

If only he had stuck to boogie-woogie piano.

Maverick is really sad. Meg Ryan tells him, "God, he loved flying with you, Maverick…He'd have flown anyway without you. He'd have hated it, but he'd have done it." What? Why would he have done it if he hated it? What???

Maverick flies bad now. He's scared. He blames himself for Goose's death. He fights with his new partner. All the while, the wretched villain, Iceman, looks on with an expression that says, "How can we build some more productive teamwork strategies?"

Iceman approaches Maverick, just to twist the knife: "I'm sorry about Goose. Everybody liked him." Curse you, Iceman! From hell's heart I stab at thee; for hate's sake I spit my last breath at thee!

The villain of this movie literally only says kind and responsible things the entire time.

Maverick decides he's going to drop out of TOPGUN, and, oh no? It's hard to care about the loss of one insubordinate and only slightly above-average pilot when I have no idea who the navy is actually fighting or what's at stake. Are we in a war? What do fighter pilots actually DO? Am I just supposed to be sad abstractly at the squandering of a great plane-flying talent? Because I'm not. Charlie takes a job in Washington and moves away. Maverick goes to see Viper and gets the classified scoop on his dead dad. I didn't pay attention to what it was. Viper tells him, "You're a lot like he was, only better, and worse." (Thanks?)

It's TOPGUN graduation day. Maverick shows up super late like an asshole and basically misses it. Iceman wins number-one top gun, AS HE SHOULD, and then all of a sudden there's some sort of…enemy…plane…situation…! I don't know what the story line of this movie is!

They have to do a real fighter plane mission like big boys. Maverick gets assigned to fly with Merlin, replacing Goose, and I gotta say I think it's really nice that they let you have a friend go in the plane with you! Not sure how Merlin's big pointy hat is going to fit inside his helmet but NOT! MY! PURVIEW! Iceman expresses some concerns to Viper about letting Maverick pilot a $30 million murder plane right now, and even that is totally reasonable! Maverick has fucked up every single fucking thing, his best friend just died, and he couldn't even show up on time to graduation!

Viper sends Maverick out anyway, and they beat the bad guys (?) (or bad girls—women can be bad!) because Maverick finally learned ONE FUCKING THING, which is not to leave his wingman. Honk honk. Then, at the end, he buzzes the tower again and makes the tower man spill his coffee AGAIN! That's what you get for stealing Merlin's tower!!!!!

Iceman and Maverick have a tender moment, and then Charlie comes back from DC to be Little Miss Mrs. Maverick. Then Maverick emotionally drops Goose's necklace into the ocean at the end, and in conclusion, I just have to say, FUCK YOU, MAN!! GIVE THAT TO HIS KID!!!!!!!

If they recut *Top Gun* with Maverick edited out, it would be a gorgeous short film about sunsets and friendship. Petition to recut real life with all Mavericks edited out.

RATING: 5/10 DVDs of *The Fugitive*.

Fabrizio's Last Meatball

I don't remember a lot of specifics about watching *Titanic* in theaters in 1997, but I was fifteen years old, which means my two primary concerns in life were 1) locating romance, and 2) not dying in a nautical catastrophe. So I think we can safely assume that *I fucking loved that movie*. I watched *Titanic* again on TV with my sister a few years later, making sure to switch it off right before the whole iceberg thingy (stressful!)—a strategy that turns the movie into a pleasant romp about two teenagers who take a perfectly safe boat ride and then bang in a horseless carriage. The end. Charming! Watching *Titanic* for a third time, for the purposes of this essay, I cannot imagine what I was thinking that second time around. I could not *wait* to get to the second half and watch all these motherfuckers drown.

Titanic is three hours and fourteen minutes long, which— fun fact—is longer than the actual journey of the *Titanic* (this is not a fact). It is sooooo ballsy to just assume people will watch your movie for three hours and fourteen minutes! Especially when everyone already knows exactly what happens in the end (spoiler: the boat is Keyser Söze). Sorry, Epcot Center, I'mma let you finish, but James Cameron's balls are like the giantest balls of all time. It would take three hours and fourteen minutes just to walk around the circumference of James Cameron's balls.

Anyway, here's what happens in *Titanic*. In case you forgot, it is terrible:

It starts out on a modern-times submarine. Bill Paxton is snooping around on the ocean floor trying to find a big necklace to impress Britney Spears. James Cameron himself has literally done this, and Paxton's character is clearly Cameron's idea of what a cool person is like—he does stuff like wear male earrings and say "sayonara" in a sarcastic voice. Awww yeeeeah. *Pretty cool.* Bill Paxton finds this old safe in the ocean, expecting it to be full of *Titanic* diamonds, but instead it's just an old doodle of some boobs. Total rip-off!...OR IS IT?

An old lady recognizes her boob-doodle on the news and goes to visit Bill Paxton on James Cameron's rock-and-roll treasure boat, where they make her watch a gruesome CGI reenactment of the *Titanic* sinking (I believe the working title is *Hey, Granny, Fuck Your PTSD*). Then she tells her story, which is extremely not pertinent to treasure-hunting, unless by *treasure* you mean *three hours of nonsense, garbage, terror, death, and Italian stereotypes*.

Turns out, that old lady used to be Kate Winslet, and one time she rode a big boat named *Titanic*. But she wasn't too happy about it! "It was the ship of dreams to everyone else," she says. "To me, it was a slave ship, taking me back to America in chains." Yes. Because generations of imprisonment, rape, and violently coerced labor are *just like* having to marry Billy Zane and live in a fur-lined bon-bon palace. (Also, it's 1912 right now, which means that *real slavery* has only been over for like...fifty years? Maybe a little too soon for the flippant slavery metaphors?) She continues, "I saw my whole life as if I'd already lived it, an endless parade of parties and cotillions, yachts, and polo matches. Always the same narrow people, the same mindless chatter. I felt like I was standing at a great precipice, with no one to pull me back, no one who cared, or even noticed." Nobody notices me! Everyone is so fake! My polo horse is the wrong color! As you can see, Kate Winslet's life is *just* like slavery. She decides to just kill herself immediately so she doesn't have to face another terrible, terrible cotillion.

Luckily, along comes Leonardo "I Am Definitely Wearing Lipstick" DiCaprio, who is traveling to America with his friend Fabrizio (Human Olive Garden Commercial). Leonardo DiCaprio rescues her from suicide, and she repays him by letting her entire family treat him like human feces for the last few days of his life. Then they fall in love.

Leonardo shows up at fancy dinner even though he is a stinky poor and Kate Winslet's mom hates him: "My mother looked at him like an insect—a dangerous insect that must be squashed quickly." After dinner, Leonardo says, "Time for me to go row with the other slaves!" Again with the slave thing. PLEASE READ A BOOK.

In an act of defiance, Kate Winslet sneaks downstairs to party with the simple folk. And look who's down there dancing a jig! "Aaaaaaaay! It's-a me, Fabrizio!" Fabrizio treats everybody to all-you-can-eat breadsticks and then invents the Mafia. Can someone tell me why this movie wasn't entirely about Fabrizio? At the very least, could I get a fan edit called *Titanic 2: Fabrizio's Quest*? (It is a quest for lasagna.)

Next there's a whole bunch of stuff that doesn't involve

Fabrizio at ALL, so I'm on strike. It's the Celine Dion part ("I'm flying!"), the boob-sketching part, and the aforementioned banging part. All of it is incredibly awkward and boring. Then Theoden, King of Rohan, drives the boat into this big iceberg and the ocean starts coming inside the boat, where the people go.

Bill Paxton interrupts the old lady's endless fucking story and is like, "BOAT SCIENCE. EXPOSITION. BOAT SCIENCE," for a while. Nobody cares, Bill!

Kate Winslet and Leonardo DiCaprio run around the boat in circles for a long time holding hands. I think we're supposed to admire Kate Winslet for having terrific moxie or something, but really all she does is yell about how no one can tell her what to do and then just does whatever Leonardo DiCaprio tells her to do. (Sometimes he tells her things like this: "You're so stupid! Why did you do that? You're so stupid, Rose!!!" and "SSSSSHHHHHHHHHHHHHH.")

Fabrizio shows up (FINALLY) to tell them that they're fucked because all the lifeboats are gone: "The boats-a! They're all-a gone!" "Where's your life jacket, Fabrizio?" Leonardo asks. "Ees-a okay!" says Fabrizio. "I've-a got this-a beeg ravioli! Abbondanza!" Then he drowns (oops).

Fortunately for Kate Winslet, Leonardo DiCaprio turns out to be the world's number-one expert in surviving ocean liner disasters—offering genius advice like, "We have to stay on the ship as long as possible! Come on!" Eventually, though, they end up in the ocean, where Kate Winslet sits on a board and cries. Leonardo makes *one* attempt to get on the board with her, but falls off, so he decides to just die instead. Kate Winslet is sad.

Finally, even though she knew Bill Paxton was searching for the necklace, and he patiently listened to her stupid story (it's like she writes erotic fan fiction about herself), that old lady just goes and drops it into the ocean at the end!!! Like, seriously, old lady? First of all, you're a dick. Second of all, that necklace belongs in a museum. Third of all, you're a dick! I wish Bill Paxton would drop YOU into the ocean at the end.

The end.

RATING: 3/10 DVDs of *The Fugitive*.

Dead Man's Pants

Ah, the holidays, when families (some families, possibly, maybe) gather 'round the hearth to enjoy the traditional Fudge Reinhold, the Peter Boyled Potatoes, the Tim Watermallen Salad, and watch Tim Allen's *The Santa Clause* (may its celluloid never decay). It's not the most important Christmas movie, nor the best Christmas movie, nor really a beloved Christmas movie, but it is technically a movie. And it's the only movie that teaches us one of the lesser-known meanings of Christmas: that putting on a dead man's pants constitutes a binding legal agreement to assume all his debts and obligations.

We open at some dumb corporate party for poseurs. Peter Boyle, soulless toy king, is honoring Midwest marketing and distribution team Scott Calvin and Susan Perry for their work shilling some sort of hideous chauvinist ice witch called, "Do It All for You Dolly." Susan gets only a few words into her acceptance speech when Scott (Tim Allen) interrupts because he has no time for thanking people like a woman, he ONLY HAS

TIME FOR PROFITS. After high-fiving Johnson from Sales for incessantly pressing his boner against his secretary, Tim Allen bails on the party and vrooms off into the night.

On his drive home, Tim Allen makes it clear that he does not give a *fuck* about holiday cheer. Eeeeew, a Christmas tree with a bear on it!?!? HORK. A children's merry snowball fight? UGH, JUST EMBALM ME ALREADY. Fuck you, bell-ringing charity Santa! VROOOOOOOOOOOOOOOOOM!

He's late for his divorced dad weekend custody drop-off snide remark summit, but it's NBD because he's not really that into his dumb kid anyway. Exactly what Tim Allen's character *is* into that makes him so single-mindedly disdainful of parenting, non-mute women, and holiday cheer is never revealed. This is a cinematic technique known as "not fucking bothering." Tim Allen is hella mad at his ex-wife's new husband, Neil (Judge Reinhold), for telling his kid, Charlie, that there's no Santa Claus, even though there obviously isn't. Judge Reinhold is a psychiatrist, and because this is the '90s, Tim Allen's character HATES PSYCHIATRISTS even more than he hates having a consistent and discernible personality. (As was scribed in the ancient texts: every movie from the '90s must include equal parts lawyer jokes, hatred for psychiatrists, and your divorced parents getting back together.)

The fact that Tim Allen only bothers to defend the wonders of childhood when it's a convenient vehicle for dissing Judge Reinhold is not lost on Charlie, who clearly can't stand being around this asshole (#NOTTIMALLMEN). Tim Allen attempts to win Charlie's love back by cooking him a phat Xmas turk, but he sets it on fire (BASICALLY IMPOSSIBLE) and has to spray it with a fire extinguisher for one hour. Instead, they go to Denny's, which apparently has two sections: the Asian people section and the sad garbage dads who don't know how to cook turkeys section. It is not hot.

After dinner, they go home and Charlie badgers Tim Allen about the physics of reindeer flight for a while, and then Tim Allen reads "The Night Before Christmas" out loud, dad-style. This seems like a good time to mention the biggest Santa Claus loophole of all, by the way: setting aside the implausibility of flying deer and the impossibility of visiting every Christian household in a single night—if there were actually a Santa Claus, every Christmas morning parents would be like HOLY FUCK HOW DID ALL THESE PRESENTS GET INSIDE MY MOTHERFUCKING HOUSE OH MY GOD CALL 911 SHARON OH GOD KIDS RUN ACROSS THE STREET TO THE FERGUSONS' RIGHT NOW THEY COULD STILL BE IN THE HOUSE. In other words, if there were a Santa Claus, we would know about it because *there would be a Santa Claus*.

Anyhooz, suddenly, there's a commotion on the roof! A clatter!

"DAD, a clatter!!!"

"Charlie, do you know how to call 911?"

"Sure, 911!"

(This movie calls that dialogue a "joke.")

Tim Allen runs outside in his underpants and discovers a fat old man clomping around on the roof. Distracted by Tim Allen's shouts, the man slips and falls off the roof AND DIES. Right there on Tim Allen's lawn. Tim Allen stands and stares at the man for several minutes, doing nothing. DUDE, YOU NEED TO CALL A FUCKING AMBULANCE. EVEN BURGLARS DESERVE MEDICAL CARE. Instead, unperturbed by the fact that there is a rapidly rigor-mortifying grandfather in his yard, Tim

Allen checks the man's ID and it's just a business card that says *Santa* on it. On the back: "If something should happen to me, put on my suit. The reindeer will know what to do." So specific. Is it that dangerous being Santa? He sounds like a sexy DA who went undercover and got in too deep on *SVU*.

A magic ladder appears ("the Rose Suchak Ladder Company"—LINEMOUTH) and Tim Allen and son discover that there's a herd of fucking caribou hitched to a fancy sled on top of their house. The two regard the caribou herd as one might look at an unusual mushroom, or some poorly written microwave instructions. Like, "Huh." They are just not that weirded out by it.

Charlie, being an idiot child, wants to hop in the sleigh and let the reindeer drag them off the roof to their deaths—"Are you gonna put on the suit like the card said? I wanna go too!"— but Tim Allen says no. "YOU NEVER DO WHAT I WANT TO DO!" Charlie laments. YEAH. JUDGE REINHOLD ALWAYS LETS ME PUT ON A DEAD MAN'S CLOTHES AND RIDE A DEER.

Then this inexplicable exchange happens:

> **Tim Allen:** Stay away from those reindeer! You don't know where they've been! They all look like they've got key lime disease!
> **Reindeer:** FAAAAAARRRTT.

And then this:

> **Tim Allen** (standing next to Santa's sleigh): There's no such thing as Santa's sleigh!

Charlie: What about the reindeer? These are Santa's reindeer, aren't they?
Tim Allen: I hope not!

How high are you guys right now.

Tim Allen, who still is not wearing pants, agrees that they can sit in the sleigh for a sec, but then accidentally says the magic words, "Let's go!" and the reindeer gallop off the roof and start flying around. (Not the most practical magic words, IMO. It's like having *ooh* as your safe word.) The frigid December air begins to pimple his naked thighs, so he finally, begrudgingly, puts on Santa's enormous pants. NOW IT'S ON. The reindeer drag him, screaming, from house to house, and at each stop Santa's magic sack sucks Tim Allen down the chimney and squeezes him out like a big red turd. Occasionally, he encounters a precocious child sleeping near the Christmas tree, and they exchange "hilarious" banter:

Child: You're supposed to drink the milk.
Tim Allen: I am lactose intolerant.

Again, if this ever happened even once in history, WE WOULD KNOW ABOUT IT because there would be a police report and many screams.

Oh, ugh, and then Tim Allen does his horrible caveman catch-phrase thing in the form of a "ho ho ho," which sucked my soul out of my mouth like a haunted cat. Then the reindeer ditch them in a frozen wasteland, which turns out to be the North Pole. Tim Allen is mad perplexed by being at the North Pole (like, waaaaaaaay more freaked out than he was about visiting every house in the world in a magic sled) until David Krumholz shows up and is like, "Yo. I am a sarcastic elf. Here's a snow globe."

Krumholz explains that Tim Allen is now required to be Santa Claus because of the "Santa Clause," a line of fine print on Santa's business card requiring anyone who puts on Santa's pants to abandon his life, career, and home, and just permanently be Santa until death because "children hold the spirit of Christmas inside their hearts" or something. I'm sorry, but UNDER NO CIRCUMSTANCES SHOULD TIM ALLEN BE REQUIRED TO BE SANTA CLAUS. You don't fucking own Tim Allen, David Krumholz! Also, aren't you guys sad about the fact that the last Santa Claus—a living, breathing man with whom you presumably worked for many decades, if not centuries—just fell off a roof and died, alone, in the snow? What is wrong with you people? Can someone at least go collect the body?

Tim Allen, somehow, still doesn't believe this is happening. He wakes up in his own bed the next morning, acting like, "Oh yeah, this all seems back to normal. Yeah, I'm wearing another man's silken pajamas, but I probably just bought them in a turk-fume-induced fugue. No big." Charlie, on the other hand, can't keep his dang mouth shut. When his mom picks him up, he's all, "Oh yeah, we totally went to this elf party, and flew a few deer, and, oh yeah, Dad's Santa now." In an even less sensical plot development, the mom hears that and goes, "OH MY GOD, THIS IS LITERALLY CHILD ABUSE." So she and Judge Reinhold begin scheming to get custody taken away from Tim Allen. For "pretending" to be Santa Claus. To his six-year-old child.

"You've got more important things to worry about," Tim Allen quips to Judge Reinhold. "Like where you're going to get more sweaters after the circus pulls out of town." What does this joke mean? What is this circus that sells sweaters? How many sweaters does Judge Reinhold require? How quickly does Judge Reinhold wear his sweaters out? Why does Judge Reinhold get his sweaters at the circus? What is it about Judge Reinhold's sweaters that indicates they are cirque-related? If Judge Reinhold needed a new sweater, why couldn't he just purchase one at a regular store? Or wait for another circus to come to town? If there is one thing to be said for *The Santa Clause*, it's that it asks more questions than it answers.

The next morning, Tim Allen awakes with a fart. AND A BEARD. The Santa Clause, apparently some sort of perverse yuletide virus, has entered its Jiminy Glick phase. No matter how much he shaves and dyes his hair and runs on the treadmill and attempts to eat a salad for lunch instead of eight crème brûlées, his body always bloops back into a fat blond goober. Plus, fat Tim Allen suddenly hates corporate toy ideas like planned obsolescence and success! He is becoming pathologically fun.

So, Tim Allen just keeps getting fatter and jollier, the ex-wife gets SO MAD about Tim Allen's magic beard that she exiles him from Charlie's soccer game, and Judge Reinhold just keeps saying, "You're taking this Santa thing a little too far," over and over again like a broken robot. Eventually, Tim Allen's custody gets revoked by an even shittier judge (WEARING RED AND BEING FAT IS NOT A SAFETY ISSUE), so he does the only logical thing—he kidnaps Charlie and runs away, leading state and local police (and possibly federal agents) on what was no doubt a monumentally expensive manhunt.

Meanwhile, Judge Reinhold and the ex-wife reminisce about when they stopped believing in Santa Claus like normal humans:

Ex-Wife: I was Charlie's age. I wrote Santa a letter every week that year. Okay. Maybe not every week, but...Boy I really wanted a Mystery Date game. Do you remember those? No, of course you don't. No one does. I don't even think they make them anymore, but...Well, anyway, Christmas morning came and oh I got dozens of presents, I got everything. Except Mystery Date. [CRIES.]

Judge Reinhold: I was three. And it was an Oscar Meyer Weenie Whistle. Christmas came, no Weenie Whistle. That's when I stopped believing.

Ex-Wife [weeping]: You were three?

Judge Reinhold: Yeah.

Yo, man, I don't want to fart on your parade here, but a whistle is not a good toy.

As the manhunt continues, Tim Allen and Charlie head to the North Pole because it's time to deliver some presents! (Wait, has it been a year?) For some reason, the elves let Charlie design some new features on Santa's sleigh—because that's really who you want engineering your aeronautical devices. Inspecting the new features, Tim Allen points at two pewter goblets sitting on a small shelf. "What's this?" he asks.

"CD!" Charlie replies.

"Compact disc! Nice!"

"No, it's a cookie cocoa dispenser!"

HOW DID YOU THINK THAT WAS A COMPACT DISC PLAYER WHEN IT IS CLEARLY TWO GOBLETS? I HATE EVERYONE IN THIS MOVIE SO MUCH.

As they get ready to take off, Tim Allen sighs, "How could I do this without you, Charlie?" And Charlie sasses, "You couldn't." Um, pretty sure he could. He can do magic and he has a child army.

Upon returning to civilization, Tim Allen immediately gets ambushed by a bunch of cops and has to get rescued by these sort of Navy SEALs but the elf version. "We're your worst nightmare. *Elves with attitude*." You are correct, movie. That phrase is literally my worst nightmare.

Eventually, Tim Allen proves to Judge Reinhold and his ex-wife that he really is Santa Claus, so she burns the custody papers and for some reason the cops are like, "Eh, bygones," about the multimillion-dollar search and rescue operation, and Judge Reinhold gets his Weenie Whistle and can FINALLY stop crying, and then Charlie tells Judge Reinhold, "I think I'm going to go into the *family business*."

I'm going to push my dad off a roof and steal his magic clothes. And then it's over.

I think my feelings about *The Santa Clause* can best be summed by this (100 percent true) sentence: it took me literally an entire day to get through this ninety-minute movie because I kept getting pleasantly distracted by YouTube videos of farmers lancing cow abscesses. Happy holidays!

RATING: 2/10 DVDs of *The Fugitive*.

Men Yelling Men Yelling Men Yelling

L ook. Is *The Rock* a perfect movie? No. But is it a perfect movie? Maybe!

Just describing the plot of *The Rock* is a lush, lip-smacking thrill, like a piece of bacon that is all fatty rind, like a bowl of Lucky Charms that is all marshmallows—so many elements that could each, alone, be too much, here combined into one film that somehow works, one great, baroque cinnamon roll that is all the middle of the cinnamon roll, *The Jetsons Meet the Flintstones*, a duck-billed platypus, a place beyond decadence, foie gras on your burger, everything you want and nothing you don't and then some more. Nicolas Cage, an unchained freak; Sean Connery, virtuosically hammy; Ed Harris, a haunted prince going down with his ship; antihero vs. antihero vs. antihero vs. the president; and gruesome chemical weapons and a heist and a mutiny and a double mutiny and family drama and Alcatraz and mine carts and fighter jets and flames and a rock, stalwart against the sea.

All that, but with none of the septic irony, the relentless

self-conscious hedging, that infects so much of our lives these days. *The Rock* does not take one single moment to look you in the eye and say, yes, we know this is a little silly, we are sorry, please know we are cool—there's no need! *The Rock* believes in itself, it commits, it is happy to be fun. Coolness is a deadly neurotoxin. Inject *The Rock* into your heart.

In *The Rock*, Nicolas Cage is some kind of...gas expert? (same, LOL) who works for the FBI...de-gasifying...stuff...that the FBI finds that has gas on it. We meet him in an underground gas lab where he is examining a plastic baby. Suddenly, the baby starts leaking gas, which really surprises everyone, though you'd assume they expected something like that since they're having a gas scientist dissect the baby inside an airtight glass cube? Oops, the gassy baby is also a bomb. Nic Cage, rapidly corroding, sums up the situation efficiently: "Okay, I've got some bad news and some really bad news. The bad news is that the gas is corrosive and it's eating our suits. The really bad news is that there's enough C-4 explosive and poison gas to blow the whole chamber and kill everybody in the building."

Like, I just, I'm so grateful for this movie.

Later that night, finally relaxing at home with his hot woman, having narrowly escaped being melted at work, Nicolas Cage finds out his girlfriend is pregnant and demanding marriage. It's a lot for one day! That's why I forgive him for saying, "Whoa, okay, marriage police, pull over!"

Meanwhile, Ed Harris and his friends are on a tour of Alcatraz, probably just having fun, right? NEGATORY. GET READY. Ed Harris is a retired general in the Marines, maybe the best general ever, who's fed up because his boys didn't get any recognition or military pensions after they died doing clandestine black ops.

"These men died for their country, and they weren't even given a goddamn military burial!" Yeah, man, that's fucked up! Ed Harris wants their sacrifices publicly acknowledged by the US government, and he wants each of their families to get $1 million. Seems reasonable!

And the ONLY WAY TO DO THAT, obviously, is to steal some rockets armed with deadly VX poison gas, take over the prison-turned-tourist-island Alcatraz with a band of rude, crude mercenary dudes, and threaten to vaporize San Francisco unless you receive $100 million out of a secret government slush fund within three days! TRULY THE ONLY POSSIBLE WAY TO GET UNCLE SAM'S ATTENTION, ESPECIALLY WHEN YOU ARE A FAMOUS GENERAL WHO LITERALLY KNOWS THE PRESIDENT. Toxic friends will say, "Call a newspaper maybe," but it's Scorpio season, okay? Cut unsupportive snakes from your life, honey!

Ed and friends set up shop in the 'Traz. They lock all the tourists into the cells as hostages, install "anti-motion trembler device[s]" so nobody can sneak up on them from the basement, and rally around Ed for a little pep talk. "Couple hundred years ago," Ed tells them, "a couple guys named Washington, Jefferson, and Adams were branded as traitors by the British. Now they're called patriots." Wow, man, makes u think.

Then Ed sends a Zoom invite to the US government (triggering, TBH) and relays his demands via video chat: "I have choked on these lies for my entire career. But here and now, THE LIES STOP."

(Seriously, though, what was this crystal-clear 1996 video phone? The closest thing to an actual video call in 1996 would have been for Ed Harris to take a bunch of pictures of his Nokia screen while he was playing snake, develop the film at the mall, staple the pics into a flip-book, and mail it to the Capitol in an envelope that he licked with his mouth because they didn't even have the peel-off kind yet. Give *The Rock* a freaking retroactive Nobel for future-predicting already!!!)

The government officials are not sure what to do here. On the one hand, Ed Harris is a famous hero, and they agree that he does make a good point about how much they blow. On the other hand, he is doing a very bad terrorism right now, and they are against that except when it's them doing it in other countries.

Ed makes it real simple: "You alert the media, I launch the gas. You refuse payment, I launch the gas. You send payment, I launch the gas. You launch the gas, I launch the gas. You pay the gas, I launch the pay. You gas the gas, I am the gas."

VX gas is really bad, it turns out—"one teaspoon of this hits the floor, it's lethal to one hundred feet"—and, bad news, Ed has a BUNCH of teaspoons. The VX gas comes in these lime-green bath beads and you know as soon as you see them that someone is getting FUCKED UP by one later. There's only one weapon that burns hot enough to destroy VX: "Thermite plasma...but it's still in the test phase." Well, great.

YOU KNOW WHAT, I'D SAY JUST GIVE HIM THE $100 MILLION, BUDDIES. I'D DO THAT OVER POTENTIALLY LIQUEFYING SAN FRANCISCO. He doesn't even want the money from the taxpayers—he wants it from the slush fund! That's what a slush fund is for! It's literally where the term came from: if Ed Harris comes and says he's gonna turn all the people into slush, then you fund him!

Instead, though, the government decides to give it one college try to stop Ed Harris's chemicals: "Who is your best chemical/biological man?"

Well, he's fucking.

Nicolas Cage and his girlfriend are having sex among one thousand burning candles in his extremely flammable rooftop shack to celebrate their pregnancy. She has put her hair in pigtails for the occasion, so Nicolas Cage says, "Oh yeah, pigtails are naughty. Naw-tayyy!!!"

Have either of these people had sex before?

His phone rings, and he picks up.

I feel like in the '90s people were *always* answering the phone while they were having sex. I remember watching movies as a kid and thinking, like, three out of four adults were probably secretly having sex when you talked to them on the phone! Honestly, I'm still not sure this isn't true! It puts me constantly on edge! This is why I only text!

Nic's boss tells him he has to come in for an emergency gas assignment, so he's like, "I gotta go!" and runs off the edge of the roof. (I mean, you could just finish having sex—it'll take like two minutes.)

Back at the government, the government is trying to figure out how exactly they're supposed to break into Alcatraz when, famously, no one has ever broken out.

Unless…maybe someone HAS! Wow, this is the best plot of any movie!

FBI director James Womack (John Spencer! My president!) is like, "No no no no no no no no no no no no no, HE DOES NOT EXIST!" and the other government guys are like, "Bad news, we know he does exist, and his name is Sean Connery, and he escaped from Alcatraz and he alone knows its secrets, and we know you know he's moldering in a secret prison right now, James Womack! Go get him!" And James Womack is like,

"We can't risk letting him out. He's a professional escape artist!" which, respectfully, is kind of the point, sir?

Sean Connery was a British spy who got put in Alcatraz for stealing a microfilm with all of the US government's dirtiest secrets, such as who shot JFK and what aliens' butts look like, which is why they hated it so much when he escaped. As soon as they caught him again, they put him in a secret dungeon and pretended he never existed—"This man has no identity, not in the United States or Great Britain, he does not exist"—so he could never tell anyone about the aliens' butts ever again!!! But now they need him to team up with Nicolas Cage and break INTO Azkaban and save San Francisco. Tell me another way! There isn't one! Experts say!

They bring Nicolas Cage in to see if he's the gas king of their dreams, and quiz him on VX gas: "It's very, very horrible, sir. It's one of those things we wish we could disinvent." (That's what I say about my *husband's socks*, right, ladies?) Nic passes the test, so they take him to the interrogation room, where they're trying to convince Sean Connery to join the team in exchange for a pardon.

Unfortunately, the FBI sent some bozo agent in to persuade Connery, but when Connery tries to tell him a sly fable about why he doesn't trust the FBI, this guy doesn't even know who Archimedes is! Dumbass! But Nicolas Cage knows about Archimedes! Behind the one-way glass, in the other room, he starts yelling out the answers like Hermione in Potions. The king put Archimedes in prison! James the First! James the First! Essence of Myrtlap!

Womack perks up, like, "Whoa, this guy does chemical weapons AND he watches the History Channel?!? A double threat!" On a hunch, he sends Cage in there to finish the negotiation. On his way out, the bozo agent tosses Sean Connery a quarter, sarcastically, breaking the first rule of FBI: Never give Sean Connery a quarter! You'll see why! (It doesn't really go anywhere, though!)

Connery can sense that Cage is not a bozo, but also not a very good FBI agent. He tells Cage that he will consider the FBI's offer, but in exchange he wants a schower, a schave, the feel of a schuit, and a schwuite at the Fairmont Hotel Schan Franchishco. Cage says okay, and Connery signs the contract without reading it or even asking what the mission is (DUDE).

When Cage leaves the room, Connery uses his spy skills to quickly turn the quarter into a knife. A GLASS-CUTTING KNIFE! He cuts through the window and scares the shit out of Womack, his nemesis. This does not seem to effect anyone's enthusiasm about the plan. Let's go!

Cage is not a field agent—he is more of a laboratory nerd who mostly works with evil dolls—so Womack tells one of the real agents to give Cage his gun. (Really? You couldn't go back to HQ and get one from the closet?) That agent is like, "A gun? For what? You're a chemical freak!" which seems like wildly bad teamwork, and Cage goes, "I'm a chemical super-freak, actually," so credit to that guy for the assist.

We're at the Fairmont Hotel Schan Franchishco in the penthouse schwuite. Connery is getting a haircut from a gay schtereotype on the balcony while the FBI guys are inside going to town on some room schervisch schandwichesh that Connery ordered to dischtract them.[9] Connery seizes the moment to tie

---

9   It feels very Jay Leno, or something, to lean in this hard on the Sean Connery accent joke, but let me tell you, when I finally rewatched *The Rock*, I was

a clothesline around Womack's wrist and dangle him off the balcony, then escape while everyone else is busy rescuing him. Connery's on the run!

> **Hairdresser, cowering in terror on the elevator:** Okay, I don't want to know nothin', I didn't see you throw that man off the balcony, all I want to know is are you happy with your haircut!

Classic gay person!

Now there's a car chase. Connery and Cage and the entire FBI absolutely pulverize San Francisco, which they are specifically in town to save. It seems like if you're Sean Connery, and your whole thing is insisting that you've been wrongfully imprisoned by the US government, maybe you should not commit many guilty vehicular homicides the second you have the chance? Or maybe it doesn't count because nobody seems to be that mad about it. "Damn! This sucks!"—streetcar conductor whose streetcar (i.e., job) just exploded. (Many of these quotes are fake, but this one is real!)

In my memory, this entire movie takes place on Alcatraz.

Counterintuitively, even though he just burned and maimed many, Connery is actually tender. He only ripped Womack's arm out of its socket and ran away from the FBI so that he could go see his daughter for the first time in twenty years and try to make

---

POSITIVELY HORIZONTAL over how much it is not even an exaggeration! I had forgotten! Sean Connery is so utterly incapable of making the alveolar sibilant [s] sound, it is possible that his name has actually been Sawn Connery this whole time! There is no way of knowing!

amends. "I'm not an evil man," he tells her. She's skeptical, and just then every cop in San Francisco drives up. Cage, intuiting the sitch, swoops in with the big save: "He's working with us."

This is a soft, healthy masculinity of which I approve! Men deserve perceptive, caring friendships with other men!

As they sketch out a plan, the FBI tries to get Connery to tell them the way into Alcatraz, but he just says he'll know it when he gets there: "My blueprint was in my head! I was underground for three days in the dark." Everybody's just gonna have to trust him.

Then, unfortunately, Connery says this: "Womack, you're between the Rock and a hard case." Somebody is still rich from writing this line! And, what the hay, I support it!

A Navy SEAL team is assigned to accompany Cage and Connery into the Rock, and *buon giorno*, look who it is! Fabrizio! Fabrizio promises Cage that he will protect him like he would protect his nonna's gabagool. Cage feels a little bit better.

They all get suited up in scuba gear—"In my day, we did it all with a schnorkel and a pair of flippersh"—and swim in through a hole in Alcatraz (that was easy). They're in!

The only way out of this room is through a big tube that is regularly blasted with a jet of flame (what is that *for*?). Sean Connery offers to roll through the flame tube and unlock the door for everyone, and it's okay because he "memorized it" sixty years ago. As soon as he rolls through the tube, the Navy SEALs start bitching, "Looks like he fucked us, Commander." "That son of a bitch jumped ship."

HOW??? EVEN IF HE DID, HE'S NOW INSIDE ALCATRAZ. HE ESCAPED YOU BY ... BREAKING INTO PRISON?????????????

He didn't, though. He opens up the door and is like, "Welcome to the Rock."

OPENING CREDITS. (JK.)

It rapidly becomes clear that Nicolas Cage sucks at breaking into the Rock. He is not good at guns, or climbing, or walking, or being quiet, or being fast, or having a good attitude. And yeah, of course he's not! He's not trained!!!! He shouldn't be there!!!!! It's like having a basketball player on your team because he's good at repairing basketball hoops!!!!!

They creep up to a manhole that will take them to the next level of the Rock. They just have to neutralize the security system first. The Navy SEAL commander successfully tricks the laser prism, but he doesn't know it's also got a wiggle detector! They're caught! Now they are completely surrounded by Ed Harris's boys. It's Marines vs. SEALs.

The Navy SEAL commander tries to reason with Ed Harris: "Sir, we know why you're out here. God knows I agree with you. But like you, sir, I agreed to defend this country against all enemies, foreign and domestic." Wow, what a morally complex situation, almost as though this movie deserves every Oscar, foreign and domestic!

MEN YELLING MEN YELLING MEN YELLING.

Right in the tensest moment, some bonehead accidentally kicks a rock and everyone flips out and shoots each other until literally all of the Navy SEALs are dead, even Fabrizio. Mamma mia. Ed Harris is sad. Nobody heard him yell, "Cease fire." He didn't come here to kill SEALs! He came here to give Marines $1 million! This sucks!

Nobody knows that Cage and Connery are still down there in the sewer tubes, a significant advantage for their mission, but unfortunately they start chitchatting so loud that the mercenaries immediately find them: "We have a rodent problem." "Flush the pipes." They start dropping bombs down there, and not the fun kind of bombs (shits).

Cage and Connery narrowly escape, then sneak into the morgue (which seems to still be fully functional and packed with vats of corpse chemicals, even though this has not been a functioning prison since 1963?) where the first three VX rockets are hidden. Sean Connery throws a knife through a Marine's neck and advises Cage, "You must never hesitate." If you see a neck, you have to throw a knife through it.

Connery covers Cage while he goes to disarm the rockets. "You're shooting too close to the rockets!" Sean Connery will not stop shooting close to the rockets. He's a maverick like that. A Marine is about to pull the pin on a grenade near the rockets, so Connery shoots an air-conditioning unit and it falls on the guy, squishing him, and yet nobody wrote or ad-libbed the line, "Why don't you COOL OFF?" Rude! Maybe I don't like this movie!

This is so stressful that Nicolas Cage finally snaps (YESSSSSSS): "Look, I'm just a biochemist. Most of the time, I work in a glass jar and lead a very uneventful life. I drive a Volvo. A beige one. But what I'm dealing with here is one of the most deadly substances the earth has ever known, so what say you cut me some FRIGGIN' SLACK?"

They escape and/or fall (I forget) into a hole and now somehow they are riding around on a mine cart in a subterranean cavern. Quick Q: Why is that in Alcatraz?

Ed Harris starts threatening to shoot civilian hostages if Connery and Cage don't stop riding around in the mine carts and messing with his rockets. Connery is like, "Okay, lemme hop out of this rolly coaster and just go talk to him." He climbs(?) up there and lays a PHAT guilt trip: "I can't see how you honor the memory of the dead by killing another million... This is not combat, it's an act of lunacy, General, sir. Personally, I think you're a fuckin' idiot." Ooooooooooooooo!!!!!!

It was a great plan, but now Connery and Cage are both locked up in the cells of Alcatraz. If only they knew someone who knew how to escape! Only fifty-one minutes until the vaporization of San Fran! Meanwhile, back in Washington, DC, the thermal plasma is ready. The president is going to plasma Alcatraz!

Sean Connery escapes from his cell, duh, and understandably tries to bail on the whole thing, but comes back at the last second to rescue Nic Cage (cute!) and also San Francisco, I guess. It's not soon enough, though—the time runs out and Ed Harris fires the first rocket! Holy shit!

Everyone braces for San Francisco to disappear, but at the last second Ed Harris changes the coordinates and makes the rocket fire into the ocean because King Triton didn't pay him one hundred million seashells.

Unfortunately, he still has one rocket left, and the mercenaries are going batshit. Ed Harris is like, "Look, it's over, they're not paying us, they're shooting us with thermal plasma, we should probably just bail." And Tony Todd is like, "The day we took hostages we became mercenaries, and mercenaries get paid," and Ed Harris is like, WHAT DO YOU WANT ME TO DO, MAN? Then the mercenaries shoot Ed Harris. It's mean!

Nic Cage and Sean Connery battle it out with the last few most evil mercenaries, who—to be clear—COULD have just escaped at this point and gone back to their regular lives but instead are determined to fire off that last rocket. They're like, "No, if I can't get a million dollars, I at least want to kill all of San Francisco!" WHY, THOUGH? What's the benefit? The whole point is that you are mercenaries driven by self-interest above all!

Cage faces off against Tony Todd.

> **Cage:** Do you like the Elton John song "Rocket Man"?
> **Todd:** I don't like soft shit.
> **Cage:** Well, I only bring it up because it's you. You're the rocket man. [shoots Tony Todd with rocket]

If you've been on the fence about this movie so far, *how about now*?

There's only one mercenary left. He and Cage grapple over the last rocket's guidance chip and—crap! The deadly VX balls spill out and start rolling everywhere. It's Michael Bay's big hot potato moment. Cage finally gets the upper hand and stuffs one of the balls into the mercenary's mouth: "EAT THAT, YOU FUCK!!!"

HOW ABOUT NOW?

With his last breath, as the VX gas leaks around him, Cage stabs himself in the heart with a special anti-chemical weapons potion that makes you immune to all chemical weapons. Sure! He sets off the green signal flare of victory, but before they see it, the Blue Angels have already dropped the first thermal plasma bomb! It's okay, though, because Nic Cage jumps in the water, and thermal plasma isn't hot enough to burn water.

Connery rescues him one last time, and they have a tender moment of nontoxic masculine best friendship. Cage knows that Connery's pardon was a sham and Womack is planning to throw him back in secret prison, so he sends him on his way: "If you can get to the Pan Pacific Hotel, there's clothes in my closet, $200 in the Bible."

Connery tells Cage to go to Fort Walton, Kansas, and he'll find a little treat hidden in the leg of a church pew.

They part.

Cage assures Womack that Connery was obliterated in the plasma explosion. Then he goes to Kansas. He finds the church. He finds the pew. He breaks open the leg. He opens the package.

It's the microfilm. Now he knows who shot JFK!

WAIT

YOU GUYS

WAIT

HOLY SHIT

IT'S LITERALLY THE PRESIDENT'S BOOK OF SECRETS.

HOW ABOUT NOW??

RATING: 9/10 DVDs of *The Fugitive*.

. . . Miami?

Real quick: Was 2003 our tackiest year, as a species? I know the competition is stiff—there was 1997's swing revival, 1998's failure to contain and exterminate said swing revival, or literally any given moment in the Trump era (for instance, the random day I'm writing this, when America's toilet king bragged on Twitter that his daily COVID-19 press briefings are a "ratings hit" rivaling even the *Bachelor* finale!).

But remember 2003, though, when girls wore those miniskirts that were like six floaty napkins stapled to a scrunchie, with perhaps an Edwardian waistcoat sewn of cobwebs as a top? Where at any moment a baby's sneeze across campus might expose Kaylee's entire bunghole and even the slouchy Western belt she wore over her three layers of different-colored camisoles couldn't save her? In case you've repressed the memory, 2003 was the kind of year where Jessica Simpson might wear rubber flip-flops to the Golden Globes, and Nicole Richie was nearly elected president on a platform of "straight blonde hair on top, long curly dark brown extensions underneath, one feather." The 2003 vibe—culturally, socially, politically, spiritually—was very "energy drink commercial directed by Mark McGrath, and not Mark McGrath in his prime, either." Millions of Americans were forced to mourn Mr. Rogers while wearing a hot-pink corduroy train conductor's hat. Never again!

Bad Boys II is a 2003 movie.

Verily, the first ten minutes of *Bad Boys II* are unimpeachable. Will Smith and Martin Lawrence are police officers in Miami who are also good boys. They are hard at work investigating a sophisticated, multimillion-dollar international ecstasy smuggling operation that for some reason is being funneled through an unincorporated community of eight wetland yokels who live in an old boot.

On the night that literally millions of dollars in pills are set to drift ashore in a rusty corn can, the swampy clods throw a Klan rally to celebrate their forthcoming bazonga paycheck and subsequent appearance on *My Lottery Dream Home* (a bigger boot!). But just as the crosses begin to flicker alight, two of the merry Klansmen doff their hoods to reveal...whoa, it's Will Smith and Martin Lawrence! Did you believe me earlier when I said they were good boys? You idiot!

These are BAD BOYS.[10] TWO.[11]

---

10   PLOT HOLE: Sometimes when Martin Lawrence and Will Smith capture a criminal, they triumphantly sing, "Bad boys, bad boys, whatcha gonna do," the theme from *COPS*, because they have defeated the "bad boys" (i.e., criminals). But then OTHER TIMES, they high-five and say, "Bad boys for life," and THEY are the bad boys! So which is it!?!!?!??!? Get it together, movie!

11   I picked *Bad Boys II* instead of *Bad Boys* for this book because a hot sequel can attain a level of hype that the first movie in an eventual franchise just can't. *Bad Boys* was a success. *Bad Boys II* was a WHOLE THING.

Smith and Lawrence, public servants paid with taxpayer dollars, then absolutely indiscriminately massacre the Klansmen using guns, explosions, a helicopter, and Henry Rollins. Which, obviously, if you have to massacre someone, make it an eager foot soldier in a white supremacist domestic terrorist organization with ties to the highest echelons of American political power working to entrench brutal inequalities and bring back slavery if they're being honest, but also, maybe it's better, as a rule, for the state to stay out of the massacre business? Does that make me a Republican? Or the opposite? Either way, Smith and Lawrence have a job to do, which is to stop kids on spring break from having too much fun dancing.

In the melee, Smith shoots Lawrence in his anus. Ten minutes of perfect cinema.

The movies were just kind of figuring out how to use computers in 2003, and nobody was just kind of figuring out how to use computers harder than Michael Bay. It's tempting to say that every frame of *Bad Boys II* looks like a TV commercial, but truly every frame looks like a print advertisement, like those Candies ads where Jenny McCarthy's taking a shit, shallow and glossy and tinged acid green. There are *four* car chases, one of which is at least fifteen minutes long. Even the most passing transitions are giddily tasteless: the camera EXPLODES out of the speedboat's tailpipe and ZOOMS across Biscayne Bay and WHAMS down the ventilation shaft in the backward sunglasses factory and SHOOMPS into the buttcrack of a raver's low-rise jeans and SPROINGS across her transverse colon and SQUEAKS through her appendix and AIRHORNS out her belly button and PLOPS into the Cuban drug lord's mojito as he shoots his favorite nephew in the head while saying, "Adios, kemosabe," or something fucking cool like that.

When faced with a choice, Bay picks "all of the above" every time. He's like a dog in one of those obedience trials who's like, "Obedience? I don't know her," and just goes buck wild on the sausages. Except instead of "obedience" it's "having a coherent plot that holds the audience's attention" and instead of "sausages" it's "explosions, Ferrari chases, and how many different cool kinds of box could a gun come in."

Which, to be clear, I support. I was twenty-one in 2003, and tasteless shit isn't just IN my blood, IT IS MY BLOOD. I crave excess! There's something else I crave a little bit more, though, which is all of the parts in *Bad Boys II* when Will Smith and Martin Lawrence are yelling at each other. More of that, please, Mr. Bay! Maybe 10 percent less car-chasing, 40 percent more bickering! It's the first rule of filmmaking: when you have Will Smith and Martin Lawrence at your disposal to do unlimited bickering, you do not NECESSARILY need to add a scene where a Humvee obliterates a Cuban shantytown, killing many hundreds of impoverished children! Smith! Lawrence! Brutally roasting each other! Make it four hours long! That's your blockbuster! NO NEED TO GILD THE LILY, BAY.

Maybe if I understood *why* the Humvee was obliterating the Cuban shantytown, this diversion would feel worth it to me, but as far as I can tell, the plot of *Bad Boys II* is...MIAMI.

?

Here's what happens, as best I can understand it. Martin Lawrence's sister, Gabrielle Union, is a DEA agent (?) who has gone undercover (?) to infiltrate...something drugs. Something has something to do with the pills from the beginning, and something to do with Russians laundering (?) money (?). Unfortunately, the "bogeys" (did not write down who that was in reference to, do not remember) do a hit on Gabrielle Union's friend (?), causing everyone to car chase for one year. A semitruck full of evil Haitians is chasing Gabrielle Union, who is chasing the bogeys (?), because they stole her Russian's $2 million, maybe. Will Smith is chasing the semitruck in his Ferrari (for seriously SO long—HOW IS THIS FERRARI NOT FASTER THAN THE SEMITRUCK?) on the surface streets of downtown Miami, occasionally firing his assault rifle haphazardly into large crowds of civilians. People are just getting STRAIGHT-UP MURDERED. And what are they trying to track down again, $2 million? Just one of these wrongful death lawsuits is going to cost the City of Miami that much, and Will Smith has killed approximately seven thousand people at this point!! Let it go, dog!

One cool thing about this movie is it's got all the kinds of criminals. It's got the Russian criminals! The KKK criminals! The Haitian criminals! A Cuban guy, I think! That's all the kinds!

The Haitians in the semitruck start dropping their cargo, which is cars, on Will Smith to get him off their tail. These Haitians will NOT stop throwing cars at Will Smith! I wish this movie would stop perpetuating the old stereotypes about Haitians constantly throwing cars.

Smith and Lawrence go back to the office where their boss (JOEY! PANTS!) yells at them for not being "subtle" and "tactical" enough (i.e., totaling twenty-two cars and a boat and uncounted human lives [never mentioned]).

Over at his weird three-quarter-scale mansion (seriously, the ceiling in this one hallway is like five feet high and it is legitimately extremely weird and nobody says anything about it, they just stoop and shuffle around???), the Cuban ecstasy lord discovers that rats are eating all his money, and then says a good line: "Carlos, this is a stupid fucking problem to have, but it is a problem." I laughed! His henchman agrees to call an exterminator.

Meanwhile, the bad boys are attempting to track down the Haitians, so they go to some Haitian guy's extremely culturally sensitive burning-candle-and-spooky-baby-doll-head shop looking for leads.

> **Bad Boy:** We're looking for someone. Haitian blond
> with dreads.
> **Haitian Guy:** Oh, Blondy-dread?

Sometimes I write fake dialogue and pretend that it's real dialogue, as a joke. The above is not one of those times.

He refuses to tell them where Blondy-dread is, so they bash and destroy his entire livelihood with a stick. Serve and protect!

They track the Haitians to a rotting apartment filled, again, with burning candles and spooky baby doll heads (like, you know Haitians are...regular human people, right?) and immediately get into a horrific gun battle. One Haitian makes the toilet water go in Martin Lawrence's mouth. Will Smith shoots another Haitian in the eyeball. Michael Bay does this shot where the camera circles around and around the wall, around and around and around and around and around, so if you accidentally swallowed rat poison earlier, you might want to check that part out. (Also, I don't know, call me an SJW, but I think it kind of matters how many Haitians a cop shoots in the eyeball in one day?) Eventually, they find a Haitian camcorder with a tape in it, which will surely tell them the ????? they need to ???????????????????.

Now, one would assume that the Miami police department

has, bare minimum, *one* VCR on one of those rolling carts they used to wheel into the classroom for movie day to perform the extremely basic task of playing the videotape that's inside the Haitian camcorder. But I guess the cops have never needed to watch a video before 2003? Instead, Smith and Lawrence go to a crowded electronics store and bully some dweeb into accidentally playing the tape on all four hundred TV screens, which is uncomfortable (and possibly a crime?) because it's completely a porno.

Then, I forget why, Smith and Lawrence go into a private room at the Best Buy for a quick heart-to-heart, but unfortunately the aforementioned dweeb switches all four hundred TV screens from the porno to a live feed of their feelings convo! Which is uncomfortable because Martin Lawrence is complaining at length about what Will Smith "did to his ass" and how his erection is now flaccid. Now everyone in the Best Buy thinks they're gays!!!!![12]

I have no idea what information they glean from the Haitian camcorder porno, but it is decided that they must go pose as exterminators to infiltrate the Cuban drug lord's rat-infested mini-mansion. But first they have to literally go to exterminator school to learn how to fight bugs, which they do *extremely badly*, THANK GOD. LESS SHOOTING AND HOMO-PHOBIA, MORE WILL SMITH AND MARTIN LAWRENCE EXTERMINATOR TRAINING MONTAGE. At the Cuban guy's house, Lawrence sees two rats having sex and he's like, "He's

---

[12] I forgot that in 2003 homophobia was normal as shit! The age of the metro-sexual, I guess! Everything was vaguely homophobic, but also OBSESSED with gay men. Sometimes it is nice to live in the future.

straight pile-driving her! They fuck just like us!" HAHAHA-HAHA!!! WOULD WATCH MARTIN LAWRENCE SEXUALLY DEGRADE A RAT FOR TWO-PLUS HOURS.

Their only job on this mission is to plant some kind of microphones in the house, or maybe tap the phones, who fucking cares, but instead of getting the job done and getting out of there ASAP, they both go tromping around the house, creepin' and peepin', until they get deeply and absolutely caught. Could you have done a worse job of this???? Will Smith discovers that the Cubans have chopped up a Russian and put him in a "tortilla bin" (what?), so they car-chase outta there in the exterminator van, presumably putting all actual employees of the REAL exterminator company, who still have to go to work tomorrow, in mortal peril. But who cares because they get away. Protect! And! Serve!

Holy shit, this movie is only HALFWAY OVER.

Next, Will Smith wears a suit that is three different shades of shiny purple with purple sunglasses. More like two-thousand-and-YEE-IKES!

Okay, there's a thing I didn't bother to tell you about earlier in the movie, but now it's important. The Cuban drug lord is smuggling the ecstasy pills into America inside corpses inside coffins that are on boats. Then, they put money inside different corpses, or maybe the same corpses, and smuggle those back to Cuba. Here is another real line from the movie and not one I made up to make fun of the movie: "We need to put my money in coffins to Cuba faster!" Straightforward!

The bad boys grab Michael Shannon from the jail where he's awaiting trial for being in the KKK at the beginning of the movie. They need him to do...something (?), so they put him in the trunk of their car and go on another car chase. Sometimes Michael

Shannon will yell something hilarious, such as, "These men are violating my rights!" It's funny when cops abuse their power!

The Cubans are driving a big van full of drugs / cash-stuffed human corpse turduckens. Smith and Lawrence chase them for so long that the corpses start falling out of the van, and it is very humorous! Haha, those are people's relatives! Will Smith runs over somebody's dad and his head pops off! Hahaha! Reminder: this is all to stop ecstasy from entering North America.

They sneak inside the Cuban crime mortuary, and Martin Lawrence accidentally eats two ecstasy pills out of a corpse's rotten body cavity. They go to their captain's house, where Martin Lawrence gets his erection back and why can't this whole movie be Martin Lawrence on ecstasy at Joey Pants's house?? Reader, it's not.

They finally intercept all the money and the drugs, but unfortunately, the Cuban guy has intercepted Martin Lawrence's sister and taken her back to Cuba. But Joey Pants won't help! So they're like, "We've just gotta do it ourselves, man."

THAT IS ALREADY WHAT YOU DO! YOU HAVE NOT FOLLOWED ONE RULE THIS ENTIRE MOVIE!

But then, all their cop buddies are like, "We are also bad boys! We will go with you!" and the entire Miami police force leaves the country to invade a sovereign nation to save Martin Lawrence's sister—who, by the way, works for the DEA! What are they doing to help? Is there truly no protocol for when a federal law enforcement agent gets kidnapped by a drug cartel? That's never happened before?

Doesn't matter because Smith and Lawrence have a "protocol" too, and it involves the phrase "throw a bag of cats and iguanas over the fence." Nothing could go wrong!

After that, all they have to do is dig a tunnel under the Cuban guy's lawn (how much are these Cuban people getting paid to dig this tunnel, BTW?), use a remote control car to distract some guys playing soccer, blow them up with a bomb, pop out of the hole in the lawn with a rocket launcher, jump out of a coffin and start shooting random landscapers, punch an elderly woman in the face, take a small child hostage, then race to Guantanamo Bay in a yellow Humvee, pulverizing the previously noted shantytown on the way. Like, those places aren't sparsely populated—they are DENSELY OVERCROWDED WITH POOR PEOPLE AND CHILDREN. I mean, I like Gabrielle Union, but......??????

Now they've got the Cuban military shooting at them from behind and the American military shooting at them from the front, so they screech to a stop in a live minefield, and I'm sorry, but EVERYONE WOULD BE DEAD.

Then Martin Lawrence shoots the drug lord in the head and Will Smith and Gabrielle Union kiss.

This concludes.........???......?.........MIAMI.

RATING: 7/10 DVDs of *The Fugitive*.

The Real Monster Is Inspections

We open on some bushes. *Scary bushes*. You can tell the bushes are scary because a bunch of dudes in jumpsuits are standing near them looking scared. The bushes are all, "Rustle, rustle. Rustle, rustle." There is *definitely* something in those bushes. Some sort of monster. "Come over here," the bushes whisper. "Try me, I'm just bushes!" Suddenly, the monster begins to emerge. The leaves part. Is it a bigfoot? Is it a dino?

No!!!

It's just some dumb forklift carrying a dumb box. The monster, it turns out, isn't a monster at all—it's a machine. The real monster, you see, *is man*. (Or else the real monster is forklifts. Unclear. Will circle back.)

Oh, except there actually are actual monsters in the box that the forklift is carrying. They're called velociraptors, and they are the world's biggest a-holes. Right away they wiggle out of the box and eat this dude named "the Gatekeeper," and then they're like, "OM GROM GROMPH. WASN'T EVEN HUNGRY—JUST ATE HIM

TO FUCK WITH YOU GUYS #YOLO." One of the velociraptors makes extended Six Sigma eye contact with this hunter dude (let's call him "the Keymaster") through the bars, like she's thinking, "I shall bookmark you for later, Keymaster." And she does.

Foreshadowing.

Now we're in an amber mine in the Dominican Republic! Try to keep up! A lawyer is there, being annoying. "Waaaahhhhh, I want inspections! Inspections are my food!" yells the lawyer. "Mr. Hammond *hates* inspections," says the guy in charge of the mine, all normal as though that isn't the vaguest thing in the world to hate. The lawyer suggests that they get a certain "Dr. Grant" to do the inspection because of "insurance." (Not sure why that's the mine guy's call, but bygones.) Mine guy isn't into it. "Grant's like me," he explains. "He's a digger." Then the miner, who's been mining this whole time BTW, gets very excited about something he's just mined. It's a piece of amber with a bug in it. The lawyer, feeling less appreciated than an old bug (and still very concerned about inspections), stomps off to sit on a tuffet somewhere and lick an oversize lollipop, probably. That's a lawyer stereotype, right?

Cut to the Badlands. Dr. Grant (Sam Neill, incidentally an Instagram MUST-FOLLOW) is digging (OF COURSE) at a fossilized velociraptor skeleton, which is just sort of half-buried in one to two inches of soft sand, like the cap to your sunscreen, or Joey in the opening credits of *Friends*. Is that how easy it is to find a velociraptor? "I hate computers," says Dr. Grant. Dr. Grant *hates computers.* Dr. Grant touches Laura Dern on the buns to establish that their relationship is caliente yet tender. Laura Dern, in double denim, is busy agitating for Dr. Grant to impregnate her with a small paleontological baby. No luck yet.

Wait, who's that talking? UGH, it's a kid. DR. GRANT HATES KIDS. They're like computers but covered in food and hair! Even worse, this kid is talking talking talking, and he has no respect for dinos. "That doesn't look very scary," the kid says, eyeing the velociraptor with disdain. "More like a six-foot turkey."

:-|

"Oh no," says Laura Dern, shaking her head. She knows what's coming. Dr. Grant is going to spill the intestines of an innocent child with his six-inch turkey claw AGAIN. (The paperwork alone!) But in the middle of his super-mean lecture about dino behavior and the fashionable disembowelment theories of the day, Dr. Grant is interrupted by the arrival of a helicopter full of Richard Attenborough's hubris. Richard Attenborough (Mr. Hammond, mentioned earlier, hates inspections, etc.) has *ruined the turkey dig*. But it doesn't matter. He's there to invite Dr. Grant and Laura Dern to inspect his mysterious new theme park. Then this dialogue happens:

> **Hammond:** There's no doubt our attractions will drive kids out of their minds.
> **Grant:** What are those?
> **Laura Dern:** Small versions of adults, honey.

Solid joke!

Then there's a scene of Newman eating breakfast. Later in the movie, breakfast eats Newman.

Foreshadowing.

Dr. Grant and Laura Dern hop into Richard Attenborough's helicopter and point the pilot toward Costa Rica. Also on board is Jeffward Goldblum as mathematician Dr. Ian Malcolm, about whom it is extremely difficult for me not to write in all caps, even though Jeff Goldblum has kind of become a played-out meme now, which I resent.

Jeff Goldblum explains that he's not a mathemagician so much as a "CHAOTICIAN. Chaotician."

Dr. Grant, being some sort of Flintstone who has never ridden in a motorized vehicle before, fumbles with the seat belts like a confounded granny in an infomercial for lids. The helicopter descends, and everyone hops into some jeeps. At this point, Richard Attenborough has flown four people *all the way to Costa Rica* without actually telling them why the fuck they're going to Costa Rica. Presumably, they've been sitting in a tiny enclosed space staring at each other in silence for hours and hours. Nobody seems to think this is weird. Nobody is yelling at all.

The jeeps rumble deeper into the jungle. "HEY, RICHARD ATTENBOROUGH, WHAT'S WITH THIS BIG FENCE?" "DON'T WORRY ABOUT IT. IT'S DEFINITELY NOT FOR MONSTERS."

Finally, it's time for the Big Reveal. There's dinos! Dinos everywhere! Dr. Grant pees his own pants, and then he pees Laura Dern's pants too, and then a butterfly pees its pants and it causes a landslide in Calabasas. "We're going to make a fortune with this place," says the lawyer, who clearly doesn't understand that greedy lines like that get you killed in Steven Spielberg movies.

"Welcome to Jurassic Park!"

Richard Attenborough leads them all into a little movie theater where he has a conversation with a piece of cartoon DNA named "Mr. DNA." Turns out, Jurassic Park scientists were able to build their own "dahnasauwwwers" by extracting blood from the stomachs of dinosquitos, putting the blood in a jar with some frog DNA and glue, and then shaking it. Or something like that. I don't know. Go ask B. D. Wong.

The dumb lawyer asks if B. D. Wong is "auto-erotica," but he means "animatronic." It is offensive how little the lawyer knows about B. D. Wong.

After watching a baby velociraptor hatch, Dr. Grant starts asking uncomfortable questions about how they control the dino populations. B. D. Wong explains that all of the animals at Jurassic Park are ladies because B. D. Wong is on top of his shit and he engineered them that way and why must you always question B. D. Wong?

Time to feed the raptors! The hunter man lowers an entire cow into the raptor cage, and they go fucking nuts. (Jurassic Park absolutely keeping the cow sling industry in the black.) Hunter guy gives a terrifying PowerPoint on how smart the raptors are, their SAT scores, their sudoku speed, their vengeful hunger for human intestines. Richard Attenborough tries to distract everyone with lunch—"Alejandro's prepared a delightful menu for us. Chilean sea bass, I believe!"—but ALAN GRANT DOESN'T GIVE A SHIT ABOUT CHILEAN SEA BASS. He just wants to stand around and worry about raptors. (Dude, Alejandro probably worked really hard on that!)

Okay. Then these kids show up. Disregarding why anyone would bring children to an uninspected monster island, everyone gets back in the jeeps and they head out for a tour.

"Hold on to your butts," says Samuel L. Jackson (Jurassic Park's chief engineer), demonstrating that he's the type of cool dude who says things like, "Hold on to your butts," possibly even *twice in one day.* (Foreshadowing.)

They don't see any dinosaurs right away, but that's not really important because Newman is busy fucking up everything on earth. See, Newman figured out a get-rich-quick scheme called "steal the dinosaur embryos and sell them to a shadowy warlock" because that's really who you want to have control of your rogue dinosaur embryos. Just the ne'er-do-welliest fool on earth. In order to get the embryos and get out of the park undetected, Newman shuts down the security system. AGAIN. REALLY PLAYING FAST AND LOOSE WITH THE DINOS HERE.

Over in the jeep, everyone is irritated that they haven't seen a *T. rex* yet and Jeff Goldblum is doing philosophy.

> **Jeff Goldblum:** God creates dinosaurs. God destroys dinosaurs. God creates man. Man destroys God. Man creates dinosaurs.
> **Laura Dern:** Dinosaurs eat man, *woman inherits the earth*.
> **MGTOW Lawyer for Sure in His Head:** MISAN-DRY!!!!!!!!!!!!!!!!!!!!

Everyone stops to help a Triceratops with a tummy ache and dig through its mammoth dump. (Fun fact: Laura Dern never goes anywhere without her elbow-length dump gloves. Both Laura Dern's character in this movie and the actual Laura Dern.)

Uhhhhh, okay, let's fast-forward. This is taking forever. The *T. rex* gets out. The lawyer tries to hide in a toilet house, but *T. rex* finds him immediately because this is the '90s, so *T. rexes hate lawyers*. Newman gets eaten by some fancy lads (GOOD), while everyone else runs around screaming, or holds perfectly still, depending on their prior knowledge of dinosaur eyeballs. They all spend a long time trying to escape dinosaurs and sometimes getting covered in boogers. Dr. Grant pulls an extremely hilarious and appropriate prank involving an electric fence and some severely traumatized children. Everything is fucked.

(Cut to the interior of the Jurassic Park gift shop. Foolish humans and your ridiculous dinosaur thermoses.)

Richard Attenborough is making a speech about fleas. He just wanted to make something that wasn't an illusion, you know? "I wanted to show them something that wasn't an illusion. Something that was real. Something they could see and touch." And get dismembered by.

Off in the jungle somewhere, in grave danger of being seen and touched, the boy-child calls the girl-child a "nerd" and she goes, "I'm a hacker! I am not a computer nerd—I prefer to be called a hacker." Then the boy-child gets fried on an electric fence and Dr. Grant dubs him "Big Tim, the Human Piece of Toast"—which also, coincidentally, is my stripper name. What are the odds.

Samuel L. Jackson decides that he needs to go reset the main power switch to fix all the crap that Newman fucked up. I think you know what that means. It's HOLD ON TO YOUR BUTTS NUMBER TWO.

When Samuel L. Jackson doesn't come back from his butt mission, Laura Dern decides it's time to hold on to *her* butt and go find him. She and Richard Attenborough have this exchange:

> **Richard Attenborough:** It ought to be me, really, going.
> **Laura Dern:** Why?
> **Richard Attenborough:** Well, I'm a . . . and you're a . . .
> **Laura Dern:** We can discuss sexism in survival situations when I get back.

ROAST HIM, DERN.

While Laura Dern runs to the switchy-hut (I am literally an engineer), the hunter man attempts to give her cover from the marauding velociraptors. It's the perfect job for him, seeing as he is the world's number-one expert on how to not get eaten by velociraptors. He immediately gets eaten by velociraptors.

Over the walkie-talkie, Richard Attenborough gives Laura Dern instructions: "You've got to pump up the primer handle in order to get the charge. It's large, flat, and gray. Like my penis."

Laura Dern manages to get the power back on, but not before being attacked by a raptor and snuggled by Samuel L. Jackson's dismembered arm.

Hey, hey, Samuel L. Jackson, MAYBE YOU SHOULD HAVE HELD ON TO YOUR ARM.

Meanwhile, the raptors are chasing the kids around the kitchen (you guys, Alejandro has to clean all that up!), and they would have gotten *so eaten* if they hadn't come across science's number-one most effective dinosaur avoidance tool: the ladle. (Laura Dern never goes anywhere without her dump gloves and seventeen ladles.)

Everyone is *almost safe*, but they just need to fix the computer so they can lock the raptors out. The hacker child runs over to help. Fortunately, it is a UNIX system (and/or Microsoft Entertainment Pack Fuji Golf), and she knows this.

Blah blah blah run from the raptors some more, and then OH SHIT, *T. REX* COMES IN AND SAVES THE DAY AND EATS THE RAPTORS AND IT IS RIGHTEOUS AS HELL. Keep this metaphor with you always—it is very useful when you have more than one problem at once. Sometimes you have to let the *T. rex* fight the raptors.

RATING: 10/10 DVDs of *The Fugitive*.

No Toucan Will Ever Make ME Have Sex!

W elcome to Africa! It's the crack of dawn, and some motherfucker is singing REALLY FUCKING LOUD. I don't
speak Zulu, but I believe the lyrics roughly translate to "WAKE
UP, ANIMALS, IT'S TIME FOR A BABY LION'S BIRTHDAY
AND NO ONE CARES ABOUT YOUR HANGOVER."

Rhino is like, "Whut." Antelopes are like, "Whut." Meerkats
are like, "Is this guy GD serious." Cheetah is like, "Let me walk
up this hill for a better view of you waking me up." Birds are
like, "Yo, really?" Mom giraffe is like, "YES, you have to go to
the birthday party. It's my boss's kid." Baby giraffe is like, "BUT
WHAT KIND OF PSYCHO HAS THEIR BIRTHDAY PARTY
AT 5:00 A.M.!?!?" Leaf-cutter ants are like, "Sorry, man, couldn't
get the day off." Elephants are cool; they love a party.

They all gather around this big rock with a lion at the top. The
lion is named Mufasa. This krazy baboon climbs up there and
hugs Mufasa like they are old bros, which probably would not
happen. Then this woman-lion is like, "Look over here, baboon,

I've got a baby!" And baboon is like, "JACKPOT!" So the baboon rubs some jam on the baby and then throws dirt in its face, and then he dangles the baby off the edge of the rock with some Michael Jackson blanket-head realness. You know, LIKE THE WILD ANIMALS DO IN AFRICA.

Meanwhile, this kiss-ass toucan goes to visit another lion named Scar, Mufasa's no-good brother, who's just chilling in a cave nursing his wasting disease. The toucan's mad at Scar for missing the baby-dangling jam ceremony. Scar eats the toucan. Luckily, Mufasa comes into the cave and is like, "Do not eat my toucan, please; I need him for blathering and ineffectual child-care." Scar's like, "FINE," and spits him out.

The baby lion is named Simba. Mufasa takes him up to the top of this rock and is like, "See *everything*? That's yours." Because someday Simba will succeed Mufasa as king...of...Africa?

I don't really understand how this form of government works. First of all, they leave out the part where Mufasa just FUCKS ALL THE LADY LIONS. Because that is *definitely* part of the deal. But second of all, what are Mufasa's administrative responsibilities? And why should the zebras and the antelopes trust him to look out for their best interests!?!?! If, *once per day*, Barack Obama killed and ate three of my cousins, I'm not sure I'd have stayed a registered Dem through the whole administration.[13]

Oh, but don't worry. Mufasa has some bullshit explanation for why it's okay to eat their constituents: "Everything you see

---

13 Hahaha, this joke was funny during the Obama administration, when it was written, but is less funny during the Donald "Inject Disinfectant" Trump administration! Hahahaha, I long for the sweet relief of a lion's jaws closing upon my head!

exists together in a delicate balance. When we die, our bodies become the grass, and the antelope eat the grass." Yeah, um, you sure the antelopes are cool with that? I mean...the elephants and the zebras *also* become the grass. Couldn't one of them be king, seeing as they've never killed and eaten a single one of their subjects? I just feel like the grass to murder ratio is a little off in your leogarchy.

Anyhoo, Simba goes running back to Uncle Scar (remember when you were too young to know which uncles were creepy?) all braggin' about how he's going to be king of Pride Rock someday. This is a sore spot for Scar, who really, really wants to be the king because he LOVES LION BUREAUCRACY, I guess. So then he decides to just *murder Simba* and resume his position as Mufasa's number two. Say what you will about Scar, but when the dude has an idea, he commits. Simba isn't just a baby, he's a KITTEN. Can you imagine if there was a kitten *that was also your nephew*? The only thing less murderable than that would be if, like, the knowledge of how to make chocolate chip cookies only existed in the mind of a mini-horse that was also your grandma.

So anyway, Scar tells Simba about this really cool forbidden elephant graveyard (kind of a misnomer—really more of an "elephant just-lay-down-and-die-wherever-yard"), so Simba asks his best friend, Nala, if she wants to "GO TO THE WATER HOLE" [WINK]. Nala's mom is like, "Fine, but take that wet blanket toucan along." On the way, wet blanket toucan casually mentions that Simba and Nala are in an arranged marriage and are definitely going to do penis-in-vagina someday. Reeling from the news, Simba sings one of the film's most popular songs: "I Just Can't Wait to Be King (So I Can Make a Law that Says NO TOUCAN CAN EVER MAKE ME HAVE SEX)."

Then the toucan accidentally flies into a rhino's asshole and the kids ditch him.

At the elephant graveyard, the kids start playing around on the bones (dood, those are people's moms!) and are cornered by Scar's three hench-hyenas. The hyenas are about to eat them until Mufasa shows up and bites the hyenas until they go away. I guess nobody explained to Mufasa that when a hyena eats a baby lion, the hyena turns into grass, and then the *antelopes eat the grass*!

The circle of life is way more complicated when everyone can talk.

Mufasa's like, "Simba, I am very disappointed in you," and Simba's like, "I was just trying to be brave like you!" and Mufasa's like, "Oh, I can't stay mad at you (for violating all the laws of our nation and placing yourself and Nala in mortal peril and desecrating Jeff's grandma's grave and almost making Scar the fucking king!)," and then bestows upon Simba the royal noogie.

No offense, Mufasa, but that went *really* quickly from punishment to noogie. Like, you need to have some follow-through here, man! If you don't want your kid to turn into a weird bug-eating recluse who lives with a warthog, you've got to enforce some rules. Real question. Does Mufasa actually exhibit any genuine parenting skills, besides having a deep voice?

Back at the cave, Scar hops out of his iron lung for a sec to be like, "WTF is you guys's problem? You were supposed to eat my nephew," and the hyenas are like, "Well, yeah, we were going to, but…" Then Scar sings the "Kill Mufasa" song, and it's probably the most boring part of the movie, *including* the part where Rafiki is just doodling in his magic tree.

Scar lures Simba to this ravine and has the hyenas kick off a wildebeest stampede. I feel like here's how long a baby lion could outrun a wildebeest stampede: "Oh no, it's a st—"

Instead, Simba climbs a little tree and waits for Mufasa to come rescue him. But as soon as he's pulled to safety, Scar throws Mufasa off this cliff like a total dildo and he gets squished by wildebeests!!! And then Simba is all down in the dust cloud like, "Daaaaaaaad!"

Dad? Are you my dad?

NOPE, WILDEBEEST. CLOP CLOP CLOP CLOP CLOP.

Scar tells Simba that it's his fault Mufasa died and everyone's going to be mad at him, so he needs to "run away and never return." And Simba's like, "That seems reasonable." And then Scar is like, "Okay, new government. Hyenas are lions now."

Simba wanders out into the desert and is about to become a buzzard's snack when he's rescued by Timon and Pumbaa, a pair of confirmed bachelors who only care about two things: denial and bugs. They're like, "Listen, kid. We know that you just witnessed your father's murder and snuggled with his corpse and then were framed by your uncle and subsequently became a homeless youth and were almost eaten alive by vultures as you wandered in the desert, but you should have a positive attitude! Similarly, Pumbaa farts a lot, but you don't see him moping around. WHAT'S A-MOTTO WITH YOU????"

Also, Timon is just constantly sticking his entire forearm into Pumbaa's nostril.

Simba grows into an adult, lovin' life, somehow eating enough bugs to sustain an entire lion, until one day when this other lion shows up. Oh, shit! It's Nala! And she's a hottie with a naughty body! And she's like, "Simba! You're the king!" and Timon and Pumbaa are like, "WHAT IS A MONARCHY WE ARE ANIMALS."

As Simba and Nala erotically lap water from a stagnant bog, their eyes meet and it's LIIIIIOOOOON ROOOOOOMAAAAAANCE!!!!!

Nala tries to convince Simba to come back to the Pridelands and fix all the shit that Scar douched, but he's like, "Nah," and she's like, "K." Timon and Pumbaa are all, "YAAAAASSS!!! BACHELORZ 4 LYFE! MGTOW!" and Simba gets ready to kick back and eat bugs until death.

Then Rafiki the krazy baboon shows up and tells Simba that his dad is still alive—which, I don't know how many of you have a dead dad, but it's a pretty fraught issue—and then when Simba gets all excited, he just points to Simba's fucking reflection in a pond and gives a speech about how dead people live forever in our hearts. Yeah, I know my dead relatives live on inside me, but fuck you, man! That's really not the same as being able to hug your dad! This is emotional monkey abuse!!

Luckily for Rafiki, who is about to get punched in his fucking tooth, Ghost Mufasa picks that exact moment to show up in the sky and lecture Simba like a dick. "Simba," he says, "you're a fuckup. You are more than what you have become. You must take your place in the circle of life. Stop eating bugs, you loser. Remember who you are. You are my son and the one true king." Then he goes back up to lion heaven to play two-on-two basketball with Confucius, Anne Frank, and James Gandolfini.

Simba decides to go challenge Scar and reclaim his throne. After running across the entire Sahara, I guess, he gets to the Pridelands where Scar has somehow managed to dry up all the water with his shitty attitude. Despite being a diabolical mastermind, Scar immediately admits to killing Mufasa for no reason, undermining 100 percent of his leverage against Simba. Simba dumps him off a cliff, while Pumbaa kills all the hyenas for fat-shaming him.

Then all the water comes back to the Pridelands, due to physics.

So, the moral of *The Lion King*, I guess, is don't push your older brother into a wildebeest stampede because someday your nephew might throw you in a hyena-infested fire? Also, the sky is full of dead lions. Being alive is a fright.

RATING: 7/10 DVDs of *The Fugitive*.

Look at Your Little Punk British Ass

I was always fascinated as a kid when an old movie star or musician would die and my parents would get sad—it was a window into their lives before I existed, and not just their lives but a whole world of lives, a breathing cultural atmosphere, a past that was as real as my present even though I couldn't feel it. These people I lived with and thought I knew had intense relationships with a galaxy of celebrities whose names meant nothing to me. They had crushes on them, they went on first dates to their movies, they saved up to buy their records and cried to their songs, and then, like, thirty years later, Lana Turner would die and I'd say, "Who?" and my dad would shake his head and say, "Oh, she was terrific." She was???? What else do you love that I don't know about!? *Who are you really, sir?*

I realized today that someday Jackie Chan will die (probably? I mean, maybe not?) and my kids will be like, "Who?" and I'll try to explain about *Rush Hour* and Chris Tucker and how when I was a kid Jackie Chan was not just famous but UBIQUITOUS, and they'll shrug and file it away under "old celebrity" just like I did with my parents—as though Jackie Chan and Chris Tucker belong in the same folder as, say, Hulk Hogan and Dustin Diamond. I need you to understand the subtle striations of my culture, children! Those who do not know Dustin Diamond are doomed to repeat him!

It's particularly galling to think about *Rush Hour* going into the memory hole because *Rush Hour* is the definition of STILL HOLDS UP. WOW, *RUSH HOUR* IS STILL SO FUCKING FUNNY EVEN IN 2020. *The Fugitive* is the only good movie, but so is *Rush Hour*.

Actually, I can't say that *Rush Hour* is perfect because director Brett Ratner is a known sex creep who has been accused of sexual assault and harassment by at least nine women, and also the ONE AND ONLY female character in the movie (other than "sexy crime waitress" and "kidnapped child") is sexually harassed literally every time she is on-screen, plus every time Jackie Chan says a punch line the score plays a gong. Whether or not to watch *Rush Hour* is the kind of sticky post-#MeToo judgment call we now have to make all the time, and there's no map other than your own personal instincts and comfort zone. Unfortunately, due to the indefatigable vileness of men throughout history, sexual exploitation and abuse of power have pervaded all of our art and media, and everything is tainted and fucked!

If you feel gross renting *Rush Hour* and having a portion of your money filter back to Brett Ratner, you definitely should not watch it. Don't make yourself feel gross!! Take care of yourself! If you do want to watch it, here are some ideas: 1) take the money you spent on renting *Rush Hour* and send double that to an organization that helps survivors of sexual violence; 2) borrow the DVD from your cousin, then send some money to an organization that helps survivors of sexual violence anyway; 3) illegally download it and then send a taunting letter to Brett Ratner; 4) remember that lots of dedicated, brilliant cast and crew members and other professionals who are not accused of multiple rapes also worked extremely hard on *Rush Hour*; 5) remember that absolutely nothing great about *Rush Hour* is great because of Brett Ratner. You can say, "Lindy, you have no way of knowing that; you have not worked on a set with Brett Ratner," but I know that Brett Ratner didn't make Chris Tucker funny and Jackie Chan charming! Sorry!

People always accuse feminists of taking the fun out of everything, but can you see how *it is actually Brett Ratner who did that*?????

Okay, anyway, we open on the last day of British rule in Hong Kong, and Jackie Chan is beating up an entire crime syndicate on a ship because they stole five thousand years of Chinese artifacts and Jackie Chan loves artifacts! He's trying to bring down the mysterious and mega-deadly crime boss Juntao, but all he finds is a henchman (Ken Leung, UNDERAPPRECIATED) who manages to escape in a lil boat. Jackie Chan is upset but still excited he got the art back. It's nice when people kick other people in the head in defense of art!!!

Jackie Chan's boss, Mr. Han, the Chinese consul, is having a dinner party to celebrate his family's big move to Los Angeles, and his friend Tom Wilkinson is toasting him warmly. I'm sorry, but if there's a British guy in a suit who talks in the first five minutes of your movie, he's the villain! If it's Tom Wilkinson, you're fucked.

Jackie Chan informs Mr. Han that Juntao and the henchman got away, but he did save the art. They decide to call that a win!

Jackie Chan says goodbye to Mr. Han's little daughter, Soo Yung, his best student, and tells her to make sure she practices her kicks and eye gouges. "Don't worry," he says, "America is a very friendly place." SOB!!!

Meanwhile, in America, Chris Tucker is friendlily buying some C-4 out of the trunk of Chris Penn's car. Man, everything in the '90s was about C-4! I heard the word *C-4* more times while writing *Shit, Actually* than I'd heard it in the last twenty years. But *less times* than I heard it in the month of April 1998 alone!

Two dumbass cops try to arrest them, but Chris Penn shoots both of them and drives off. Chris Tucker, who is actually an undercover cop (GOOD JOB), shoots the car and the C-4 blows up. Then he's like, "Yeah!" and does a dance. While I appreciate the dance, this situation does not warrant it!

Mr. Han, now settled down in the Chinese consulate in LA (which is... Downton Abbey?), promises Soo Yung that he will pick her up from school and sends her off with a chauffeur and a bodyguard. On the way, Soo Yung is singing along to Mariah Carey, having the fricking time of her life in the back seat, and for some reason the driver and the guard are rolling their eyes and barfing in their own mouths, and I'm not saying I'm *glad* that five seconds later they get murdered by Ken Leung, but I think we can all agree that their hands aren't exactly clean!!!!!

Soo Yung almost gets away, pulverizing the kidnappers' domes with her wicked kicking just like Jackie Chan taught her, but she gets grabbed right at the end. The FBI begins an investigation, but Mr. Han only wants one man on the case: JACKIE CHAN. (Same, TBQH! In real life for all real crimes!)

Over at the police station, Chris Tucker is in big trouble for doing a terrible job on the C-4 sting operation and getting the two dumbass cops shot for no reason. His colleague from the bomb squad, Johnson (Elizabeth Peña, RIP), lectures him about how he wouldn't fuck up so hard if he had a partner. "I work alone," he says. "I don't want no partner, I don't need no partner." Dramatic irony! I think![14] Then he sexually harasses her for eight to nine minutes.

The FBI is absolutely incandescently enraged, to a truly baffling degree, about Mr. Han bringing Jackie Chan, an esteemed Hong Kong police detective, to LA to help on his daughter's kidnapping case, which involves a Chinese crime syndicate. Sounds like maybe he could be helpful, but I'm just a cashier with an English degree!

They're so mad Jackie Chan is coming, they decide that as punishment they're going to team him up with the most annoying guy at the LAPD, Chris Tucker. Just normal adult police behavior and excellent mystery-solving when the child of an important diplomat is in mortal danger!

(I am very smitten with the fact that Chris Tucker was one of the highest-paid movie stars in the world, and then one day he was just like, "Sorry, I only like one thing now, and it's church." And now all he does is go to church. His only scandal is that he once got a speeding ticket because he was late for church! And he had a $2.5 million tax lien, probably because he gave too much money to church, or he went to church so hard he forgot to pay his taxes. Either way, he's perfect.)

---

14   Wow, this just sent me plummeting down an existential spiral about how if I have one expertise it's literature and I can't even remember if Chris Tucker announcing he will never have a partner in a buddy cop movie counts as dramatic irony and my English degree means literally nothing and is merely a class signifier so that a certain kind of person will feel comfortable hiring me for a certain kind of job and wow wow wow I think college might be fake and toxic!

Chris Tucker's captain tells him he has a very special classified assignment with the FBI, and at first he's jazzed, but then he finds out it's just "babysitting" Jackie Chan. "What the hell am I supposed to do with him, take him to the zoo?" <—another movie I would watch!

I should mention that in this movie there is a LOT of Chris Tucker making fun of Jackie Chan for not speaking English perfectly—most famously, "DO YOU UNDERSTAND THE WORDS THAT ARE COMING OUT OF MY MOUTH?"—and the only redeeming thing I can say about that is that it didn't happen as much as I remembered?

Chris Tucker takes Jackie Chan to Mann's Chinese Theater on Hollywood Boulevard and is like, "Look familiar? Just like home, ain't it!?!?" which...SIR.

Jackie Chan escapes on a sightseeing bus, and Chris Tucker chases him all around the town. The FBI will not even let Jackie Chan in to say hi to Mr. Han, and for some reason he does not have his cell phone number? Like, I didn't have a cell phone in 1998, but they existed! This guy is the Chinese consul! He lives in a castle!

Since they're both being shut out by the feds, Tucker and Chan decide to try to solve the case themselves by using the buddy cop's most potent tool: bickering (q.v., *Bad Boys II*). And for all of its moments that didn't age well, there's just no denying that Chris Tucker is a big bright shining star and one of the most naturally funny and watchable human beings to ever live and Jackie Chan is a narcotically lovable model of masculine warmth, and some things are just greater than the sum of their parts on a level that is magic!

Jackie Chan manages to get inside the consulate and tell

Mr. Han that word on the street is that "there's a badass dude in town from Hong Kong" who's buying up all the guns and bombs. Just then, the kidnapper calls! And, PRAISE JESUS for the comedy, Chris Tucker answers! The kidnapper demands $50 million for the return of Soo Yung. They trace the call to a (pre-revitalization) building in downtown LA, a rotting industrial space that's actually a Sweetgreens now!

Once they get down there, Jackie Chan has a bad feeling. He tells the FBI, "You must pull your men back!" and they're like, "GET THIS CLOWN OUT OF HERE!" I truly do not understand the FBI's animosity toward Jackie Chan, who has been nothing but cordial and professional this whole time, but apparently it would kill them to take him seriously for even one single second. So the building explodes, killing the entire FBI.

Jackie Chan runs into Ken Leung on the street after the explosion and recognizes him from Juntao's crime crew! Ken Leung looks terrified to see Jackie Chan right there in Los Angeles because Jackie Chan is famously the Dumbledore to Ken Leung's Lord Voldemort—the only wizard Ken Leung was ever afraid of! He thought he was dealing with Cornelius Fudge over here. Jackie Chan chases Ken Leung down a dank, slimy alley (that alley is actually also a Sweetgreens now!) and up into a haunted theater that is actually Timothée Chalamet's loft now! Ken Leung gets away, but he drops a mysterious device. A clue!

They go to see Johnson and ask if she knows what this thingy is, and at first she's like, "Oh, now you want to work with me? Hell no!" Which I'm sympathetic to because there is only ONE woman in *Rush Hour*, and all she does is be a bitch and get hit on, but SORRY, YOU DO HAVE TO DO THE POLICE JOB FOR WHICH YOU ARE PAID. If you have a problem you should go to HR, Johnson! She tells them it's some kind of remote control and they leave.

Then they go visit Chris Penn in jail (he survived the car explosion), and he tells them that the mysterious guy buying up explosives is named Juntao, and they can find him at the Foo Chow restaurant in Chinatown. Then there's a very long scene where Chris Tucker teaches Jackie Chan to dance to "War, What Is It Good For?" and I'm not entirely sure what's going on or how that was even written into the script, but I don't mind! Then Jackie Chan buys them a snack from a Chinese food stall and says it's "eel and camel's hump," and it is blowing my mind that "Chinese people eat cra-a-a-a-zy stuff!" was a socially acceptable punch line until I was a full adult! That's wild! The only upside to this xenophobic vignette is that Chris Tucker thinks the eel and camel's hump is really good, which is probably true!

Chris Tucker gives Jackie Chan his LAPD ID and tells him to pretend to be LAPD if anything goes sideways in the Foo Chow restaurant. Jackie Chan looks at the ID with Chris Tucker's picture on it and says, "This won't work—I'm not 6'1"!" And that's just a gorgeously structured classic joke.

It is absolutely unclear what the fuck their plan is going into this restaurant, but what happens is that Chris Tucker gets a table and asks for camel's hump, then tells the waitress he wants to see Mr. Juntao. She goes upstairs and we see…Mr. Juntao is Tom Wilkinson!!!!! ADOYEEEEEEEEEE.

Chris Tucker gets caught and Jackie Chan has to rescue him and they end up blowing up the restaurant, which a family of immigrants probably poured their lifeblood into for many years. They get in huge trouble with the FBI because they fucked up the ransom drop, and Mr. Han puts Jackie on a punishment plane back to Hong Kong. Now the ransom is increased to $70 million!

Undeterred, Chris Tucker gets Jackie Chan off the plane by pretending to be an airplane mechanic. (Again, you could just...call a person? Or go into the airport and talk to him at the gate? This is pre-9/11! You don't need to be sneaking on to tarmacs potentially causing mayhem and death!)

Tom Wilkinson goes to visit his "friend" Mr. Han—what a dick!—and advises him to just pay the ransom. Now the drop is going to take place at a big party for the Chinese art Jackie Chan rescued at the beginning of the movie. Mr. Han has to be the emcee for some reason even though his DAUGHTER IS CURRENTLY KIDNAPPED, and if that ever happens to me and I don't get at least one day off I'm talking to HR for sure!!!

Chris Tucker causes a scene at the gala and forces Tom Wilkinson to reveal himself as Juntao. Juntao tells Mr. Han that Soo Yung is in a van outside with C-4 strapped to her, so Chris Tucker goes and gets her and starts screaming at Tom Wilkinson to use the remote control to blow her up. Go ahead! Blow up this little kid! "Come on! Push the button!" Tom Wilkinson wavers. YES. YES, CHRIS TUCKER. FORCE THE BLOODTHIRSTY RICH TO PUT A HUMAN FACE ON THEIR VIOLENCE.

Everybody loves "never touch a Black man's radio" the best, but right here Tom Wilkinson runs away and Chris Tucker yells, "Look at your little punk British ass!" and I can feel it in my pelvic floor. Johnson defuses the bomb. Jackie Chan runs around trying to beat up all the guys AND save all the art, which is a 10/10 formula.

Juntao is getting away with the money suitcase! He's climbing and climbing the scaffolding up to the roof so he can meet his helicopter and fly away. But he doesn't understand that Jackie Chan is the fastest ladder-climber in Hong Kong! They grapple on a catwalk, and Tom Wilkinson falls to his death. Then Jackie Chan falls too, but Chris Tucker saves him. NOW THEY ARE TRUE BEST FRIENDS AND THEY GO ON A BEACH VACATION TOGETHER TO HONG KONG.

Rush Hour is a flawed thing, a creature of 1998, and it is not my jurisdiction to dismiss its faults. But complicated love is still love.

RATING: 8 / 10 DVDs of *The Fugitive*.

All the Kissing in the World Could Not Save It

When *Garden State* came out I was a twenty-two-year-old naïf who knew little of "critical thinking" or "not liking a movie just because it has kissing in it" or "maybe straight middle-class white guys have gotten to tell their stories enough times and there are many, many other stories that have never been told and seeking and amplifying those stories, thereby humanizing those underserved communities to otherwise incurious privileged audiences, is an ethical imperative for those who believe, as you claim to, in ending oppression," so I think my review went something like, "ADEQUATE!!!!! MORE KISSING NEXT TIME!!!"

As I learned in my exploratory rewatch, *Garden State* is not adequate. It is a doodoo movie, and it stinks like doodoo. All the kissing in the world could not save it. Also, I just noticed for the first time that Zach Braff has a perfectly round mouth like a lamprey, which makes the kissing parts kind of weird, not that there's anything wrong with lampreys. #RoundMouthPositive

So, Zach Braff is on a crashing plane, and everyone is freakin', but not Zach Braff because Zach Braff cares naught for plane crashes! Due to this modern world, Zach Braff eats many pills per day to destroy his emotions, *even the emotion that makes you care about dying in a plane crash*, which psychiatrists agree is a pretty big one.

Turns out, though, it was only a dream, and Zach Braff wakes up safe and sound (IF THE HOLLOW MUNDANITY OF HUMAN EXISTENCE CAN REALLY BE CALLED "SAFE AND SOUND") in his apartment, which is white and blank and full of pills just like his emotion-hole. Then his dad calls and is like, "Yo, your mom died, you should probably come to New Jersey now."

And Zach Braff is like:

:-|

Except really it's more like:

:-o

Because #lamprey.

Before he can go to New Jersey, though, he has to go to his job at the Vietnamese restaurant, where today's special is MALAISE,[15] and his boss threatens to give his job to Todd Swanson from Duluth, Minnesota, who apparently is some sort of internationally renowned Vietnamese-food-serving wunderkind. Man, fuck you, Todd Swanson.

So, he flies to New Jersey and goes to his mom's funeral, which is fine, and reconnects with his high school friend Peter Sarsgaard, who, for the record, is foine. Some lady makes him a shirt out of wallpaper, and he's a real dick about it.

---

15 Note for the writers of 2026's *Garden State* reboot: Missed opportunity to have him work at a MALAISE-ian restaurant, IMO! Be the change.

Then his dad, Bilbo Baggins, is like, "Son. Come over here; I need to withhold some emotions from you." And ZB is like, "Hey, Dad, I'm having these headaches, am I dying?" and Bilbo is like, "Who do I look like—Radagast the Brown!??!?!?!" and ZB is like, "Kind of, TBH."

He goes to a party with Sarsgaard and this terrible Velcro magnate, and everyone is like, "You're some big movie star now!" They do not know it, but really he is small. Just a small movie star in a white apartment full of medicine cabinets. Truly the greatest American tragedy.

The Velcro magnate talks about how he got too rich selling his patent for "silent Velcro" (WHAT NEED DOES THAT FILL[16]), and now he's terribly, terribly, terribly bored and alone with only his mansion, his friends, his hot babes, and his anything-he-wants-in-the-universe, and I'm pretty sure we're supposed to knit our brows and nod and feel like we learned something profound about the world because IT'S SO HARD BEING A RICH WHITE MAN SWIMMING IN VELCRO MONEY. Except it's not. It is *objectively easier* than being most other things that a person can be. It is definitely easier to be bored, empty, depressed, and rich than to be bored, empty, depressed, and poor! If you're so fucking bored, invent something else. God.

Meanwhile, ZB gets grinded on by a hottie and feels nothing. Too basic.

He wakes up at Sarsgaard's house and Jim Parsons is there dressed as a knight, which is moderately interesting for thirty

---

16   I get that this is part of the joke/satire, but I still hate it!

seconds, and then everyone sits around petting dead cats for three to four hours.

Suddenly, Braff remembers about his headache appointment with Radagast! Oh no! He's late! He throws the dead cat aside and it miraculously reanimates, validating my long-held and widely ridiculed theory that Zach Braff's crotch is a pet sematary.

He rushes over to the clinic, where he immediately gets humped by the world's most incompetent seeing-eye dog and *cannot figure out* how to get its red penis off him. Just an idea I'm workshopping—how about: "HEY, LADY, GET YOUR DOG OFF ME."

Enter Natalie Portman.

Natalie Portman's character claims to be a human being but is actually a genie that exists entirely within the mind of Zach Braff's dreaming penis. Much has already been written about this, so I will not rehash it in great detail. She tap-dances. She lies. She emcees somber hamster funerals. She introduces strangers to her blankie. She figure-skates in a crushed-velvet alligator costume. She wears an epilepsy helmet just long enough to facilitate a wise and bittersweet moment and then never wears it again. She walks over to her record player and opens the lid but doesn't put a record on just to make sure you know she has one.

Here are some words that Zach Braff wrote down for Natalie Portman to say throughout the course of the movie:

"My hair's blowin' in the wind."

"Can we have code names?"

"You know what I do when I feel completely unoriginal? [WORST THING EVER HAPPENS] I make a noise, or do something that no one has ever done before. Then I can feel unique again, even if it's only for a second."

"If you can't laugh at yourself, life's going to seem a whole lot longer than you'd like."

"I'm weird, man."

Oh, are you? Tell me more.

They hang out in the graveyard while Peter Sarsgaard robs graves and then ZB and NP watch a French bulldog masturbate. At this point, the accumulated quirkiness has blocked out the sun and the crops have failed. All's lost, all's lost.

Peter Sarsgaard says he has a surprise for Zach Braff, but first they have to go watch porno in a closet with Method Man (<———MAKE THIS YOUR ENTIRE MOVIE NEXT TIME). When ZB begins fretting about dirty porno getting all over NP's delicate sensibilities, she retorts, "I'm not innocent." And he goes, "Yes you ARE, and that's what I like about you."

OH, FUCK OFF, MAN.

Sarsgaard leads them to this quarry in Newark, which is a metaphor for GUUUUUHHHHHHHHHHHHHHH, where they find a bloviating Pilates instructor who lives in an old boat.

Ugh, you live in an old boat in the bottom of a quarry in Newark? How pedestrian. MY junkyard guru lives in an old tampon box in the bottom of a witch's well in San Antonio.

He gives Sarsgaard a package and then, famously, everyone screams into the abyss to represent the battle against overmedicated twenty-first-century millennial ennui, and it is so fucking stupid that now I AM an abyss. Then ZB sort of tenderly lips NP's face like a gorilla investigating a pair of bifocals.

Sarsgaard finally gives Braff his secret present, which is his dead mom's "favorite necklace," and is like PS, YOU'RE WELCOME, I ROBBED YOUR MOM'S GRAVE FOR YOUR BIRTHDAY. I DUG UP HER COFFIN AND UNBUTTONED HER BLOUSE

AND LIFTED HER CORPSIFIED HEAD AND TENDERLY UNDID THE CLASP AND STOLE THIS NECKLACE AND NOW I'M GIVING IT TO YOU. SORRY ABOUT THE SMELL. AND THE CURSE.

And Braff is, like, jazzed about it. Like that was a real solid thing to do.

He and Portman go celebrate by sitting in the dry bathtub where his mom died, and he goes, "When I'm with you, I feel so safe. Like I'm home."

OH, THANK GOODNESS. BY THE WAY, SHE HAS LITERALLY NOT ONCE SAID HOW SHE FEELS FOR THIS ENTIRE MOVIE.

Then he goes to the airport and then he changes his mind and comes back from the airport because he realizes that without his presence she would simply wink out of existence because she is a fucking shell of a person, a marionette, an agency-free boner-golem.

"You changed my life," he explains. "You changed my life, and I've known you four days. This is the beginning of something really big [MY PENIS]."

And then they penis. The end.

RATING: 2/10 DVDs of *The Fugitive*.

Auf Wiedersehen,
Kinderbjorn!

L ook, sorry to knock your socks off with this brave confession, but I, an iconoclast, never saw any of the Terminator movies before watching *Terminator 2* for this book. It wasn't on purpose, although it IS true that I am too sophisticated for popular things. I just accidentally never sought out Terminator stuff or watched it or asked anyone what it was about or thought about it. I do not know why. I knew that there was a Sarah Connor and a John Connor and that a possibly good or possibly not good robot was going to "be bock," but that's it.

And that's really all you need to know to believably fake Terminator discourse for your entire life! I was able to bank those two hours and thirty-six minutes like an efficiency queen, and you all have been two hours and thirty-six minutes behind me this whole time. Until now.

It's Los Angeles, 2029 AD (LOL @ the idea we'll make it to 2029!). Seems like a normal day. The sun is shining, people are sitting in traffic, kids are swinging on swings (safety tip: never let your kid swing on swings at the beginning of a movie!). Uh-oh! A white-hot blast, three billion human lives lost, the swing set has been nuclearly broken to shit. As it happens, humans are on the losing end of a war against an army of machines ruled by an intangible collective robot brain named Skynet, and they just got Judgment Day'd.

Skynet! Huh! Skynet's a Terminator thing! Heard people talk about Skynet my whole life, never knew what it was. Sometimes internet trolls would say things like, "Lindy West is what happens when PIE-net becomes self-aware!!!!!" and I was impervious to the burn because it meant nothing to me. Watching *Terminator 2* has now weakened me in that way. Hmm.

The machines are really hard to fight because some of them are planes, some of them are bombs, and some of them are like if a skeleton were a tank. They are so good at fighting! We should not have made them like that! "We should not have made them like that" is, I think, what this entire franchise is about (?), so let's see how things unfold.

Man, remember when FLAMES on METAL were really cool? No offense because this is actually a compliment, but the opening credits of *Terminator 2* look like the opening credits of *Guy's Grocery Games*. A metal skull emerges from the flames. Oh no! It's the mayor of Flavortown! And he's come to TERMINATE CHEESE. *Hasta la vista, gravy!* <—I am not sorry!

Cut to a parking lot at night. A portal through time opens up and look who plops through it! It's Arnold, squatting in a custom time-traveling Glassybaby. He's bock, and, schwing, the time travel has terminated his pants! Arnold clomps to a nearby country biker bar with his bockwurst hanging right out there, and the horny cougars of the bar love it. Hey, though! Why would they give the Terminator a dick!? What's he supposed to use it for? Also, *why is he Austrian?* Call me old-fashioned, but I think it's weird not to explain why your robot is Austrian and has a dick.[17]

Arnold approaches a tough biker and tells him, "I need your clothes, your boots, and your motorcycle." The biker, reasonably, refuses, so Arnold griddles his face on the flat top, then impales his friend on the pool table, then steals all their stuff. (Terminator! You are the asshole here!) The bar owner follows Arnold outside with a shotgun and is like, "I can't let you take the man's wheels, son," which is bafflingly kind of him. Arnold walks right up to the guy and you think he's going to terminate him, but instead he takes the shotgun and—B-B-B-B-B-B-B-BAD TO THE BONE—the guy's bitching Oakleys too. Now Terminator is a biker boy!

The lack of taste it takes to actually play the song "Bad to the Bone" right here belongs in a museum!

Meanwhile, somewhere else in LA, another time portal opens up, and another naked robot bloops into the '90s. This time, it's Robert Patrick a.k.a. T-1000 a.k.a. Robot Patrick a.k.a. a liquid metal absolute bitch. A cop notices him and is like, "10-4, uh, we got a liquid metal guy," but Robot Patrick kills him easily and takes his clothes. OF COURSE liquid metal guy is a COP.

Basically what's going on, I think, is that in *Terminator 1,* the

---

17   It's possible this line of questioning reveals a lack of faith, on my part, in the creative imagination. Just as Pollux Troy gave his mega-bomb "Sinclaire" the persona of a cartoon woman with outrageous sky-high naturals, perhaps the creator of the T-800 too wanted to imbue his metal son with something personal, a signature of sorts, the accent of a beloved grandfather, maybe, or the dick of another beloved grandfather. Not everything has to have utility, Lindy!!!!! Some things are just art!

T-800 (Arnold) was sent to the '80s to terminate Sarah Connor, so that she could never give birth to extremely effective anti-robot resistance leader of the future John Connor. But it didn't work (don't know why, never seen it, not my purview), so now in *Terminator 2*, Skynet has sent a different, more advanced Terminator back in time to terminate John Connor as a child, while future John Connor sent a reprogrammed, nicer T-800 (that he STILL DECIDED TO MAKE AUSTRIAN AMERICAN) back in time to protect his child self from T-1000.

T-1000 looks up John Connor's personal info in the cop car computer and, like, you didn't have that already? You're from the future! Print it out before you come!

John Connor is chillin' out with his best friend, Bobby Budnik, riding his bike around town and not cleaning his room in a month. This is back when everybody liked the same things: bein' bad, not cleaning your room, and pizza. John lives with his foster parents, who need to get a divorce but otherwise seem nice.

Sarah Connor, meanwhile, is confined to a mental hospital because she won't stop trying to warn everyone about the upcoming nuclear robot apocalypse, and also she "blew up a computer factory" (fair).

Officer T-1000 swings by John's house and asks his foster mom for a picture of him, for police business. "Do you mind if I keep this picture?" Yo, you don't even have a picture of him? HE IS STILL ALIVE IN THE FUTURE WHERE YOU COME FROM. You have a computer for a brain!

T-1000 locates John at the arcade and starts chasing him around without even stopping to say hi to the video games, which are at LEAST his in-laws. In a back hallway, just when he's about to get terminated, John runs into Arnold, who's carrying a dozen long-stemmed roses in a box—isn't that nice? He must have known that John Connor is having a tough day, what with being chased by a liquid metal guy. But Terminator's roses are actually a gun! Terminator inconveniences T-1000 by shooting him about a million times, but, unfortunately, you know, he is liquid metal. They manage to get away on a motorcycle while T-1000 oozes his body (INCLUDING GENITALS—HE HAS THEM TOO) back together.

T-1000 can't catch them on foot (why would there be a limit to how fast a liquid metal man could run?), so he carjacks a big truck and starts chasing them through Burbank. On the one hand, how does he know how to drive? They don't drive 1984 Freightliner FLA heavy-duty commercial trucks in the land of the machines! On the other hand, why isn't he better at driving? He basically is a car.

T-1000 looks stressed. Why is Arnold so much better at being a Terminator than he is? *He's* supposed to be the newer model! *He's* the one who can turn his arm into a pizza cutter! Why is this happening to him? It's not fair! But, as Freckle tells us, sometimes things that are expensive are worse.

Eventually, T-1000 smashes into an overpass, and his truck blows up. He walks out of the fire, still dressed as a cop (if he can generate any outfit he wants out of liquid metal, WHY DID HE NEED TO STEAL THE COP OUTFIT THE FIRST TIME?), but Arnold and John Connor have already gotten away. They are safe, for now.

Eddie Furlong as a child has the energy of an old Kristen Stewart.

Arnold tells John they have to get out of town and avoid the authorities, which is why he chose such a subtle, low-profile look. John insists on calling his foster parents first, to warn them that a psycho robot from the future is probably coming over.

> **John:** Look. Todd and Janelle are dicks. But I've got to warn them. Shit. You got a quarter?
> **Terminator:** I AM A QUARTER.

Janelle picks up the phone, but it's actually T-1000 who has shape-shifted into Janelle! Arnold is suspicious, so he performs the Wolfie Test, a complex tactical maneuver wherein you ask a woman whom you suspect of being Robot Patrick, "What's wrong with Wolfie?" and if she says, "Nada, amigo, he's my good boy," then you know she has most likely just turned her arm into a big metal knife and impaled your foster dad through the face. If she says, "Our dog is named Max, do you need to go to the brain hospital?" then you can continue to love her. Janelle fails.

> **Terminator, to a child:** Your foster parents are dead.

As they scram outta town, Terminator explains the plot holes to John:

T-1000 can imitate anything it touches, or "samples," which is why it now has a permanent sexy policeman costume for skin.

"But only an object of equal size."

But what about mass and density?

Don't worry about it.

"But why doesn't it just become a bomb or something?"

"It can't form complex machines. Guns and explosives have chemicals, moving parts. It doesn't work that way."

HUMANS HAVE CHEMICALS AND MOVING PARTS.

"It can form solid metal shapes—knives, stabbing weapons."

Disrespectfully, what the fuck is the point of a futuristic robot that can only become a knife? A robot is already like a gun! You had to make a robot *less like a gun* to make it a knife.

John tells Terminator that they have to go break his mom out of the mental hospital before T-1000 gets there and kills her or takes her hostage. "Negative," says Arnold. "This does not help our mission." Then John discovers that since technically he built the Terminator and sent it into the past to rescue himself, he is the Terminator's boss and the Terminator has to do what he says! It's PIZZA PARTY TIME! He immediately abuses this power, and has Terminator "prank" a couple of jocks by almost murdering them.

John Connor: Jesus, you were going to kill that guy!
Best line in the movie: Of course. I'm a Terminator.

T-1000 disguises himself as the floor so he can sneak into the hospital and get Sarah Connor, braless icon. He becomes a security guard and pokes the real security guard to death, and I know, I know, let the plumber fix the sink, as my president Sam Irby would say, but that really doesn't seem the best way to terminate someone during a stealth infiltration of a hospital! It's really conspicuous![18] Just keep being the floor!

Sarah kills her molestery nurse and steals his keys and

---

18   Also, I know that T-1000 is technically very skilled at mimicking the exact body and voice of a person, but here's a harsh toke: Terminators have bad personalities and are obvious robots no matter how much their perm looks like your mom's! Sorry!!!

nightstick, and then runs into Arnold in the hall, who she understandably assumes is there to kill her, since he is purpose-built for that one single exact thing and the last time she saw him he was unbelievably uncool. Instead, he's like, "Come with me if you want to live," and her kid's like, "Ditto, cowabunga," which has to have been a lot to process for her! They run away from T-1000 and manage to escape into the elevator, but then T-1000 turns his finger knife into an elevator spreader! Shit! Terminator shoots him right in the head,[19] which takes him a second. They escape.

Now that they have some downtime, John Connor decompresses a little and starts to cry. "What's wrong with your eyes?" says Terminator. "Why do you cry?"

> **John:** It's when there's nothing wrong with you, but
> you hurt anyways. Get it?
> **Terminator:** No.

Then, like literally the next second, Terminator starts sewing up Sarah's wound, and she asks, "Do you know what you're doing?" and he's like, "I have detailed files on human anatomy."

Oh my god, then why don't you know what crying is?????????????????????????

To kill time, John teaches Terminator the traditional human rituals of thumbs-up, down low / too slow, plus some slang so he can be "not such a dork all the time." They cover the five most vital English phrases:

---

19   Why do you keep shooting him? That just gives him more metal for finger knife!

"Eat it."

"Later, dickwad."

"Chill out."

"No problem."

And, most important, "Hasta la vista, baby."

Watching them, Sarah Connor realizes that the Terminator is the perfect dad. "This machine was the only one that measured up." Wow, horny!

Sarah Connor has a nightmare about everyone burning up on Judgment Day, so she abandons John and Terminator and drives off to blow away Miles Dyson, who was just about to invent the microprocessor that would become Skynet—which, incidentally, he reverse engineered from dead evil Arnold's severed arm from the end of *Terminator 1*, which seems like the kind of logical loop that would melt space-time? Having to think about time travel should be the punishment we give to criminals instead of prison.

Terminator thinks blowing Dyson away is a pretty good idea, but John explains that you can't just go around killing people even if it's to prevent a nuclear holocaust that you know is definitely going to kill three billion people.

COUNTERPOINT: MAYBE YOU CAN!

They chase Sarah to Dyson's house, where she's absolutely torturing this poor man and his wife and child but not killing anyone because it turns out it's actually hard to just blow some-one away in front of their kid when they haven't even invented Skynet yet.

Arnold deescalates the situation, but then instantly reescalates it by cutting some of his flesh off to show Dyson his metal bones and explain that he needs to stop building evil robots. Dyson is like, "EXCUSE ME?" But he agrees to take them over to

Cyberdyne Headquarters and obliterate his life's work. (Hey, do you have to have the only Black guy in the movie be responsible for three BILLION deaths??) Man, it would have been way harder to prevent Judgment Day if they had had the cloud in 1991. Instead, they just have to go down to the office and smush all the floppies. Easy, right? Not really!

They break in and plant explosives to destroy all of Dyson's research, but the cops arrive and there's a very big gun battle. (Another thing everyone liked in the '90s was saying, "We've got company.") While Dyson sets up the bombs, Terminator uses his big guns to terminate all the cop cars in the parking lot. He has a little counter on his Terminator Google Glass that tells him "Human casualties: 0.0," so he can make sure he doesn't violate John's no-murdering rule. But why is there a decimal, though? In case you kill 0.25 of a person? In case you kill a person's spirit and leave their body alive but depressed? In case you terminate the kid from *Two and a Half Men*?

The cops enter the building and are shooting everyone real bad. A badly injured Dyson hides behind the office equipment like, "WOW, I'm glad we bought these bulletproof fax machines! People said I was crazy!" With his dying breath, he manages to detonate the bombs and fireball the lab. Man, can you imagine if you sacrificed your life and legacy to save humanity, and then just twenty-five years later, they elected motherfucking Donald Trump to be the president? The 2016 election was disrespectful to Miles Dyson most of all, IMO!

T-1000 FINALLY shows up at the lab and rides his motorcycle up the stairs???? There's no way that's the fastest way! Arnold zooms away in a police car, so T-1000 rides his motorcycle onto a helicopter and then turns into a wiggly snake.

BUT OH MY GOD, WAIT: Wouldn't the Terminator and T-1000 both disappear once you destroyed the lab??? How do they exist if Skynet was never developed??????? Please, I'm crying.

One big draw of *Terminator 2* was that, in the '90s, it was really exciting to hear a kid say, "Shit."

T-1000 chases them to a steel mill, and Arnold crashes a liquid nitrogen truck into him. The liquid nitrogen briefly freezes T-1000 solid, so Arnold says, "Hasta la vista, baby," which is precious because he learned it from his dad-son-boss and now he's all grown up, and then he shoots T-1000 with a gun and explodes him into little pieces.

A lot of people don't know this, but making *hasta la vista, baby* his catchphrase was huge for Arnold Schwarzenegger's political career. *Hasta la vista* got him the Latino vote, and *baby* got him the baby vote! He won the governorship in that moment.[20]

Arnold and John stand around feeling good about themselves for a minute, but then the steel mill's river of hot lava thaws out the T-1000 and he starts to re-form. Dude, that's why you gotta get the dustpan! Sweep that shit up! Now T-1000 is POed. If there's one thing he hates, it's being frozen and then blasted into little pieces and then thawed by lava.

T-800 and T-1000 have an epic battle all over the steel mill. At one point, T-1000 takes Sarah hostage and tries to get her to call out to John because apparently he only knows two impressions: Janelle and the mental hospital security guard!? Eventually, T-1000 thinks he has squished Arnold to death at last, but then

---

20 It was way more successful than his previous catchphrase, "Auf wiedersehen, kinderbjorn!" Unrelated: I do not speak German.

Arnold's alternative power activates and he blasts T-1000 into the lava for good.

John can't wait to go home and start a life with his mom and new robot dad, but Arnold is like, "No. Dere is one more chip." Sarah and John will have to terminate T-800 or else scientists could still use his brain to create Skynet. (Presumably, also Sarah will have to go to prison now for her many murders? Does John have to go back to being a foster kid? WTF?)

As Sarah lowers Terminator into the lava because he cannot "self-terminate" and she read a lot of books about how to operate smelting equipment in the mental hospital, I guess, he raises his arm above his head, and just before his hand sinks below the surface.........he gives John a thumbs-up!!!!!! And I can't BELIEVE NONE OF YOU EVER TOLD ME ABOUT THAT, SIMULTANEOUSLY THE WORST AND BEST MOMENT IN ALL OF MOVIES, THE CORNIEST AND THE TENDEREST, UNBEARABLY DORKY YET INTOXICATINGLY ENTERTAINING, A COMMITMENT TO PURE ENTERTAINMENT THAT I WOULD LIKE TO INJECT INTO MY VEINS TO COUNTERACT THE UTTER VACUUM OF CARE IN WHICH WE ARE ALL GASPING OUR LAST BREATHS, THE PLAGUE OF DISINGENUOUSLY IRONIC CRUELTY AND FASCIST INDIVIDUALISM THAT INFESTS THE DECAYING RUIN OF TWENTY-FIRST-CENTURY AMERICA, THE TRUE RISE OF THE MACHINES (US). I DO NOT KNOW WHY OR HOW THIS ROBOT LOVES THIS TERRIBLE LITTLE BOY, BUT IT KINDLES IN ME A HOPE THAT ONE DAY WE MAY LOVE ONE ANOTHER AND OURSELVES.

I'm getting a dog.

RATING: 7 / 10 DVDs of *The Fugitive*.

Manual for Shitheads

F ew things have shaped my existence more profoundly than the realization, courtesy of the 1994 film *Reality Bites*, that there are two kinds of women—Janeane Garofalos and Winona Ryders—and that I would never, ever be a Winona, the only kind that really matters. I wrote about this in my last book, *The Witches Are Coming*. That line of thinking fucked me up until I was about twenty-seven.

Rewatching *Reality Bites*, I nearly cried when it dawned on me: I can't *believe* I ever thought I'd rather be Lelaina than Vickie. Not that I don't still love (/hate) Lelaina the impossible saucer-eyed night-elf, but Vickie's the only non-dickwad in this entire dang movie! I know you're not really supposed to identify with these characters (I *hope* you're not really supposed to identify with these characters) because *Reality Bites* is a commentary on '90s slackerism or whatever, but I identify with funny, second-fiddle, lost-at-sea Vickie, and I'm pretty sure those teen feelings have had a tangible effect on how I turned out as an adult. I be'd the

Vickie I wanted to see in the world. And you're not going to trick me into wanting to be Lelaina by dangling that Ethan Hawke–shaped carrot in my face because Troy is a petroleum-jelly-dipped turd and I make plenty of those already with my butt.

Anyway, Vickie aside, everyone else in this movie is the fucking worst, and the worst thing about them is the stuff they say. (Oh, my bad, Sammy. You're fine too.) But oh my GOD, as a '90s teen, did I ever want to sit on a fourth-hand couch in a smoke-choked apartment and have these conversations and then eventually get "picked" by an emotionally abusive band guy!!! I had never come across *any better thing* to want. So, in honor of my long-deceased naivete, let's take a look back at all the garbage words we thought were profound when we were twelve. (Spoiler: most of them come out of Troy.)

> **1. Lelaina:** I know this sounds cornball, but I'd like to somehow make a difference in people's lives.
> **Troy:** And I'd like to buy them all a Coke.

Hey, Troy, I get that it's part of your anti-consumerist schtick, and was likely the apex of wit in 1994, but do you ever say *anything* that isn't just a corporate slogan parroted back in a sarcastic voice?

> **Troy:** [begins nihilistic seashell poem]

NOPE, DON'T EVEN WORRY ABOUT IT.

> **2. Troy** (when Lainey's dad tries to give her a BMW): Yeah, just think about all those starving children in Africa who don't even have cars.

Lainey's mom: Troy, does your father give you gifts like that?
Troy: Well, actually, my father's dying of prostate cancer, so I don't really trouble him much for gifts.

Jesus fucking Christ, Troy, could you be normal for *one second*? These grown-ups are just trying to have a conversation with you because their asshole daughter brought you along to family dinner (without asking, probably). They don't actually give a shit about what you think—YOU'RE A TWENTY-THREE-YEAR-OLD UNEMPLOYED POET—they're just being nice. They have mortgages.

3. Lelaina: He's so cheesy I can't watch him without crackers.

This is kind of a good line if you're Bugs Bunny in 1952.

4. Vickie: Welcome to the maxi pad.
Sammy: Yeah, with new dry-weave, it actually pulls moisture away from you!

Look, Sammy, I know you hang out with Troy a lot, but it doesn't have to be like this. You can just do you.

5. Lelaina: I finally figured out what your problem is.
Troy: What's that—I'm not a pepper?

Seriously, it's like a verbal tic at this point. It doesn't even make sense.

6. Lelaina: Troy, aren't you excited?
Troy: I'm bursting with fruit flavor.

:-|

7. Sammy: I don't understand why this moment has to be Memorexed.

LOL, "Memorexed."

8. Troy: Lelaina. You know the punishment for premature evacuation.

What does that even MEAN!!? I see that you're doing a pun on "premature ejaculation" because it rhymes and stuff, but how does "evacuation" apply in this context? You mean evacuating the apartment? But what's the "punishment"? You just sitting there some more? Her not "getting" to hang out with you for the rest of the night? Because that was kind of the idea. Seriously, Troy, I think you have some significant style-over-substance issues you'll need to deal with if you really want to be a professional, um, whatever it is you're into. (Just a reminder: Condescending Guy Covered in Oil is not a job!)

9. Lelaina: The most profound, important invention of my lifetime. The Big Gulp...I guess it really doesn't take much to make me happy.
Lelaina and Michael: Blah blah blah blah blah blah...
Michael: I should have stayed in college and got a degree in astronomy or something.

Lelaina: Oh, god, I love astronomy.

Michael: Really?

Lelaina: Yeah. I just—the math, though. It was the math that just, like, got me every time.

Michael: I loved astronomy too, and I got into class, and it was like, everything was three-squared times pi equals the root of pi. And I just wanted to look at the stars.

This movie's like a Shithead Manual.

10. Troy: I am really in love with you.........PSSSSHHHHHHH!!!! Is that what you want to hear? Well, don't flatter yourself.

Okay, so clearly Lelaina should have never spoken to Troy again starting from this moment AT THE ABSOLUTE LATEST. And I'm supposed to be happy that they end up together at the end?[21] Nobody's happy in the long term with someone who's this much of an emotionally abusive, weird, manipulative, controlling, wet snake. Boooooooo. Or, as Troy would put it, "Easy, breezy, beautiful. Cover girl."

11. Troy: It's all just a random lottery of meaningless tragedy and a series of near escapes. So I take pleasure in the details. You know, a Quarter Pounder with Cheese. Those are good. The sky about ten minutes

---

21 My horrible secret: I AM AND I CAN'T ESCAPE IT.

before it starts to rain. The moment where your laughter becomes a cackle. And I sit back and I smoke my Camel Straights and I ride my own melt.

It's possible that I hate Troy more than any other fictional or living human. I know he's broooooooken, or whatever, and he's scaaaaaaared, and twelve-year-old me is horrified/bewildered by this entire sentence, but "broken and scared" and "not being the most unbearable blowhard on earth" are not mutually exclusive. And twelve-year-old me is still mad that Jo didn't end up with Laurie, so what does she know?

> **12: Lelaina:** I'm not going to work at the Gap, for Christ's sake!
> **Vickie:** Shut up.

That line's not embarrassing. That line is fucking boss. VICKIE 4 LIFE.

> **13. Troy:** [runs hand through hair]

TAKE A SHOWER. YOU LOOK LIKE A BARBECUE MOP.

> **14. Troy:** What happened to your normal clothes?
> **Michael:** Wow!... You look like...
> **Troy:** A doily.
> **Lainey:** I'm gonna change.
> **Michael:** No, don't change.
> **Troy:** Don't go thinking for yourself either.
> **Michael:** Come on. Let's go. You don't need this.

Troy: You don't know what she needs.

Michael: I think I know what she needs in a way that you never will.

Hey! Or maybe you could actually treat her like a human being? Nightingales R people 2!!! This is approximately the thirtieth time in the movie when you're like, "Oh, you should not be talking to these dicks anymore."

15. Lelaina: They're just videotapes, right?

Yeah, kinda, actually.

16. Lelaina: I worked so hard on them, you know?

Did you? I mean, did you really? Are you sure you have a solid perspective on what "worked hard" means? Because it seems like mostly you just hung out and got drunk with your friends and carried around your Memorex.

Man, there's nothing America loves more than a really pretty woman who *kind* of tries. That's the most sympathetic thing in the world. A really pretty girl who tried a little bit.

17. Lelaina: I just don't understand why things just can't go back to normal at the end of the half hour like on *The Brady Bunch* or something.

Troy: Well, 'cause Mr. Brady died of AIDS.

I hope Troy dies of GLIB.

18. Michael: I just feel like maybe I deserve another shot here.

Troy: Yeah, this girl is kookoo for Cocoa Puffs.

YOU'RE JUST FUCKING WITH ME NOW, RIGHT?
FROZEN EMBRYOS > HEY, THAT'S MY BIKE.

19. Lelaina: I win the big commitment cook-off and you just run away!!!?!

You see, what's going on in this scene is that Lainey won the big commitment cook-off, and in response Troy has run away.

20. Troy: I'm sorry, Lelaina, but you can't navigate me. I might do mean things, and I might hurt you, and I might run away without your permission, and you might hate me forever. And I know that that scares the shit out of you, because I'm the only real thing that you have.

Lelaina: Yeah? Well, that ain't real much.

At this point in the rewatch, you realize that you are nearly a decade older than these characters, and what you're watching is a movie about children yelling nonsense at each other.

21. Troy: What happened was that I kind of got this arcane glimpse of the universe, and the best thing I can say about that is...I don't know. I have this planet of regret sitting on my shoulders, and you have no idea how much I wish that I could go back to that morning

after we made love and do everything different. But I
know I can't do that, so I thought that I would come
here and tell you something. And what I wanted to tell
you was that I love you. And, uh, I just wanted to make
sure that was clear so that there wasn't any confusion.

If these weren't attractive white people, they'd definitely have to
explain how a couple of jerks who hate jobs got a free house
at the end.

I absolutely love this movie.

RATING: 7/10 DVDs of *The Fugitive*.

Never Boring, Always Horny

One thing you can say about *Twilight* is that it is not boring. There are a billion characters, they're always saying some crazy shit, and they're SO HORNY! *Twilight* feels like it was written by an AI that *almost* gets it. Something is just 2 percent off about every line and every interaction, which, taken cumulatively, is like a window into one of those dimensions where everything is identical to ours except cats and turtles are switched and Prince never died. *Twilight* took me out of my body in a way that did not give me pleasure but did give me fascination, and when it was over, I couldn't believe it, but I felt compelled to watch the next one just to continue the satisfying, itchy glitch of it all. *Twilight* kept me awake, which honestly is more than I can say for *Top Gun*, peace be upon Tony Scott (I stan *Déjà Vu*).

For instance, this is the opening line of the movie, delivered in sullen voice-over by Bella (Kristen Stewart): "I've never given much thought to how I would die, but dying in the place of someone I love seems like a good way to go."

WHAT??

How is that a "good way to go"!? There are zero versions of that "way to go" that don't involve some sort of violent hostage situation and/or dystopian fascist cull. How about a "good way to go" is dying of old age gently and simultaneously with every-one you love while lying on a quilt and holding hands in a big circle and reminiscing about the time you reversed climate catastrophe and squashed the global Far Right together? If you're picking a hypothetical "way to go," pick something that doesn't include your life and the life of a dear one being leveraged against each other in some zero-sum villainous endgame! What!?!? You weirdo!

The thing about that line is that it is both semantically ambig-uous in a way that obscures its meaning, AND it turns out to be borderline cyborg argle-bargle anyway!!! That's *Twilight*.

When we meet Bella she has just moved from Phoenix, Arizona, where she lives with her mother, to Forks, Washington, where her father is the chief of police, because her mom wants to "go on the road." You can tell this is Bella's childhood room because it's still decorated with her old childhood construction paper hand turkeys, you know, like kids love to make for them-selves and show off to other kids on their walls year-round (SEE? ALIENS).

Her dad gives her an old truck that he bought from their neighbors, and the neighbor kid is like, "Hi, I'm Jacob. We used to make mud pies when we were little." Bold intro, also, "mud pies" is one of those phrases people casually throw around that I feel like is not tethered to any foundational meaning. I'm not talking about "mud pie" as a euphemism for a dank dump; I'm talking about when people use it *not to mean that*, which they absolutely do! It's, like, a pervasive child stereotype! Why do I know the phrase *mud pie* but don't know what it is? Is it just a…pile of mud? What do you do with it? Eat it? Am I the only one who didn't grow up slapping mud into a patty and going hog wild on it? Anyway I think Jacob meant the dump kind.

Bella goes to her first day of school, and all the kids glare at her like, "Who's the dweeb with the truck?" because if there's one thing teenagers hate it's an extremely gorgeous new girl. Now, most movies would be content with giving Bella two to three friends at school, especially since they are shooting on location in FORKS, WASHINGTON, but *Twilight* gives Bella seventy-five distinct friends who all have names and personalities and LINES (which = MONEY), and they're all flirting and doing slapstick comedy and kissing one another on the face and falling down and taking pictures of Bella for the school paper ("It's like first grade all over again, you're the shiny new toy" <—WHAT) within the first ten minutes of the film and it is truly, truly bonkers.

Then the Cullens arrive, and Bella is like, "WHO are THOSE???????"

Her new friends explain that the Cullens are a family of wealthy and mysterious foster children who are also all dating one another—THIS IS THE REAL PLOT—because the dad, Dr. Cullen, is "like this foster dad slash matchmaker." (Foster! It's Australian for incest!) To recap, this teenager is saying that a local doctor legally adopts pairs of teenagers that he thinks would be romantically compatible, and makes them date, which they do. Absolutely no one acts like this is weird at all, Bella takes it completely in stride, and everyone forges ahead.

Bella has a class with one of the Cullens, Edward, and when she walks into the room, he vomits (blood, I guess?) into his mouth. He cannot stop staring at her and gagging for the entire period, and then tries to switch out of the class to get away from her. When the registrar won't let him switch, he says, "Fine, I'll just have to endure it," and then stops coming to school ENTIRELY because Bella stinks so bad. Hahahahaha.

Bella goes out for a Gardenburger with Dad and does such a bad job with the ketchup bottle it seems like she should go to the hospital. She's still thinking about Edward and how he hurt her feelings: "I planned to confront him and demand to know what his problem was. But he never showed."

Bella's dad tells her that the security guard at the mill got killed by some kind of animal.

> **Bella:** Animal?
> **Dad:** You're not in Phoenix anymore.

Yeah, they definitely have animals in Phoenix, sir!

It's not a spoiler if I mention that the Cullens are obviously vampires using the seamless and extremely low-profile cover story of "weird incestuous foster family," right? Because I cannot wait one more second to talk about how fucking bananas it is that any of these old-ass sexy corpses still go to HIGH SCHOOL. You don't have to keep going to high school!!!!!! If a Forks, Washington, truancy cop comes up to you and says, "Shouldn't you be in high school right now?" just be like, "Yeah, I'm twenty-five, haha, yeah, I know I look young." DONE!

Regardless, Edward returns to biology class and is assigned to be Bella's lab partner. Which is a fucking huge win for her, since he's already taken biology 179 times. His first year of biology, they dissected humans.

Bella tells Edward that she doesn't really like cold, wet things [*twitch twitch*], which is awkward because he's a cold, wet thing.

> **Edward:** If you hate the cold and the rain so much, why did you move to the wettest place in the continental US?
> **Bella:** It's complicated.
> **Edward:** I'm sure I can keep up. I've been alive for seven hundred years. I've read EVERY BOOK.

They twitch at each other for the rest of class.

From this point on, Edward is just constantly staring at Bella around corners and peeking at her from under manholes and disguising himself as a potted plant so he can watch her pee. Heads up: your children think that is romance now!

One day one of Bella's friends is leaving the school parking lot in his van when he skids on some ice and almost crushes her. (Then Bella's dad threatens to take that Black teenager's driver's license away, for revenge, which is extremely fucked up!) Edward zooms over there using wizard speed and stops the van with his boday.

> **Bella:** How did you get over to me so fast?
> **Edward:** I was standing right next to you, Bella...Bella, you hit your head. You're confused...Nobody's gonna believe you.

Gaslighting! Vampire gaslighting!!! Later that night, Bella wakes up and thinks she sees Edward *inside her room watching her sleep.* But he's not. OR WAS HE? (Yes!!!!!!!)

"That was the first night I dreamt of Edward Cullen."

Bella and Edward become more and more erotically enthralled, but they're teens (well, one teen and one EX-TREMELY ELDERLY MAN), which means lots and lots and lots and lots of staring, and Edward constantly walking up to her and saying stuff like, "Bella, we shouldn't be friends," and "If you were smart, you'd stay away from me." Dude, YOU CAME OVER HERE.

Bella invites him to go to the coast with the regular kids, but he's like, "What if I'm not the hero? What if I'm the bad guy?" so, that's a no, I guess.

At the beach, she runs into Jacob "Mud Pie" NeighborBoy and his friends, and this is as good a time as any to mention that this character is Native and they should have cast a Native actor! Bella asks, very rudely, "What are you, like, stalking me?" and Jacob says, "You're on my beach, remember?" and Bella's like, "What did your friends mean about 'the Cullens don't come here,'" and Jacob reveals that his tribe has an ancient legend about the Cullens SPECIFICALLY. An ancient legend about the group of foster children who go to her high school. "If they agree to stay off our land," he explains, "then we won't expose what they really are to the palefaces." Oh! Okeydokey!

Bella decides to pop over to Port Angeles to get a book about Quileute legends so she can learn more about HER LAB PART-NER. In the dark and twisting alleys of Port Angeles, Bella is menaced by some Port Angeles rapists, but then Edward appears and rescues her in his lil vampire hatchback! He casually drops that he can read minds and then takes her out for mushroom ravioli. (Waiter: "You're sure there isn't anything I can get for you?" I don't know, do you have a BOWL OF BLOOD??)

Edward tells Bella that he feels very protective of her, and also he can read the mind of every human in Forks AND Port Angeles except her. "It's very frustrating."

> **Edward:** I don't have the strength to stay away from you anymore.
> **Bella:** Then don't.

Their hands touch, erotically, and his is cold as ice. Because he's dead. And old. Dude, Edward. Come on. All the other vampires are with other vampires! What could you possibly have in common with this teenage girl?

Yo, girl, lemme play u my favorite song.

[Gregorian chant]

Bella looks up vampires on the internet and finds out that they're called "THE COLD ONES," which freaks her out, so now she's scared of Edward and hurts his feelings at school on purpose. Who's the cold one now????

He follows her into the woods, and she confronts him with her suspicions: "You're impossibly fast and strong, your skin is pale white and ice cold, your eyes change color, and sometimes you speak like you're from a different time. You never eat or drink anything, you don't go out in the sunlight. How old are you?"

If I had a dollar for every time I had this exact fight with my exes!!!!!!!!!!!

Edward tosses Bella on his back and runs up an entire mountain in fast-motion, which is funnier than any intentional comedy I've ever seen. (Also me when they restock the toilet paper at Walgreens, right???)

Up above the clouds of Forks, Bella learns that vampire skin sparkles in the sunlight, a detail that would go on to sell many thousands of dollars in glittery dildos!

> **Bella:** It's like diamonds. You're beautiful.
> **Edward:** Beautiful? This is the skin of a killer, Bella.

And this is the peacoat of a killer.
  I'm wearing a killer's socks.
  This is the hair gel of a killer.

> **Edward:** I am the world's most dangerous predator. I am designed to kill.
> **Bella:** I don't care.
> **Edward:** I've killed people before.
> **Bella:** It does not matter.
> **Edward:** I wanted to kill you. I've never wanted a human's blood so much in my life.
> **Bella:** I trust you.
> **Edward:** Don't.
> **Bella:** I'm here. I trust you.

BELLA.
GIRL.
YIKES.

> **Edward:** Your scent, it's like a drug to me. You're like my own personal brand of heroin. I call it Pale Eddie's Heroin.
> **Bella:** I'm not afraid of you. I'm only afraid of losing you. I feel like you're going to disappear.

Edward: You don't know how long I've waited for you.

Then they're about to kiss, maybe, but the camera pans up to the sky all kooky because I guess the cameraman found his own personal brand of heroin. Bella and Edward lie down on the grass and stare at each other, which is how you can tell this movie wasn't written by someone from the Pacific Northwest—there are only three days a year here when the grass isn't wet. Enjoy your soggy asses!

I do need to pause and say that Kristen Stewart and Robert Pattinson perform the frick out of these goofy-ass roles, and you know what? I love them both. I do! I think they are good! Sue me! Take me to Taste Court!

Edward tells Bella that Dr. Cullen turned him into a vampire in 1918 while he was dying of Spanish influenza (PLEASE no one let Donald Trump watch *Twilight*), and that the Cullens "think of ourselves as vegetarians." He invites Bella over to meet his whole family, and she's like, "But what if they don't like me!?" Dude, they go to your school! And one of them's your doctor!!!!

Bella shows up, and Edward's mom is like, "Bella, we're making Italiano for you!" like a FULL ALIEN. "We're using this as an excuse to use the kitchen for the first time!" Then Edward plays the piano for Bella while she looks ill. Man, that's the best song you learned in one hundred years?

Meanwhile, Bella's dad is investigating the "animal" that killed the guy at the mill and another guy. He finds a footprint and it's...HUMAN!?!?

Bella's mom wants her to come to Jacksonville, but Bella refuses because she's fallen in love. Bella's mom is PUMPED: "What is he? Jock? Indie? Is he smart? I bet he's smart." Well...he's 107 and he watches me sleep.

They finally kiss but then Edward is like NO, NO, WE MUSTN'T, MY BONER IS 2 POWERFUL (this is also a real story line), so then they just have to TALK ALL NIGHT! And he learns about snuggling! Now THAT'S what I call a movie made for women by women!

The idea that a man born in 1901 wouldn't have any fucked-up gender role shit or extreme racism going on is iffy. Wait, what am I saying, he does have fucked-up gender role shit. He is a human fucked-up gender role! I'll make a call on the racism when I see him interact with ANY BLACK PERSON EVER.

Bella's mom was actually right about one thing, though— Edward is kind of a jock. It's raining, so he picks Bella up at her house because his whole family is going to play vampire baseball! And you just *know* it's gonna be dumb!

You might want to lie down for this, in a grave, and never get up again: the Cullens can only play baseball when there's a thunderstorm going on *because they hit the ball so loud.* I can't. How loud could you... you know what? I'm not doing this one.

Anyway, Bella doesn't even get to play. She has to be the umpire. In the rain! And they throw, hit, and run too fast for a human to see! Wow, fun!

In the middle of their baseball game, some other vampires show up. (Of all the weird shit Stephanie Meyer wrote in this series, "all vampires love baseball" is absolutely the weirdest. Did you know a vampire can smell one drop of baseball in a million gallons of old growth forest?) Oh shit, it's the bad vampires who have been munching the townspeople this whole time! Everything seems like it's going to be cool, but then one of the bad vampires, James (Cam Gigandet, who you might remember from *The O.C.* but I prefer to remember from the Lifetime

Original Movie *NANNY CAM*), sniffs Bella and is like, *"Ooooooh, oh boy, Daddy's num nums, don't mind if I dooooooo!"*

They manage to get Bella away from James, but Edward offers this extremely convoluted justification for the whole rest of the movie: "James is a tracker...I read it in his mind. I just made this the most exciting game ever." Since James is a "tracker" and he smelled Bella, now he *will not chill* until he gets Daddy's num nums!!!

The Cullens are like, "She's part of this family now, and we protect our family" (they've been on ONE DATE), and they help Bella make a plan. In order to keep her dad safe, she has to tell him she hates Forks and she hates him and he's fucking pathetic and she's moving to Florida to be with mom. It's honestly way harsher than it needed to be! Just tell him you're going on a vacation, dude! Then she drives to Phoenix because she believes James has taken her mom hostage in her old ballet studio, but, duh, it's a trap!

James takes Bella prisoner and decides to make a video of himself eating her to make Edward mad. But Bella pepper sprays James right in his low-rise jeans! And Edward shows up! And the two hot vampires fight over her—EVERY WOMAN'S BIG DREAM.

James is stronger because he eats the human meat, and he manages to bite Bella, but then all the Cullens show up and they rip James into small pieces and set him on fire. Then Edward has to suck James's vampire venom out of Bella's body without greedily sucking all her blood out and making her a vampire, but it's a big job, so Peter Facinelli comes to help too. Love 2 suck venom erotically from my girlfriend side by side with my dad! Anyway, Bella is fine.

Edward tries to tell Bella that she needs to move to Jacksonville "so I'll stop hurting you," and she says, "WE CAN'T BE APART! YOU CAN'T LEAVE ME!" So instead of setting some boundaries in their wildly codependent relationship, Edward takes her to the prom: "Prom's an important rite of passage."

This is his eighty-ninth prom.

RATING: 5 / 10 DVDs of *The Fugitive*.

Speed 2 **Is Not Canon**

W e open in the basement of an office building. Some big dork is down there, a security guard or something, wandering around like he's going to survive this opening scene. Yeah, right! Dennis Hopper is there too! If you ever find Dennis Hopper in your basement, DO NOT APPROACH HIM. Dennis Hopper is extremely territorial. This Einstein doesn't know anything about Dennis Hopper Safety, though, and he interrupts Dennis Hopper right when he's trying to do terrorism, so Dennis Hopper murders him. You know, it's always a tragedy when Dennis Hopper murders some reckless, irresponsible basement security guard, and then Dennis Hopper Control puts Dennis Hopper down, when he was just out there in Dennis Hopper's habitat doing what Dennis Hopper does. I mean, what did you expect? Truly, *we* are the virus.

Upstairs, a bunch of business boys get into an elevator. (Somebody coughs in the elevator, and I have an anxiety attack. Loved watching this during the cataclysmic global plague!)

Dennis Hopper sabotages the elevator and all the business boys are trapped in there. Time to call Keanu Reeves and Jeff Daniels: ELEVATOR COPS!

Jeff Daniels drives dangerously to the business boy tower—what traffic laws? There's elevator crime, and it's *going down*[22]—where Miles Dyson from *Terminator 2* is waiting in the lobby to fill them in on the scoop (guess he survived extremely blowing up at Cyberdyne HQ! Kudos!). There are like one hundred cops just standing around doing nothing because for some reason only Jeff and Keanu can handle this one. They have to climb thirty-two motherfucking flights of stairs, which I suppose would become the sole qualifying criteria to be an elevator cop. Can you climb thirty-two motherfucking flights of stairs? In less than an entire day? Congrats, you're an elevator cop! (This is why most elevator cops are rascally old alley cats.)

They locate the trapped elevator and call out to the hostages. Some guy inside is like, "What are you doing up there?" FUCKING SAVING YOU, MARK.

While they're working, Jeff Daniels gives Keanu a pop quiz (it's a cute little thing they do):

> **Jeff Daniels:** Airport, gunman with one hostage. He's using her for cover; he's almost to a plane. You're a hundred feet away.
> **Keanu:** Shoot the hostage. Take them out of the equation.

---

22   USE THIS LINE IN THE REBOOT!!!!!!!!

It was around the *Speed* era, I think, when people used to constantly make fun of Keanu Reeves for being a "bad actor." Are you kidding me with that? I love Keanu Reeves! I love him. He is a really good actor, you fucks. Did you ever think that maybe you're a bad actor??

I do think, though, that there is something unnatural about Keanu's vibe in *Speed*, probably because his character is supposed to be a kind of hard-edged utilitarian robocop and Keanu can't help being a freaking lamb to his core!!!!! Keanu would never "shoot the hostage," unless the "hostage" was a **H**og-piece-of-shit-republican-governor **O**pening **S**tates **T**oo-soon **A**gainst-COVID-19 **G**uidelines-in-order-to **E**xterminate-the-poor! Sorry, can you guess what month it is when I'm typing this?????[23]

Keanu smells that something taint right, and he needs to make sure that this elevator car is safe as hell. He goes up on the roof and finds exactly what he was looking for—a crane with a rope on it! That might seem like a convenient coincidence, but if you put good out into the world, good is what you get back. Keanu can have whatever he wants. He dives down into the elevator shaft and hooks the crane rope to the car, just in case.

Just in case is right! Right then, Dennis Hopper literally yells, "DON'T FUCK WITH DADDY!" and detonates a bomb that sends the elevator box hurtling toward the ground where it will surely smoosh all the lil finance sausages in there. But Dennis doesn't know about Keanu's secret crane rope! The crane is like crooooooooooaaaaaak, but it hangs in there just long enough.

Keanu and Jeff run down to the floor closest to the elevator, pry

---

23 MOTHERFUCKING APRIL 2020!!!!!!!!!!!!!!!!!!!!!!!!!!!!!!! WOW, A TIME!!!!!!!!!!!!!!!!!!!!!!!!!!!!!!!

open the wall, and start pulling people out one by one, making sure to show the female passengers' entire pantied asses. (Wait. That was an option? How come no one else was doing that while K&J: Elevator Geniuses were up on the roof playing with the crane? There were literally one thousand cops downstairs just staring at the ceiling that whole time!) The rope snaps and the elevator falls JUST as they haul the final lady out of the box.

All the cops are packing it up, high-tenning, and getting ready to go, but Keanu's like, "Hold on." Keanu has the best 'stincts in LA, and he has a feeling Hopper is still in the buil'. He and Jeff go to check it out.

They find Hopper hiding in the freight elevator with a bomb, and not only does he take Jeff hostage, he's also like, "POP QUIZ, HOT SHOT," which is so rude because pop quiz is, like, *their thing.* Hopper tells hot shot that he wants $3 million or else. Keanu shoots Jeff in the leg to "take him out of the equation," and I'm not sure exactly how that helps because Jeff is still a) alive, b) a hostage, and c) in Dennis Hopper's arms except now he can't walk, but I didn't go to Bomb Sexpert Elevator Academy, so what do I know?

Regardless, it works. Hopper kind of waddles backward into the parking garage going, "Hahahahahahaha!" and then explodes. OR DOES HE?

Jeff Daniels is one of those guys that seems fat, but then he's not.

Keanu and Jeff receive police medals in some sort of televised police medal ceremony—yes, very common, we've all watched them. And you know who else is watching? Dennis Hopper! Totally alive at his house! Turns out he did not blow up, and he's really mad.

The next morning, Keanu goes to his local coffee shop and says hey to his favorite bus driver, and…did buses really look that antique in 1994????? Am I…old? If you asked me to date that bus I'd be like, "Sure, as long as it's not a SAGITTARIUS"—HAHAHAHAHAHAHAHA—no, I'd be like, "Uh, 1963?" but apparently that is a full-on 1990s bus like I rode to the bead store before piano lessons every Tuesday.

Does anyone else feel like everything was 1970 until 2008 and then it abruptly switched to 2015 until 2017 when it became 2020 and has been ever since?

Half a block away, the bus absolutely explodes! Keanu runs over and discovers a pay phone ringing next to the burning dead bus. He answers it and, pop quiz, hot shot, it's DENNIS. That was always happening in the '90s—a pay phone ringing and on the other end is a psychopath who's about to explain the plot. There's nothing as creepy as that and now we can't do that anymore because pay phones were canceled! I hate the 2000s!

Dennis informs Keanu that he's actually put *another* bomb on *another* bus, and now he wants $3.7 million: "It's my nest egg, Jack. At my age, you have to plan ahead." (Bro, you're old! Didn't you already miss "ahead"?)

Spoiler alert, but I need to skip forward and address something. They figure out eventually that the reason Dennis Hopper made this extremely overcomplicated weird bus bomb is because he used to be a police bomb sexpert supercop just like Keanu. Unfortunately, his hand got fucked up in the line of duty, and now he's mad that his pension isn't luxurious enough. Can you imagine that story line being presented as a comprehensible motivation for terrorism in the year of our lord two thousand and twenty????? Hahahahaha! To a kid born in, say, 2001 that's like a fish threatening to blow up the ocean because he's thirsty. You're an already-comfortable yet inexplicably enraged middle-aged white guy in 1994 *with a government pension* who's prepared to kill a bunch of working-class people on public transit so you can squeeze millions of dollars of fun-money out of the US taxpayer coffers *because you want it*? LOL. Is *Speed* an allegory for the twenty-first-century GOP????? I hope so because at the end Dennis Hopper is decapitated to death by a subway lamp! (My hope is *allegorical*, of course!!!)

Dennis tells Keanu that there's a bomb on a bus, and it's rigged so that the bomb will arm when the bus goes above fifty miles per hour, and then it will explode if the bus dips back below fifty miles per hour. I feel like the one thing thrillers never take into account is that in real life all people are very, very lazy and no one would ever do this.

Keanu figures out which bus it is and starts chasing the bus. He has to stop it before it goes over fifty miles per hour! There is a joke about LA traffic that I could make here but I will not!

When the bus passengers notice Keanu chasing them, they say things like, "He really wants to get on this bus!" and "That man sure has a hard-on for this bus." They don't understand that he just has a hard-on for saving their dang lives! Also porno.

Keanu spies a random cool guy driving a speedy convertible with a vanity plate that says "TUNEMAN," and decides it's just what he needs for chasing down this bus. Keanu steals TUNE-MAN's convertible, and in the process he also steals TUNEMAN! TUNEMAN is more exasperated than terrified, even though he is nearly liquefied many times by Keanu's gonzo driving styles. That's probably because this whole carjacking thing is making TUNEMAN late to either creating or listening to TUNES (it's never specified). "I gotta get on that bus," Keanu explains. "Yeah, yeah, you get on that bus."—TUNEMAN, over it.

TUNEMAN has a car phone, so Keanu is able to alert the cops about the return of Dennis and his pointlessly baroque speed-based bus bomb. He has TUNEMAN take the wheel, and then he leaps on to the bus! Then TUNEMAN crashes, but that's not Keanu's problem.

The bus passengers are reasonably freaked, so Keanu explains that he's a cop. A small-time criminal, assuming Keanu is there to arrest him, pulls out a gun! Coincidentally, then Keanu tells him exactly the thing I say to myself every night before bed: "I don't care about your crime. Whatever you did, I'm sure you're sorry. So it's cool now. It's over. I'm not a cop right now. We're just two cool guys."

Just when the situation is almost deescalated, some construction man gotta be a hero and tackles the guy with the gun, accidentally shooting Sam the bus driver. Great. This is not what Keanu needs right now!

Keanu tells Sandra Bullock to take the wheel so he can try to find the bomb, and then they have this exchange, which is really all you want from a movie:

> **Sandy:** I should probably tell you that I'm riding this bus because I had my driver's license revoked.
> **Keanu:** What for?
> **Sandy:** Speeding.

Sandra Bullock is an unmatched charm powerhouse, and I feel like nobody acknowledges that anymore because she made too many comedies for women, and men can't stand that. Watch

Sandra Bullock in action. Watch Sandra Bullock in *Speed* and then tell me you don't want to frame your spouse for a crime so you can marry her instead! Watch *While You Were Sleeping* and try not to send Sandra Bullock a thank-you card with $4,000 inside. I DARE YOU.

Keanu inspects the bomb and calls Jeff, who's back at the office trying to dig up dirt on Dennis. Keanu tells Jeff that "there's enough C-4 on this thing to put a hole in the world," and also mentions that the timer on the bomb is a cheap gold watch—the kind of shitty watch the bomb cops get when they retire! (Can you imagine being this pissed about getting a comfortable retirement, a lifetime of unconditional hero worship, *and a present*??)

There's heavy traffic ahead, so they have to exit the freeway to stay above fifty, and here begins one of the great mysteries of the movie *Speed*: WHY DOES SANDRA BULLOCK HAVE TO DRIVE THE BUS? Keanu—a highly trained police officer dispatched to handle this extremely dangerous situation—just kind of hovers over Sandy B.'s shoulder, occasionally gabbing to Jeff or Dennis on the phone, while she—A RANDOM CIVILIAN—navigates crowded Los Angeles surface streets in a bus going fifty miles per hour. What if she runs someone over? What if she is bad at driving? Who is accountable for all of the human lives on the bus when they are put into the hands of a person who doesn't even have a driver's license?

Sometimes Keanu and Sandy take a little time to flirt as Sam bleeds out behind them and they hurtle toward death.

Sandy has to make a hairpin turn at top speed in order to get back on the freeway. (See, not to be one of those analog bitches, but this is all I need from an action movie. Just an exciting bus turn! I do not require Transformers!)

Dennis told Keanu that nobody is allowed to get off the bus, and he'll know if they do because he is monitoring them via secret video. Keanu convinces Dennis to let Bus Driver Sam get off so he doesn't die, because I guess mayors never give $3.7 million to terrorists who let one bus driver die, but they do sometimes give $3.7 million to terrorists who didn't. He gets the big beefy construction worker to help him move Sam by saying, "You! Gigantor!" (Hey, how about *sir* when you want someone to do you a favor?) The cops pull up alongside the door of the bus on a trailer and Keanu and Gigantor, I mean *sir*, pass Sam over to them in a way that definitely seems like everyone would die.

Even though Keanu just explained that only Bus Driver Sam is allowed to get off the bus, the temptation is too great for another passenger, Helen (the great Beth Grant), and she tries to jump off after him. Dennis was ready for this, and he activates the Helen Contingency, a smaller Helen-shaped bomb right under the door of the bus, which he put there in case any Helens try to escape. Helen blows up and gets run over and is dead. Now it's not so fun being on the Speed bus anymore! Adventure? More like I'm-sadventure!

Oops, turns out the freeway isn't finished. (Nobody knew that???) There's a fifty-foot gap coming up in three miles. Keanu thinks about it and decides that they'll have to fly the bus over the gap. It's the only way. Really, you can't exit and go around it? There's not an exit for the next three miles? In Los Angeles? OKAY!

Keanu tells Sandy to floor it (again, why isn't he just driving?! Abolish the LAPD!), and they accelerate toward the gap and fly over it effortlessly, you know, like a real bus would. It definitely wouldn't 100 percent absolutely tip straight down into the pit and accordion into a bloody, clattering disc!

Hey, if you guys had a flying bus this whole time, why didn't you get off the fucking freeway instead of causing four hundred car accidents?

Keanu directs Sandy (STILL DRIVING) to LAX so the bus can circle around and around on the tarmac without endangering other drivers, and so that the news choppers will stop broadcasting their every move straight to Dennis's TV. Now it's time to defuse the bomb.

Keanu slides underneath the moving bus on a little skateboard attached to a rope. He scoots down to where the bomb is and tries to dismantle it while Jeff gives him instructions over the phone. It makes total sense that Keanu has to personally do this. Did you know there's only one guy in the LAPD?

Keanu can't figure out the bomb and then starts careening out of control underneath the bus. In order to not die, he has to stab the fuel tank with a screwdriver and cling to the bottom of the bus like a lil spider, until Sir Gigantor opens a hatch and pulls him up into the bus. Wow, this is a beautiful movie about teamwork in adversity! If I'm making Dennis Hopper an allegory for mediocre white male greed, then truly the bus is an allegory for human tenderness and teamwork during COVID-19! I feel strengthened by this.

Meanwhile, Jeff Daniels locates Dennis Hopper's house, but unfortunately, the house is a bomb! Jeff goes there and explodes.

Which, like, I hate because I love Jeff. But also, you guys didn't suspect anything? You didn't suspect any funny business from the evil bomb mastermind?

When he hears that Jeff is dead, Keanu freaking LOSES IT, and only Sandy B. can bring him back to earth: "I can't do this by myself!"

YEAH, SHE REALLY CAN'T.

NOR SHOULD SHE BE EXPECTED TO.

Dennis tells the cops they need to drop his money in a garbage can at Pershing Square. The bus is losing fuel and also has a flat tire. They need to get these people off the bus fast. Keanu finally figures out how Dennis knows everything about what they're doing: he's hooked into the surveillance camera from the bus! The cops make one of the nearby news vans record thirty seconds of everyone sitting still on the bus and loop it. With Dennis now in the dark, they finally get all the people off the bus except for Keanu and Sandy.

Again, SHE SHOULD HAVE GOTTEN OFF THE BUS AS WELL! SHE IS A CIVILIAN BUS PASSENGER! HE CAN DRIVE! WHAT THE FUCK!

Then the two of them escape by using the hatch in the bottom of the bus as a sort of surfboard and sliding into some cones, while the bus drives into a cargo plane and explodes. Sorry, you didn't clear the airport? At any point in this whole thing?

They lie on the ground for a moment in a sensual embrace, and then Sandy B. says something that has haunted me for the rest of my life: "Relationships that start under intense circumstances, they never last."

Is that true?????? What is that based on? I saw this movie when I was way too young to have a concept of what a relationship is actually like, and I definitely filed this away as conventional wisdom. Better not start a relationship under intense circumstances, idiot! They never last! But what qualifies as "intense circumstances"? Is there really a scientifically significant data set on the divorce rate among couples who met when trapped in a bus that would blow up if it went under fifty miles per hour?

What if you meet on a roller coaster? Or a haunted elevator? My husband and I met at a very stressful and off-putting party full of cool snobs. Does that count? Are we doomed? I hate it when people just say things!!!

Anyway, Keanu tells Dennis they're going to make the drop, and Dennis is still watching the looped video like a dumbass so he doesn't realize that the bus blew up. Apparently, the news (which he is obsessively watching) didn't report "massive explosion at LAX," even though you could definitely see that smoke from downtown. Look out the window of your derelict mannequin factory, Dennis! Then he spies a glitch in the loop, realizes the ruse, and heads to Pershing Square to fuck these cops up.

For some reason, the LAPD makes Sandy B. come along with them and sit in an ambulance while they finish arresting Dennis Hopper. What???????? Can't she go home??? Why on earth does Sandy have to go to the drop? She lives in Venice! It's not even like downtown is on the way back from LAX!

Of COURSE she instantly hops out of the ambulance and runs into Dennis, who is dressed as a cop and takes her hostage. Good job, cops!

The cops, like a million of them, wait and wait for Dennis to come get the package out of the garbage can, but he never does. Because it turns out he squizzled a hole 'neath the can so he could squeak up and bungle it away with his great twiddly sneak fingers!

They eventually figure out the hole trick and, for some fucking reason, Keanu jumps down in there alone—because who needs these eleven thousand trained snipers (who are literally already there!) when you're going to confront the murderous and tricky bomb king? Keanu is overconfident, he thinks he has the upper hand on Dennis—"Pop quiz, asshole!"—but, shit, it's actually Sandy, and she is COVERED in bomb.

"A bomb is made to explode," says Dennis eccentrically. "That's its meaning, its purpose. Your life is empty because you spend it trying to stop the bomb from becoming."

They're on the subway. Now it's *Speed* on a train. Dennis makes Sandy hold this trigger device so he can murder the train driver and check out his loot. He opens the money bag and it squirts purple paint in his face and all over the money. "My money!!!" You can't buy a Jet Ski with purple money! Everyone knows that!

Keanu and Dennis climb up onto the roof of the subway where they fist-fight. Yo, Dennis, no offense, but you are one million years old. There's no way you can beat up Keanu! And, indeed, he does not. He gets his head whacked off by a lamp on the subway tunnel roof. THAT'S YOUR PENSION NOW, BITCH!

Even worse for Dennis, Sandy asks Keanu what happened to Dennis and he says, "He lost his head." A freaking ruthless roast!!!!!

But it's not over yet! Dennis also broke the train so they cannot stop it, and now the subway track is finished. Keanu knows what to do, though—he's gonna fly the train like he flew the bus! The thing about Keanu is that he learned stuff from what happened before!

He cranks up the speed, sits down sensually with Sandy to snuggle while they die, and I tell you that train pops right up out of the street like the snake I just found in my peanut brittle! Keanu and Sandy skid to a halt amid the rubble and make out HARD. They are troublingly horny considering how recently they decapitated a dude!

Keanu: I've heard relationships based on intense experiences never work.

Sandy: Okay, we'll have to base it on sex, then.

Keanu: Okay, ma'am.[24]

Then all the Hollywood tourists high-five and take pictures because they love two hot, dirty people kissing in a burning subway car that just exploded out of the earth like a Tremors worm.

This is the greatest love story ever told. RIP, Helen.

RATING: 9/10 DVDs of *The Fugitive*.

---

24   It has come to my attention that in *Speed 2: Cruise Control* Sandra Bullock is in a "relationship" on a "boat" with Jason Patric, but experts agree that *SPEED 2* IS NOT CANON. THE COMMITTEE DOES NOT RECOGNIZE THE VALIDITY OF *SPEED 2* OR BOATS.

The Shawnsnake Redumptruck

The Shawshank Redemption is a movie about how prison used to be pretty bad (like, at least 4–5 percent more bad than it is now, I think!). Tim Robbins is Andy Dufresne, a fancy banker who is falsely convicted of his wife's murder in a kind of Night-the-Lights-Went-Out-in-Georgia-style whoopsie-daisy, and gets two consecutive life sentences. (So *that's* how you put a banker in prison! #topical)

Over at Shumptruck State Priz, Morgan Freeman is not getting paroled, AS USUAL. He explains, folksily, that he's the guy who smuggles in contraband such as cigarettes, pornos, and geological fieldwork equipment. "Yessir, I'm a regular Sears and Roebuck." (Pretty sure the cigarettes/porno/rock hammer Sears is a specialty branch.) He is also the narrator of the prison.

When Andy shows up, prison's like, "Hey, welcome to prison. We hired Clancy Brown to be mean to you." Not a terrible crime reduction tactic, TBH!

While the guards hose and flour all the new inmates, Morgan

Freeman and his prison friends—Richie Aprile, the Grim Reaper from *Bill & Ted's Bogus Journey*, an old guy with a bird in his shirt, and three to four Tom Waits cosplayers—place bets on which one of the new guys is going to cry first. Turns out, it's the fat one, OF COURSE (can fat people be afforded no dignity?), who starts screaming for his mommy as soon as they turn the lights off. Everyone has an early morning of pointless toil, gallows humor, and grimacing, so Clancy Brown murders the crying fat man with his Clancy Brown Murder Stick.

At breakfast the next day, Andy finds a maggot in his porridge, so he gives it to the dude with the shirt-bird who's like, "Jake says thank you!" NO, HE DIDN'T. I WATCHED THE WHOLE THING. HE SAID, "CHEEP CHEEP." #GASLIGHTING

During his post-breakfast shower, Andy is approached by a red-haired fellow who is one of the FBI agents who is mean to Chris Tucker in *Rush Hour* and also indicates that he would like to initiate a sexual relationship: "Hey, anybody come at you yet? Anybody get to you yet? Hey, we all need friends in here. I could be a friend to you. Hey. Hard to get. I like that." (Yo, guy, read *The Rules*. Neediness is a turnoff.) Morgan Freeman advises Andy to "grow eyes in the back of [his] head," which I'm pretty sure is impossible, but apparently some people in prison can speak bird, so what do I know. Andy fails to grow the extra eyes in time and is horrifically beaten and raped. It is the worst.

Andy asks Morgan Freeman to get him a rock hammer, and Morgan Freeman is like, "What is that, weirdo?" and Andy's like, "My hobby is hitting rocks with a hammer?—just get me one," and when it arrives, Morgan Freeman is all, "LOLOLOL, THIS IS A VERY TINY HAMMER," and Andy is all, "You do you, me do me!!!" The downplaying of the hammer's power becomes very important for a later switcheroo. Note it.

One day, all the guys are tarring the roof of the license plate factory when Clancy Brown starts going on and on about how he's inheriting $35,000 from his dead brother, but he doesn't want to pay a bunch of stupid dead-brother taxes. "Uncle Sam," he gripes, "he puts his hand in your shirt and squeezes your tit till it's purple." (Sir, real quick, do you mean Uncle Sam the fictional patriotic dandy? Or do you have an actual abusive uncle named Sam? Oh my god, *is that how your brother died*?) Andy tells Clancy Brown that he's a banker and offers to fix his tax problems if Clancy Brown will give everyone beer. And here's why Andy is so cool: he DOESN'T EVEN WANT THE BEER. (Andy, please, have a beer. You're in prison.)

After that, Andy and Morgan Freeman decide that they are best friends.

Back in his cell one night, Andy is playing around with his rock hammer when a huge chunk of wall just glops off into his hand. Hey, prison, what the fuck is your wall made of? *Ehhhhh, cookie dough.* Pretty sure your main job is walls. You did it bad.

Now that Andy is frenemies with Clancy Brown, he finally has some protection from the rape gang. Goodbye, super unpleasant subplot!

Everything is really coming up Andy during this period. He is no longer being violently assaulted on the reg, he gets a job working in the library with Shirt-Bird, he starts doing all the guards' taxes and memorizing their secrets, and the warden doesn't mind if he does his stupid rock carving as long as he keeps pretending to care about Jesus. He is truly the best at being a prisoner ever.

UNTIL. Shirt-Bird gets paroled, even though he is two hundred years old and hasn't been outside prison since a car was called an "electric horse." He goes to live at a halfway house and gets a job bagging groceries, and he is very lonely and it is very terrible. Plus, for some reason, he decides he HAS TO *HARRY AND THE HENDERSONS* HIS BIRD. (Dude, I don't know how it was in the 1870s, but they have birds outside prison now! I'm sure there are mad grubs in the halfway house gruel.) So then, since they won't let him go back to prison and bird never even calls anymore (dick!!!!!), Shirt-Bird kills himself and it is the saddest, worst thing ever to happen in any movie. Until the other worst thing that happens later in this movie. Ugh, this movie!

Andy is feeling sassy in the aftermath of Shirt-Bird's death. So, one day, he barricades the bathroom door while his guard is *shooting some brown bullets into the porcelain yard*, and commandeers the prison loudspeaker to play a Mozart song. Every single one of the downtrodden, defeated inmates turns his face to the sun, soaking up, with his full body, this fleeting scrap of the achingly brilliant human audacity so long denied him by cold prison walls—as though humans do not need art as surely as we need oxygen, as though we do not bleed beauty as freely as blood.

"I have no idea, to this day, what those two Italian ladies were singing about," Morgan Freeman intones.

Meatballs, probably.

Andy starts laundering money for the warden's nefarious extortion schemes, which is a pretty cool prison job. It also brings him ever deeper into the warden's inner circle, which is not that cool because the warden is a big turd.

Case in point: One day, Billy from *Ally McBeal* shows up in prison and reveals that—mega small world—he used to be cellmates with the guy who actually murdered Andy's wife! When Andy takes that hot goss to the warden, hoping to get a new trial, the warden throws him in the hole for two months AND THEN MURDERS BILLY FROM *ALLY MCBEAL*. (Not sure why Andy expected the murderous warden for whom he's been laundering millions of dollars to be like, "Yes, I'll totally help you get out of prison so you can go tell everyone about my mad felonies!" but yeah. You're totally the *smartest guy in prison*, Andy.)

At this point, Andy is officially FED UP with this shit. He tells Morgan Freeman that he plans to move to Mexico one of these days, and that if Morgan Freeman ever gets out of prison, he should just go to Buxton and look under the special volcano rock and then he can come live with Andy in his Mexican she-shed. And Morgan Freeman is like, "Ooooooooookay. Go lie down, kookaburra."

Now everyone's freaked out because Andy's been "talkin' funny" and it seems like he's planning to self-harm out of grief over the death of Billy from *Ally McBeal* (I know the feeling). AND THEN HE DOES. Only he does it with like a laser or some shit because when the guards open his cell in the morning, dude is STRAIGHT VAPORIZED.

What actually happened is that Andy spent nineteen years tunneling out of the cookie castle with his rock hammer, concealing the tunnel hole behind Raquel Welch's boobs, and when it was finally done, he yoinked the warden's outfit and shoes (which seems dubious because the warden appears to be a small little pocket-pal and Tim Robbins is a ten-foot 'squatch, but okay), and crawled through a half mile of poopoo to get out. Then he tattled on the warden to the newspaper and headed to Mexico with $375,000. WHO'S KOOKABURRA NOW, MORGAN?

Cops show up at Shawshank and take Clancy Brown away, and he's all a-bloo-bloo-bloo-bloo-bloooooo and then the warden shoots himself and then Morgan Freeman is like, "Some birds aren't meant to be caged. Their feathers are just too bright. And when they fly away, the part of you that knows it was a sin to lock them up does rejoice." (Hollyweird Fun Fact: that line wasn't in the script—it's just something Morgan Freeman said to his assistant when she brought him a salami sandwich in the voice-over booth.)

Then Morgan Freeman has his parole meeting and he NAAAAAILS IT! He gets out of prison and goes to work at the grocery store where Shirt-Bird worked and lives in the same dumb apartment where Shirt-Bird lived and the same shitty white ladies are all, "Um, DOUBLE BAGS," and his boss is like, "STOP TELLING ME ABOUT YOUR URINE," and he just doesn't know how to fit in in this non-prison world. "All I do anymore," he says, "is think of ways to break my parole so maybe they'd send me back."

Until, one day, Morgan Freeman remembers that Andy left him a present under some fucking rock in Buxton! And do you know what the present is? IT'S LITERALLY A TON OF BUX!

So Morgan Freeman takes a bus to Mexico and finds Andy on a beach and he's so excited that he doesn't even care that his only hat falls in the ocean and the two of them scrub boats together forever. And that's why *Sharktank Rondonald* is the first great American bromance. Eleven out of ten. Your mom was right.

RATING: 11/10 DVDs of *The Fugitive*.

Know Your Enemy

I know that gen Z has it tough—they're losing their proms and graduations to the quarantine, they're on deck to bear the full brunt of climate catastrophe, and they're inheriting a carcass of a society that's been fattened up and picked clean by the billionaire class, leaving them with virtually no shot at a life without crushing financial and existential anxiety, let alone any fantasy of retiring from their thankless toil or leaving anything of value to their own children. That's bad. BUT, counterpoint! Millennials have to deal with a bunch of that same stuff, kind of, PLUS we had to be teenagers when *American Pie* came out! Fuck/marry/kill: Rudolph Giuliani, Stephen Miller, the guy behind you in chemistry saying, "This one time? At band camp?" nine thousand fucking times per hour for FOUR YEARS MINIMUM. You know you would fuck Stephen and marry Rudy if it meant you got to murder that motherfucker!

What I'm saying is that suffering IS a contest and I DO stand by that and straight teenage boys losing their virginities IS worse than not having breathable air. Okay??????

American Pie absolutely captivated a generation because my generation is tacky as hell. "I have a hot girlfriend but she doesn't want to have sex" was an entire genre of movies in the '90s. In the '90s, people loved it when things were "raunchy" (ew!). Every guy at my high school wanted to be Stifler! Can you imagine what that kind of an environment does to a person? To be of the demographic that has a Ron Burgundy quote for every occasion, without the understanding that Ron Burgundy is a satire? This is why we have Jenny McCarthy, I'm pretty sure, and, by extension, the great whooping cough revival of 2014. Thanks a lot, jocks!

It's not that I hate every '90s teen sex comedy. Believe me, as a teen who was *not* having sex in the '90s, I needed them to live. I just think a lot of them are bad, and have bad morals, and did bad things to boys' and girls' brains, but that doesn't mean I can't *like them*. I was a *Can't Hardly Wait* girl myself, and that shit is absolutely radioactive with incel energy. This tension is the stuff of life.

American Pie was the big one, though, and I never got it. I just always thought it was the least charming of the bunch, Eugene Levy and Natasha Lyonne notwithstanding.[25] That said, this franchise has made a collective *$1 billion*. So change my mind, rewatch!!! (Spoiler: it won't!)

American Pie is about a group of high school boys who make a pact to lose their virginities before they graduate.

Jason Biggs is our main guy, whose problem is that he cannot stop masturbating in front of his parents, which is

---

25   I confess it! I also like Chris Klein!

weird because if there's one thing I know about teenagers, it's that they are masters of secrecy! When I was in high school, if I was going to steal an extra Dorito after my mom told me I couldn't have any more Doritos, I would memorize the exact topography of the Doritos in the bag and the bag's placement in the snack drawer and I would SILENTLY Jenga a single Dorito out of there and snap the chip clip back in the exact right position *to the millimeter* and then backflip out of the kitchen like motherfucking Sydney Bristow! Yet Biggs "accidentally" masturbates in front of his parents...three? Four times in this movie? And god knows how many more times later in the franchise! I haven't watched any of those, but it would be bad storytelling to have your protagonist overcome the defining struggle of his life at the very beginning of his hero's journey, and for Jason Biggs, that's masturbating in front of his parents. One might argue that masturbating in front of his parents is Jason Biggs's entire personality. And one would be almost right, except that he is also 1 percent ruthless objectification of women and 4 percent battery. Jason Biggs looks like a battery.

Chris Klein is a lacrosse jock with a tender heart who is constantly being harassed by Stifler (class clown/bully/sexual success) about how he needs to be pulling chicks the old-fashioned way: by insulting and tricking them.

Kevin(?) has a beautiful girlfriend, Tara Reid, who is not ready to have sex because she wants it to be "perfect" and because Kevin(?) won't say *I love you* back. Who even remembered that Kevin, one of the four main characters in this movie, was even a character in this movie? Not me! Is his name actually Kevin? I will not look it up!

Finch is the old soul of the pack, which you can tell because he has fine tastes such as "mochaccinos,"[26] lying, and hiding.

Did you realize that only twenty years ago, it was still socially acceptable to make ensemble comedies of all white men who look exactly alike even though one of them is a battery?

Stifler is having a party tonight, and the four pals are sitting around wondering if this will be the night they finally coerce a girl into intercoursing them. Biggs asks what "third base" feels like, and Chris Klein tells him it's "like warm apple pie." *Is it, though*???? Oh yeah, you know, crusty and mushy!

Klein isn't going to the party because he has a date with a college chick, and he's been practicing his lines for sex-convincing.

Kevin(?) wonders if tonight is the night that Tara Reid will finally let him break through her flaky crust.

The fourth guy, I forget what he does.

The party opens with a truly virtuosic full-minute-long take of Stifler walking around being a dirtbag, exactly like the car chase in *Children of Men* but with more Barenaked Ladies. Biggs and Kevin(?) can't believe it when Sherman, a guy they think is worse than they are, tells them he's had sex before. The Shermanator is

---

26 Hey, when will "mochaccino" die as a joke? Like, I get it, your high school shop teacher needs a way to be vaguely homophobic on Facebook, and drinking anything but the shittiest black coffee in existence is extremely homosexual and Marxist, but for FUCK'S SAKE, coffee snobs are not ordering "half-caf extra-hot no foam triple-pump rooty tooty fresh 'n' fruity crème brûlée for a day fudgy white extra whip coconut mochaccinos" at Starbucks!!! Are you nuts? I actually live in an effete liberal urban center, and we dicks are drinking single-origin pourover from coffee shops that don't even believe in milk. If you want a really good "mochaccino," you gotta go outside the city limits to Red State Real America because they're using heavy whipping cream, they're giving you 128 ounces of it, and they're sticking Almond Joys and Oreos and whole cherry pies and other smaller mochaccinos on top, hail Satan. "Mochaccino" is a self-own, please stop.

supposedly worse because he is an unappealing chauvinist nerd who wears ugly big jeans, whereas our heroes are...different from that. Biggs tries talking to his crush, Nadia, but beefs it. Meanwhile, on his date with the college girl, Chris Klein tries out the sex line he prepared for 100 percent guaranteed sex: "Suck me, beautiful." (Jesus, who's your dating coach—Castor Troy?) The college girl laughs in his face and tells him she's majoring in "postmodern feminist thought," which, in the '90s, was a punch line. Haha! Thinking about feminism! *Postmodern*—does that word even *have* a meaning?? She suggests that if he wants to have sex with a woman, he should try being less like a Ying Yang Twin and more like a human being who is normal, nice, and enjoys talking about shared interests or the news of the day. Yeah, right! Nice try, Lorena Bobbitt.

At the party, Tara Reid and Kevin(?) go up to one of the bedrooms where she sucks his dick and then he jizzes into a beer. Stifler kicks them out so he can try to have disrespectful sex with a girl named Sarah in there ("I don't know if I want to be doing this"—Sarah, hilariously!), but then just when he's about to successfully badger her into accepting his penis, Stifler accidentally glugs the jizz beer! Guk guk guk right down! And then he realizes that it was jizz beer because it tastes like the inside of Kevin(?)'s balls, so then he supersoaks Sarah with a fire hose of vomit that is also jizz. I'm sorry, I don't like it either, but it's all we had for entertainment in the '90s!!!

I forgot that *American Pie* popularized the term *MILF*, and that they made John Cho do it, which is a microaggression. Also, later, Stifler calls the guys *cucks*! Did *American Pie* really mainstream both *MILF* and *cuck*? Can you put a movie in jail?

The guys wake up, hungover, in Stifler's living room the next morning and ratify the terms of their four-boy sex pact (god, straight guys are SO GAY):

> "Here's the deal. We all get laid before we graduate."
> "Together, we are the masters of our sexual destiny."
> "This is our very manhood at stake."
> "No longer will our penises remain flaccid and unused! We will fight for every man out there who isn't getting laid and should be!"
> "We will make a stand! We will succeed! We will get laid!"
> "Prom is our last chance."
> "All the parties afterwards? Chicks are gonna want to do it!"

That's the vibe that killed us all, by the way! Buncha white boys sitting around like, "We will fight for every man out there who isn't getting laid and should be!" Oops, that's it for the species. Not to get all "postmodern feminist thought" major on you, but the idea that straight white men "deserve" some degree of unfettered access to other people's bodies and if they don't get it, they are being robbed of something that *intrinsically belongs to them* is white supremacist patriarchal capitalist imperialism, dog! People have inherent value regardless of their usefulness to you, sorry! Being able to squeeze as much pleasure or profit as you want out of somebody else's life or body or labor (or out of any weaker party, any nation, any system, any natural resource), regardless of their security or consent, is not a right, sorry! My bad, but kill every billionaire, metaphorically, I swear! Sorryyyyyyyyyyyyyyyy!

Alas, the horny-boy sex quest continues. They buy SO MANY CONDOMS. Biggs makes an online dating profile, gets no hits. Klein wonders, "How the hell am I supposed to become this Mr. Sensitive Man?" and then joins jazz choir. Kevin(?) seeks advice from Natasha Lyonne, who tells him, "If you want to get her in the sack, just tell her you love her. That's how I got duped." She also says he should try to cause Tara Reid to have an orgasm, and we, as a society, should probably pause and think about how wild it is that men need that info delivered to them as sex advice. Hahaha, Ed Harris, please neurotoxify us ASAP!

Turns out, Chris Klein is actually really into vocal jazz—understandably because singing in a choir teaches you how to connect with others on a profound level, to subsume your ego and truly listen, to create something beautiful out of a collective using only your bodies and your shared understanding of human emotion and the concept of time. Also, another good point, "This place is an untapped resource. I mean, check it out, these vocal jazz girls are hot!"

Klein tries to pass along his newfound wisdom to Stifler:

"All you gotta do is just ask them questions and just listen to what they have to say and shit."

"I don't know, man, that sounds like a lot of work!"

He is a horrible person, but there is something soothing about Stifler's complete self-actualization. Stifler knows who he is and he knows what he wants and he does not question himself. He lives effortlessly within the contours of the life he has chosen. I admire Stifler in this way. I yearn for the kind of certainty that seems to come so naturally to him. May we all someday find the serenity of Steve Stifler, but with, I don't know, not so many up-skirt video schemes.

Eugene Levy corners Biggs for a father-son sex chat and gives him some sex magazines to teach him about pussy: "Okay, so, uh, this is the female form, and they have focused primarily on the breasts." I don't listen to a lot of podcasts (Harry Potter audiobooks aren't going to listen to *themselves* on a ceaseless and frankly worrisome twenty-year loop!!!), but I would pay upward of $7,000 per episode for Eugene Levy Describes Shaved Centerfolds.

Finch pays Natasha Lyonne to start a rumor at school that he's "equipped" because that's what teen girls are into—huge cocks! These girls are positively IN HEAT over Finch's rumored dong!

Kevin(?) calls Casey Affleck to get sex tips, and Casey Affleck bequeaths to him "the bible," a handwritten book of sex information passed down from senior to senior for generations. "Now it's full of all kind of stuff guys have added over the years" (jizz). Kevin(?) goes and finds the book in its secret hiding place in the library, and first of all it is SO BIG, WHY IS THAT BOOK SO BIG, but second of all, you guys know there are just books about sex in the regular library, right? And they're probably better, because they were written by adults who have actually had sex? You absolutely do not need to do any of this.

Chris Klein is not just surviving but thriving in jazz choir. He is wearing a cardigan. He is feelin' it, and he lets the music take control: "Scooby dooby do bop!"

"That was good!" says the choir teacher.

No, it wasn't!!!!!

"The state competition's a few weeks away, so keep on it!" says the choir teacher.

They are not going to win the state competition!!!!!

Klein starts flirting with Mena Suvari, one of the choir hotties. She was pretty impressed earlier when he went, "Scooby dooby do bop," and she can't wait to see what other steamy surprises this scat king has in his pants!

Uh-oh. Jason Biggs gets home from school and his mother has left a fresh apple pie on the counter. Biggs immediately gets an erection. He pulls down his pants. He clambers up on to the kitchen island and begins making full horizontal love to the hot pie using his penis. In the kitchen. Of his parents' home! TAKE THE PIE UP TO YOUR ROOM, JASON! This is literally so disrespectful. Do you know how much work it is to make an apple pie from scratch????

Of course, Eugene Levy comes in and finds his only child inseminating a pastry, moaning and twitching and stuff. This is a horror movie. In some weird gesture of male solidarity, Levy's like, "Well, we'll just tell your mother that we ate it all." But, I'm sorry, as a married couple, your first allegiance is to each other. If my husband came home and our son was fucking a pie that I made and he didn't IMMEDIATELY TELL ME so we could laugh and vomit and call 911 together, divoooooorce!

Mena Suvari asks Chris Klein to prom, but then she sees Stifler doing a sex motion and high-fiving Klein on the lacrosse field, so then she UN-asks him to prom. "I saw you making fun of me with your lacrosse buddies. You are just a jock. No, wait, you're a jerk." Nice one.

Kevin(?) gives Tara Reid an orgasm using "the infamous TONGUE TORNADO," which he learned about in the secret sex bible. (Another entry says, "Know your enemy," with a picture of a vibrator. Very cool for women!)

Eugene Levy tries to have a postmortem talk with Biggs about the pie incident: "I want to talk about masturbation."

The purpose of this conversation, Levy explains, is that he

wants to make sure that Biggs wants a sex partner and isn't just content with masturbation for the rest of his life. Is that a real problem? Teenage boys not wanting to fuck enough? Anyway, who cares, it brought us this dialogue:

"I did a fair bit of masturbating when I was younger. I used to call it *stroking the salami*. You know your uncle Mort? He pets the one-eyed snake five, six times a day." SAVE IT FOR THE PODCAST, EUGENE.

Back at school, the rumors about Finch are getting sexier than ever. "He's the guy with the tattoo, right? You know, the eagle and the blazing fire, and all that stuff? Well, if you see him later, will you tell him Courtney says hi?"

Nadia, the exchange student Biggs is darkly obsessed with, asks him if he will help her study. "I have ballet practice; perhaps I could come to your house afterwards, I could change clothes at your place?" A woman changing clothes in the same building as you while you don't watch? In some cultures (orc, badger, Mar-a-Lago) that makes her your wife! Might as well do whatever the fuck you want to her!

"There's gonna be an Eastern European chick naked in your house and you're not going to do anything about that?"

"What am I gonna do, broadcast it over the internet?"

"Yeah!"

"You can do that?"

NO, YOU CAN'T!!!! YOU ABSOLUTELY CAN'T!

This is one of the most fucked-up things to happen in any movie. It is so so so so so so so so so so so fucked up. *Porky's* is bad, but at least peeping through a hole is purely analog sexual exploitation. Jason Motherfucking Biggs nonconsensually livestreams Nadia's naked body to everyone he knows, AND he "addressed the e-mail

wrong" so it went out to "every mailbox in the East High directory"
INCLUDING BLINK-182 AND A MONKEY.

THE NAME FOR THIS IS CRIME.

Biggs sets up his webcam, and Nadia comes over. Biggs shows
Nadia to his bedroom so she can change. Nadia takes off her
clothes. She does a little dance. Then she starts going through
Biggs's stuff. She finds his sex magazines. She lies down on his
bed to read the sex magazines. She starts masturbating on his
bed to the sex magazines! WHO WOULD DO THIS IN SOME-
ONE ELSE'S HOUSE!? It's almost as though this character is not
remotely a person!

The guys urge Biggs to go back in there and "seduce her."

"If you ever had a chance with Nadia, this is it."

"Go over there and ask her if she needs an extra hand."

He barges into the room and instead of, I don't know,
screaming and crying and apologizing for nudely masturbating
in the bedroom of an acquaintance??? What would be a normal
response to this absolutely alien situation that has literally never
happened without the presence of methamphetamine? Instead
of anything like that, Nadia is just naughtily titillated and tells
Biggs, "You have seen me, now it's my turn to see you," and
makes him do a striptease. Yeah, okay. "More, more, you bad
boy!" YEAH, OKAY.

Then Biggs jizzes in his pants and the monkey cannot believe
it. Blink-182 cannot believe it. Nadia cannot believe it the most.
She thought she was going to get some of that lil 9-volt copper-
top! Biggs begs for a second chance (reminder: everyone he has
ever known is watching this and masturbating) and Nadia is like,
"Well, I do like your dirty magazines." Then she says the word
shaved, so he jizzes in his pants again.

THEN NADIA GETS SENT BACK TO THE CZECH RE-PUBLIC BECAUSE HER HOST FAMILY WATCHED HER NONCONSENSUAL WEBCAM PORNO AND WOMEN MUST ALWAYS BE PUNISHED FOR THEIR OWN EXPLOITATION.[27]

Biggs is moping around because the whole community, including Mark Hoppus, saw his Mark Hoppus (and let's just say it *wasn't a Tom DeLonge*), when he stumbles upon the one person in school who seems unaware of his no-hands jizz video. It's Michelle, a flute geek who everyone hates because she is always talking about things that happened at band camp. It's annoying when people have interests and feel joy! Biggs asks her to the prom.

Mena Suvari visits Chris Klein at his job, and she discovers that not only is he a jazz god, he's also a working-class hot dog boy. But then Klein realizes that he has a big lacrosse game on the same night as the vocal jazz state championships! An angel torn between two worlds! Suvari says it's okay, but you know that IT IS NOT OKAY.

Stifler's prom date cancels on him because she thinks Finch might ask her instead and let her touch his tattooed XL johnson, so for revenge Stifler slips "a little something in his mochaccino." It's poop juice! Finch is gonna shit like crazy!!!!!

Stifler steers Finch into the girls' bathroom, and he's just about to release his bowels when a bunch of girls come in giggling about how Finch is a bad boy that they just HAVE to lick. Oh no! This is his demo! They won't want to munch his boy meat anymore once they learn that he is an organism that metabolizes food into energy and waste! Unfortunately, he cannot hold it

---

27   Kinda seems like Shannon Elizabeth was ALSO sent back to the Czech Republic just for playing this role! Has anyone seen her?????

in anymore and diarrhea just starts rocketing out of his asshole while he screams and screams. The girls shriek and run out of the bathroom, and then when Finch comes out, the whole school is gathered to laugh at him. Now he will never have sex! Girls only fuck guys who hold all their shit inside!

Klein's heart is just not in the lacrosse game, so he bails and gets to the vocal jazz competition just in time. Mena Suvari can't believe her eyes!

"You're missing the game for us?"

"No, I'm missing the game for you."

(The first one would have been better, but okay.)

Then the choir director gives Chris Klein his solo back, which is absolutely not fair to Albert,[28] who's been working really hard on this solo and actually showed up.

FINALLY, IT'S PROM NIGHT. There's a prom.

They go to Stifler's lake house for the after-party. Mena Suvari and Chris Klein sensually undress each other in a gazebo. Michelle loves Biggs's nasty story about Stifler drinking the jizz, and he starts to wonder if she is in fact nasty. Kevin(?) asks Tara Reid if she wants to do the missionary position, and she says only if he says, "I love you," so he does, and so they do. Finch is feeling nihilistic so he goes through a door that says "Please Keep Out," and finds Stifler's mom in there, bein' horny.

Stifler's Mom: I've got some scotch?
Finch: Single malt?
Stifler's Mom: Aged eighteen years, the way I like it.

---

28   Eric Lively, brother of Blake Lively and, more important, ROBIN LIVELY.

Out of nowhere, Michelle is like, "Oh, and this one time at band camp, I stuck a flute in my pussy," and then, "Are we gonna screw soon? Because I'm getting kinda antsy." It turns out, Michelle is the horniest and nastiest girl of them all! She tells Biggs to wear two condoms so he doesn't jizz too early (don't tell kids to wear two condoms!) because it turns out she DID see the webcam video after all, but she LIKED IT.

While they're having sex, she starts screaming in Biggs's face: "What's my name? SAY MY NAME, BITCH!" This would be my ringtone if those existed anymore.

After all that, Tara Reid dumps Kevin(?) because she doesn't want a long-distance boyfriend in college. Kevin says he wasn't lying when he said, "I love you," during missionary, and she's like, "I know." OH MY GOD, WHO CARES ABOUT THIS?

Biggs wakes up and Michelle is gone because she is a free, libidinous woman who takes what she wants.

Stifler catches Finch fucking his mom and dies.

Biggs goes home and strips on the webcam for Nadia, who is not mad AT ALL about him broadcasting her tits to the entire school and getting her kicked out of her exchange program. She knows it was all worth it because there is nothing on earth, LITERALLY NOTHING, more important than some mediocre boner.

RATING: 1/10 DVDs of *The Fugitive*.

Acknowledgments

My dear Ahamefule watched every single one of these movies with me, even when he was stressed, even when he would rather be watching *Naked and Afraid*, even the ones he knew he would hate. Some of the best jokes in the book are his, but I will never say which ones. I love you, Aham. None of my books would exist without my literary agent Gary Morris, who has been encouraging and advising me for over 10 years now, who waited SO LONG for me to write *Shrill*, and who I don't think I've ever properly thanked. Thank you, Gary! I'd be lost without you! Thanks to my family, especially my mom, Ingrid, who always knows what to do. Thanks to Hachette, as always, particularly Krishan Trotman, Michelle Aielli, and Mary Ann Naples. Thanks to Mauro DiPreta for buying this book in the first place. Thanks to Rafil Kroll-Zaidi for reading it and telling me it was funny (and which parts were not funny)! And thanks to the movies for being goofy as hell! I love you so much! And NO THANKS AT ALL FOR DEVLIN-MACGREGOR. BYE.